Service Disrupted

My Peace Corps Story

Service Disrupted

My Peace Corps Story

TYLER E. LLOYD

No part of this book may be used or reproduced by any means, graphic, electronic, or mechanical, including photocopying, recording, taping, or by any information storage retrieval system without the prior written permission of the copyright owner of this book except in the case of brief quotations embodied in critical articles and reviews.

The views expressed in this work are solely those of the author and do not necessarily reflect the views of the publisher, U.S. Government, the Peace Corps, or the Government of Burkina Faso.

Service Disrupted: My Peace Corps Story is a memoir. The author has made every effort to remain true to his experience. In some instances, names have been changed and, in the interest of clarity, some characters are combined.

Because of the dynamic nature of the internet, any web addresses or links contained in this book may have changed since publication and may no longer be valid.

Copyright © 2017 by Tyler E. Lloyd

All rights reserved.

ISBN-10: 0-692-92220-2
ISBN-13: 978-0-692-92220-0

DEDICATION

This book is dedicated to my parents, Kim and Eddie Lloyd. Without them, I would not have the drive to explore and experience all that life has to offer.

CONTENTS

SPECIAL THANKS TO:

Medrena Wand
Steven Von Gerlachter
Nicole Berckes
Kary Hill

Dear Reader,

Someone's life story is a series of short stories, told and retold to friends and family members. For a Peace Corps Volunteer, the remarkable experiences had during two years living abroad are tied together by long lackluster episodes of life where nothing worth writing about happens. After one year in the Peace Corps, I began to contemplate writing a Peace Corps memoir, but I didn't know how I would tie my individual stories together. Then, a series of events took place that would represent the best, and worst, of my Peace Corps experience, turn my world upside down, and help me to tell my story.

As I started and stalled, wrote and rewrote this book, I questioned my ability to put my story into words. I've tried to stay true to my experience and opened myself to judgment, rather than carefully handpicking the stories that show me in a positive light.

I hope you will enjoy this vignette of my two years in Burkina Faso.

Sincerely,
Tyler

Me, Tyler, wearing a traditional outfit and celebrating my birthday in village, during my second year in the Peace Corps.

Map of My Peace Corps Story

This story spans a three-week period at the end of my Peace Corps service in Burkina Faso and includes flashbacks to events throughout my experience. Below is a map to help orient you as I travel across Burkina and reflect on my time in the Peace Corps.

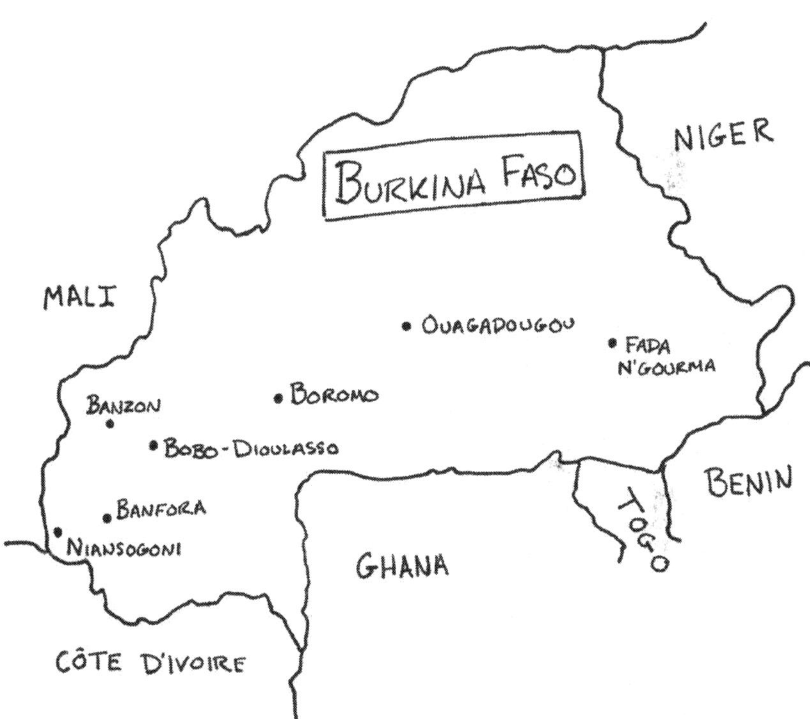

Chapter 1

May 29th – C.O.S

I sat in the Peace Corps transit house, staring blankly at my laptop, waiting for a website to load. The transit house was where volunteers stayed in Ouagadougou, the capital of Burkina Faso, Ouaga. The two-story communal house contained two large rooms filled with rows of bunk beds, men's and women's dormitory style bathrooms, a large kitchen, a large living room, a balcony, a wrap-around screened-in-porch, and a cubby room lined with lockers. I sat in the large living room amongst other volunteers. The room's furnishings consisted of several old couches, two long wooden dining room tables surrounded by chairs, unorganized bookshelves packed with paperback novels, and an assortment of eclectic art pieces cast off by former volunteers.

The transit house, which sat next door to the Burkina Faso Peace Corps office, was intended for volunteers who were either staying in Ouaga on official Peace Corps business, were in the capital for medical reasons, or were in transit across the country. Several fellow volunteers and I were in town for our Close of Service medical exams. Three other volunteers were closing their service (COSing)—completing the Peace Corps and heading home tomorrow. Many more were passing through town, hanging out, or here to say goodbye to those leaving.

It was Ascension Day, a Christian holiday observed by the

Burkinabé government. Offices across Burkina Faso were closed, including ours. Today was a free day to lounge around the house, idly waiting for web pages to slowly load. A group of friends talked about going to the pool in the early afternoon, and afterward many of us would head to one of Ouaga's fancy restaurants, a goodbye dinner for the three departing volunteers.

After spending a large chunk of our monthly income on one delicious meal, we would undoubtedly move to Dinario's, a local bar with pool tables and, more importantly, cheap beer on tap. Lastly, the night would end at a dance club. I thought it was going to be a good day.

Surrounding me sat several volunteers of my training group, Group 26. Nearly two years ago, we came into our Peace Corps service together and we were now preparing for our departure. It didn't feel like two years. The day I arrived in Burkina, a volunteer who was days away from completing her service gave me words of wisdom. She told me, "The days will be long, but the months will be short. It will be over before you know it. Enjoy it."

She was right.

I spent countless days in my village, where the clock seemed to stand still. No matter what I did to fill my time with work, projects, and chores, I would arrive at 11:00 a.m. and wonder, *Is it too early for a nap? Maybe I'll have an early lunch.*

Out of nowhere, September became October, and then I woke up two years in the future, unsure of where the time had gone.

For the past two years, I served as an agriculture and small business volunteer in Banzon, a rural village in Southwest Burkina Faso. For my primary assignment, I worked with a women's cooperative that processed and packaged locally harvested rice. My job as a Peace Corps Volunteer, however, was hard to define. Day after day, I searched for ways to make a difference in my community.

Over the 24 months as a volunteer, I led malaria prevention trainings, held maternal and early childhood nutrition workshops, weighed and vaccinated newborn babies, conducted classes on hygiene, built handwashing stations, helped plant more than 10,000 trees, developed a garden training program, started a youth karate club, and taught a group of women how to make soap. Yet, most days were spent slowly passing the time in village, desperately searching for anything that could provide me with a sense of importance or accomplishment.

You could tell that the group around me was ready to move on from the Peace Corps and on to the next chapter of their life. We had had a positive experience overall, but two years, even if passing quickly, were still two years. We were gradually checking out, focusing on the end of our service. Some of us would head to grad school, others would find jobs, and a few would take time to travel and delay having to choose between grad school or a job.

Suddenly, I was pulled from my reveries, back to the present by another volunteer.

"Hey, Tyler. Crystal has been trying to get ahold of you."

"Huh? What?" I asked, looking up from my laptop. Anna hobbled into the room, wearing her foot brace. I didn't remember how she'd injured herself, but she'd been wearing that boot for a month.

"I just came from Crystal's office. She said she wanted to see you and has been trying to get ahold of you all morning," repeated Anna.

Crystal was one of our Peace Corps Medical Officers (PCMOs), the doctors who helped us get through two years of service in West Africa. Why would Crystal want to see me? The office was closed today. I looked down at my phone, which was next to my laptop, and found it turned off.

I turned my phone on and instantly received two messages:

Tyler, call me when you get this.

Please stop by my office.

"Why does Crystal want to see you?" chimed a volunteer sitting in the living room.

"I don't know."

"That can't be good," inserted another.

"Maybe. We'll see," I said with a smile and a playful shrug, "Wish me luck."

I thought about the day before when I had the first part of my Close of Service medical exam. Dr. Patel, the other PCMO, reviewed my medical history over the past two years, drew my blood for several tests, and performed a head-to-toe physical exam to document anything that would require further follow-up. Something was wrong.

I checked out of the house with the security guard and turned left out of the gate, walking a hundred feet down the street to the Peace Corps office. I slid my ID card under the protective glass barrier to another security guard, who then buzzed me into the building. I quickly bounded up the stairs to the second-floor medical offices.

I knocked on Crystal's door. No response. I knocked again. Still no response. Impatiently, I cracked the door and inquired, "Crystal?"

"Oh, come on in. I can't hear when anyone knocks on that door," she replied. Her door was padded and upholstered to resemble the back of a cream-colored couch—a peculiar design choice.

I entered her office and sat across from her at her desk.

"How are you doing, Tyler?" she asked.

"I'm doing well. Yourself?" I replied, trying to get comfortable in the rigid office chair.

"I'm good. I sent you several messages and tried to call you, but I think your phone was off," responded Crystal.

"Yeah. I don't know why it was off. Anna told me though. You wanted to see me? What's up?" I asked calmly, even though my mind anxiously raced through the possible reasons for this meeting.

"Well, I got a call late yesterday evening from the Embassy lab. Your test results. Your HIV screening test came back positive," Crystal quickly stated, followed by an uncomfortable, lingering silence.

"Okay," I returned numbly, "what does that mean exactly?" My mind sat still as a high-pitched ringing faintly reverberated in my ear.

Crystal realigned herself in her chair and awkwardly shifted a paper on her desk before saying, "Well, it was only a screening test for HIV, not a final, conclusive test. Another test will have to be run to confirm the screening test. I was called yesterday evening and told that yours had come back positive. Since then, I've been reading more on HIV testing protocols, speaking with the regional PCMO in Senegal and others at Headquarters, planning out our next steps."

"Okay," I mumbled, leaning forward in my chair. "So, what now?"

"I've been trying to figure that out actually. The Embassy lab can't run the additional tests. Your blood could be drawn and then sent off to France for testing, but I have yet to figure out how to properly send the sample. Our best option is usually DHL, and it doesn't look like they can do it. The sample needs to be kept at room temperature and arrive within 48 hours. There is a lab here that is part of the Ouagadougou Hospital. It is a World Health Organization HIV lab. We've never used them, but Dr. Patel is confident in them."

"Okay. So, you'll draw my blood today and send it to the WHO lab?" I questioned.

"No. It would need to be drawn tomorrow. Since today is a holiday, they aren't open. We still haven't decided what course of action to take though. I'll be figuring that out today."

"So, draw my blood tomorrow. Send it somewhere. Sounds good."

"Yes…Tyler, are you okay? You're not reacting how I thought you would. How *I* would."

"Yeah. Doing as well as I can be, I guess. Not really feeling anything," I replied.

It was true. I had heard what Crystal said. I tested positive for HIV. I was very aware of what that meant. Yet, I didn't feel anything other than my body as it sat in front of the doctor, still, eyes locked forward.

I continued, "It's just that there isn't much point in freaking out. It won't make anything better."

"No, no it won't. Do you have any reason to think you would test positive? Sex with prostitutes? Intravenous drug use? Unprotected sex? High-risk individuals?" nudged Crystal.

Prostitutes, no. Intravenous drug use, no. Unprotected sex, however, but it had been with other volunteers.

"Nope. All good," I lied. Oh, shit. I started to feel something. Then I felt a lot, hitting me like a wave crashing down. I was engulfed in thought, gasped for air, surfaced, and quickly recomposed myself in a matter of half a second.

"And Tyler, there are the stitches you received in Bobo after your bike accident. The facility was reviewed and approved by Peace Corps, but there is a possible risk there. The needle used for stitches is solid and disposable. The syringe used for your anesthetic, however, is hollow and could transmit HIV if reused, but those shouldn't be reused. It is unlikely, but it is something that I've considered," proposed Crystal.

Chapter 2

Bike Wreck

Patrice had come to my house two days earlier to suggest exploring a cave he knew of outside the village. I was down. I was always down for an adventure or new experience, a quality that helped me make the most of my Peace Corps service.

My best friend Issouf, however, didn't have confidence in Patrice—understandably. Patrice was short with a very muscular build, thin dreadlocks, and best defined by his laugh and the happy-go-lucky way he typically carried himself. He was a musician, dancer, and a Rastafarian. Patrice also drank a lot. On more than one occasion, he would stumble to my house in the morning, smelling of alcohol, to say hello and see what I was up to. We'd chat for a bit, and he would then pull out two small whiskeys from his pocket and start drinking one while holding out the other one to me. I would either decline or, not wanting to be rude, accept the gift but say I would save it for later. Later being sometime not in the a.m.

As happy and goofy as Patrice usually acted, if you got to know him you started to see the pain and frustration held behind his bloodshot eyes. He was a talented musician with an ability to play any instrument he laid his hands on. He was also an accomplished dancer and acrobat who had spent time traveling across Europe performing and teaching African dance.

I remember the first time Patrice told me about his time in Europe. Initially, I couldn't believe it. I lived in a rural West African village, in a country most Americans don't know exists, and here was a guy telling me that he had been to Europe, on two different occasions, while we sat on wooden benches in a thatched lean-to. But, he had in fact traveled Europe as a dancer. He had the photographs to prove it. When Patrice talked about his career, you could hear a mix of nostalgia and regret. He knew that he had a once-in-a-lifetime opportunity, twice.

From Patrice's photographs, stories, and the gossip of others, I pieced together his past. Patrice's older brother, who was a successful businessman in Ouaga, helped Patrice join a dance troop, as well as finance the endeavor. His first tour to Europe, through France and Switzerland, was a successful trip filled with street and stage performances, as well as dance classes comprised of what I imagine were groups of uncoordinated Caucasians spastically moving to drums.

Patrice and the dance group would showcase different styles of West African dance, and Patrice would rotate between dancer, acrobat, and musician. After his first trip, he returned to the village for a short period before heading back to Europe for his second tour with the dance troupe, high off his success as a bona fide performer.

Back in Europe, Patrice started to pursue music more, his main passion. I saw the pictures of Patrice in professional recording studios, standing behind keyboards, playing guitars, and singing. In conjunction with his new musician lifestyle, Patrice began to party, drink, smoke weed, and explore other drugs.

My big brother in village told me, "Patrice started using cocaine. Eventually, he took something more than cocaine. It was mixed with something else. That's what messed up Patrice's mind. Turned him crazy."

While I didn't know the exact details of Patrice's story, I knew that he was now back in village and had been for many years. He was a talented performer who was troubled and longed for another chance to make it as a musician. He and I would play music together, and I would record videos of him playing guitar and singing for him to share with others. Regardless of his past, he was a good friend to me and had a big heart. He looked out for others and wanted to put a smile on your face.

Aside from Issouf's apprehension of Patrice, he also feared that there would be something dangerous in the cave. Issouf wasn't afraid the we'd find a poisonous snake or another dangerous animal, but rather an evil spirit. As well as being my best friend, Issouf was a sorcerer. He practiced magic, made traditional medicine, and communicated with genies. Yet, I didn't think any of this was strange. It was the culture and tradition of Issouf's family. Plus, I enjoyed learning traditional medicine, magic, and lore from him.

I didn't, however, heed Issouf's warning. My mind was set on going out to the cave. Patrice arrived at Issouf's shop where I was waiting, and we set off in the direction of the cave. As we parted, Issouf asked for our safe return, "Allah ka sira diya – *May God make the route good!*"

The cave was approximately 10 km outside my village. I rode my Peace Corps mountain bike, which was built for the terrain. Patrice rode an old, rickety, undersized single-speed, but he was flying down the path. At the rate we were going, we'd arrive in half an hour.

Zipping down the path, winding back and forth, I was having a blast. Patrice would hit bumps and come crashing down on his shockless, steel frame bicycle. I would follow and try to gain more airtime with each proceeding ridge. I was a little worried about the speed, but I wasn't a stranger to being reckless on my bike. During my service, I had already snapped a front tooth in half and gained a few scars. Funny enough, however, those injuries happened at slower speeds and were caused by absent-mindedness and a runaway donkey rather than thrill-seeking.

Bombing down the path, we hit a patch of sand and my back tire swung out from behind me. I quickly whipped the tail of the bike back around, re-correcting, and pushed on, invigorated by a rush of energy from the near spill.

I scanned ahead and readied myself to jump a natural ramp formed by compacted dirt and an exposed tree root. Hitting the bump at full speed, I pulled the bike into the air and took flight, relishing in the momentary weightlessness as I glided through the air. As I landed hard on the bike, my front tire exploded and I fought to keep the bike upright. I stayed vertical for less than a second before turning sideways to dump the bike, sacrificing my left side to road rash rather than going head-over-heels. Instantly, however, my bike caught another tree root, and flipped my bike and me into the air in a series of somersaults.

I crashed down hard on my side, but promptly popped back up, and began to assess the damage. I hadn't hit my head…good. My tongue glided across my teeth to check if they were all accounted for. No newly broken teeth…good. I hadn't landed on my back, which was also good, for my back and the camera in my backpack. I took a big deep breath to simultaneously calm myself and check for broken ribs. I hadn't cracked anything…good. Scanning my arms from the shoulders to my fingertips, I only saw a minor scrape on my right forearm.

Holy shit! I had a horrible wreck, tumbled through the air, smashed into the ground, and I was fine. *Awesome!*

Patrice, who led the way, braked to a skidding halt, threw down his bike, and turned to run to my aid.

"Tyler! Tyler! Are you okay?" Patrice yelled in a panic.

"Don't worry. I'm fine," I said with a smile. I beamed from ear to ear, riding an incredible adrenaline high.

"Oh God, Tyler. No, you're not okay," Patrice shuttered as his pointed down to my right foot.

"Oh, shit!" I said aloud as I looked down to see the pool of blood forming at my feet.

Without pause, I grabbed a bottle of water and doused my foot to clear the blood and get a better look at the damage. I don't care for blood. It makes me squeamish. But luckily, when in times of real need, my gag reflexes shut off and my basic first aid reflexes kick in.

This wasn't good. I had sliced the instep of my foot very deep, about two inches wide, and at an angle to produce what I would later describe as a 'meat flap.' Blood continued to pour out of my foot as Patrice paced in a tiny circle, repeating his mantra, "Oh God. Tyler, this isn't good. Oh God. Tyler, this isn't good."

I reached for my backpack, opened the front compartment, and pulled out sterile gauze, medical tape, and hand sanitizer. I had accepted long ago how accident-prone I could be and thus, tried to be prepared. Using more water to flush out the wound and clear bits of dirt and grit, I began to prep the wound. I gritted my teeth and squeezed a sizeable portion of hand sanitizer into the wound. Zero pain—endorphins were still keeping the pain at bay for the time being.

I gently lifted and replaced the displaced portion of my foot into its original position and tore open several packages of sterile gauze to sandwich on top of my wound. I tightly secured the bandage with rounds and rounds of medical tape. Blood still seeped through. I added more gauze and bound my foot as tightly as I could to slow the blood flow. It seemed to be working. My foot was back together, somewhat.

I looked up from my field triage unit, surrounded by empty gauze packages and covered in blood. Patrice had stopped pacing in circles and now stood silently, inhaling a cigarette as if his life depended on it. I washed my hands and pulled myself off the ground. My foot was as good as it was going to be here, but I needed medical attention and stitches.

I took out my phone and was ecstatic to see that I had a signal way out in the bush. I dialed the Peace Corps Medical Emergency number and waited calmly while it rang.

"Hello, *Medical Emergency* phone. How I can I help?" Crystal answered, stressing the words 'medical emergency.' The doctors had this phone on them all the time and were regularly called and bothered for the most minor of issues. Some volunteers called at the first hint of a headache or stomach trouble.

Oh, do I have a medical emergency for you, I laughed to myself before I bombarded her with, "Good morning, Crystal. This is Tyler. I am about three miles outside of my village, and I just had a bike wreck. I sliced my foot open very deeply, and I've lost a good deal of blood. I have cleaned the wound with fresh water, added sterilizing solution, and bound the wound with medical tape and gauze. I've stopped the bleeding, but I am going to need several stitches."

"Okay, we will send a driver to your village to come get you," replied Crystal. "You said that you are three miles outside village? Can you make it back?"

"My bike has a flat tire, but I don't know if I could bike anyway. I think I can find a way back to village though," I replied. I would limp if I had to, but ideally someone on a motorcycle would pick me up. Motorcycle use wasn't permitted, but this had to be a warranted exception.

"Okay, I will call Vincent in Bobo and he'll leave immediately to come pick you up."

"Thanks. Talk to you soon."

I hung up the phone, and at that very moment, the adrenaline had run its course. My body became weak, my foot was throbbing, and I felt like vomiting. I had to get back to village though. The Peace Corps driver in Bobo, the closest regional capital city to my village, was on his way to pick me up.

"Patrice, that was Peace Corps. They are going to send someone to village to take me to Bobo, but I have to make it back to village first," I said, finally acknowledging Patrice after ignoring him for what felt like a half hour. He also looked weak and ready to vomit, possibly more so than me. I didn't think he would be of much help.

As I began to limp and apply pressure on my foot, it became apparent that walking wasn't an option unless I wanted to arrive sometime the next day. Then, I saw how I would get back. My form of transportation was bouncing down the path in our direction.

The donkey cart arrived and Patrice told the woman who steered the donkey that we were commandeering her wagon. I asked him to explain that I was injured, unable to bike or walk, and needed to get back to the village. Patrice loaded my bike onto the cart, calmly asked the woman to get off, and told her that she had to walk back to village. She willingly accepted and looked very concerned for the tall, bloody foreigner. I mounted the cart and the donkey began to saunter back to village as Patrice slowly rode his bike next to us.

Twenty minutes after I arrived at my house, giving me enough time to unload my bike, pack a bag, and inform my family what happened, Vincent pulled up and we headed to Bobo. The doctors in Ouaga had arranged for me to have the stitches done in Bobo. It was much easier to get stitches there and then move me to Ouaga afterward for further consultation.

I had the stitches as planned. Then, I traveled to the Peace Corps office days later and spent the next three weeks taking progressively stronger doses of antibiotics as I waited for my foot to heal. After I returned to village, I showed off my new gruesome scar and told everyone that it would make a great souvenir, an idea they did not understand.

Issouf never trusted Patrice again and never wanted me to

associate with him.

Later, when Issouf and I recounted the story, we realized something. The village near the cave was called Sinfara. In Dioula, my village's primary local language, "Sen fara" would translate to "to tear a foot." Sinfara had torn my foot. "Sinfara sen fara." This funny coincidence gave us an afternoon of amusement.

What if I contracted HIV when getting my stitches?

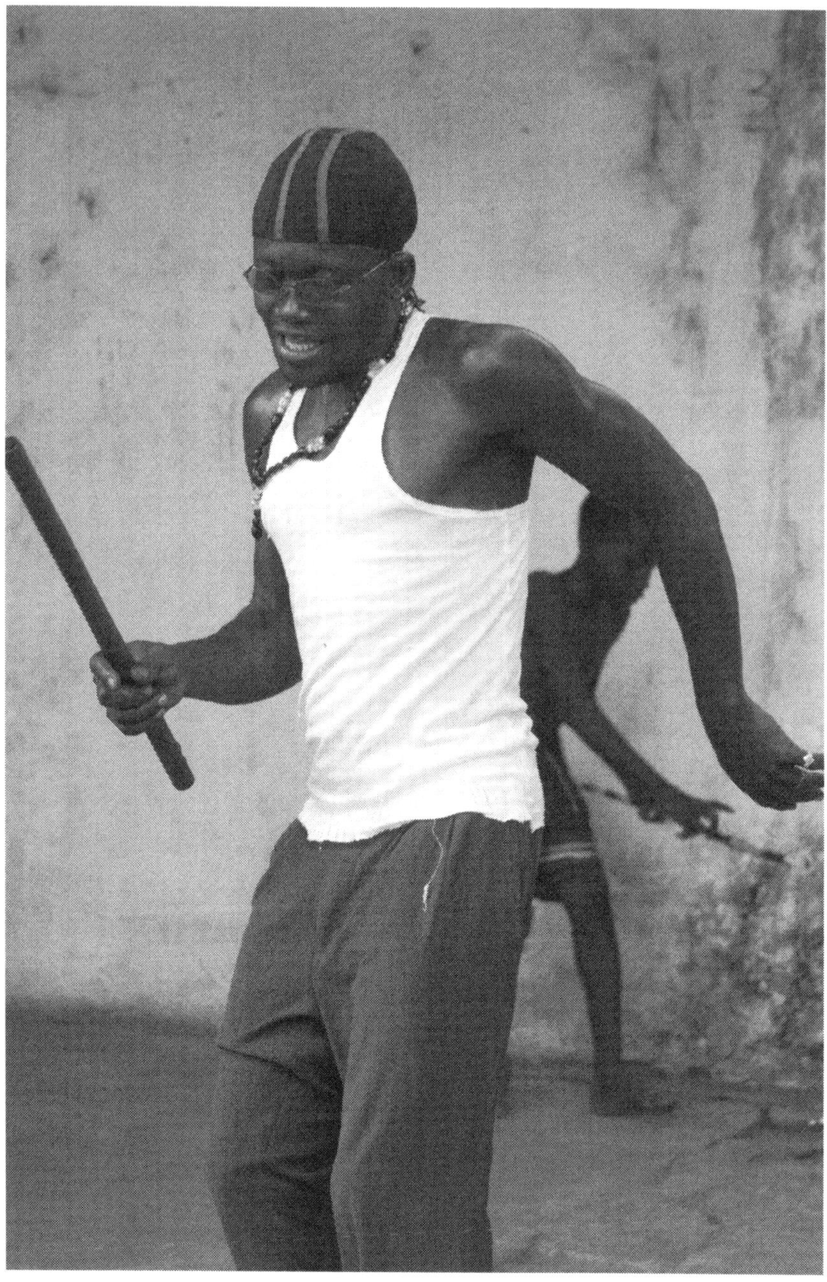

Patrice, teaching a dance class to schoolchildren for Banzon's annual cultural celebration.

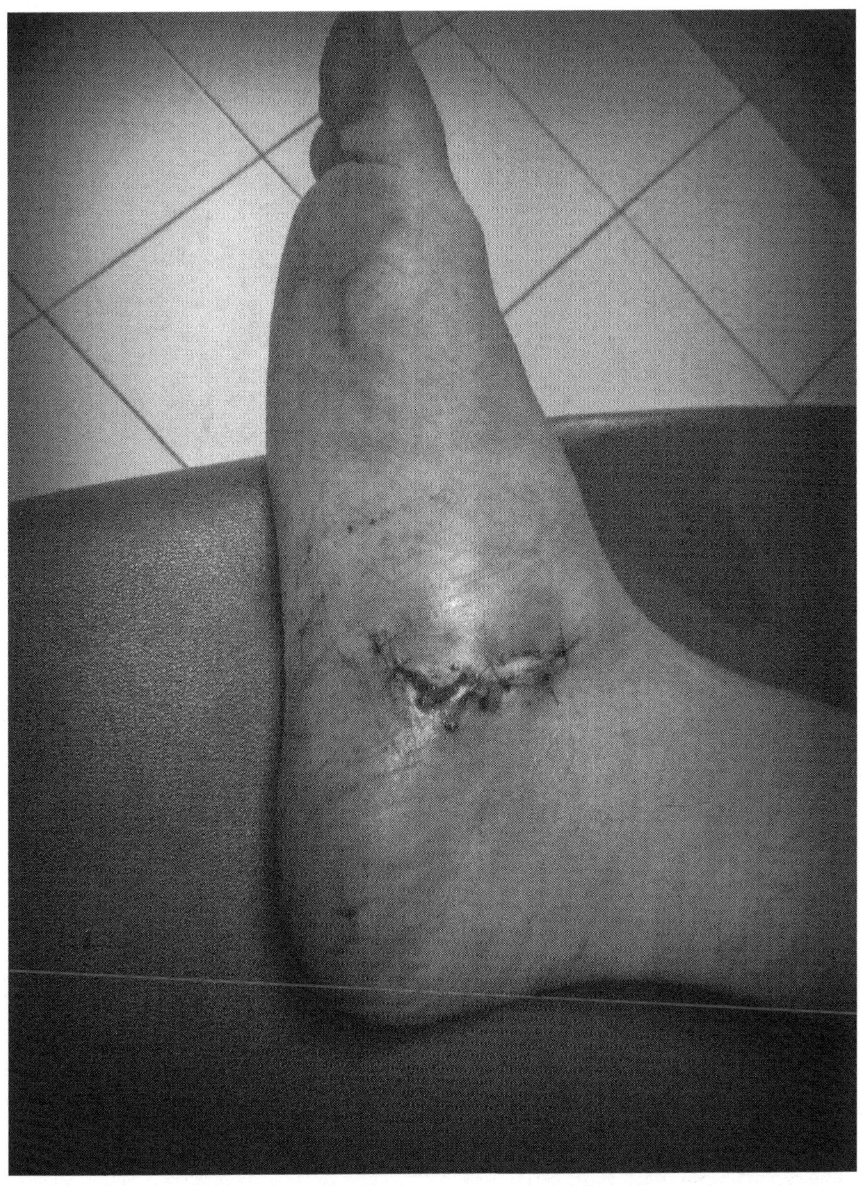

Photo of my stitches, taken by Crystal the day after my accident, once I was moved to Ouagadougou. My feet were still dirty, not cleaned since the bike wreck.

Chapter 3

Positive?

"Should I tell any recent partners about the test results?"

"No. No need to tell anyone until we have the results of a confirmation test. And, you can have a representative of Peace Corps handle that if it comes down to it," replied Crystal.

"What if one of them is about to get on a plane tomorrow and go home? I would hate for them to celebrate their homecoming and do something that couldn't be undone. If, you know, the confirmation test comes back positive," I proposed.

Hyper-logical Tyler was kicking in, as per usual when I found myself in a crisis. Maybe I was overthinking things, but my brain was now purring along, and there would be no stopping it. I would rather be safe now, even if I hadn't been in the past.

"That's a hard decision, but it's one that you'll have to make."

I sat there and considered. This wasn't an easy choice. None of this was easy. It was becoming very real and very hard to sort through the mess of what I knew to be true and unconfirmed details. I slowly started to feel my logic turn into panic.

"Crystal, I would like to talk this over with someone else. Get their opinion. Could we meet in your office?"

"Sure."

"Could you text Andy for me? I don't have any credit on my

phone and I want to text him so he can come over here without anyone knowing why."

"Yes, I can," Crystal replied and began composing a message on her phone. "How does this sound? 'Andy, can you come to my office? Tyler would like to speak with you. Don't let anyone know. Thanks, Crystal.' Does that work?"

"Perfect. Thanks."

"I take it that Andy is a close friend?" inquired Crystal.

"Yeah. He is the one person I would want to consult about something like this, and luckily he got into town about thirty minutes ago," I replied.

Andy and I were in the same training group and I held a deep respect for him from the moment we met. He was a few years older than me, and those years had provided Andy with assurance in himself and his actions. Andy could seamlessly transition from consummate professional to class clown to life-of-the-party and back again without skipping a beat or being at odds with himself.

Andy and I bonded over many long weekends in Ouaga while serving on the Information Communication and Technology committee, which managed the Peace Corps Burkina Faso website and produced numerous multimedia projects. He and I shared a love of learning, being challenged, the outdoors, and most importantly, whiskey. Andy had an extremely level head. He was logical while remaining compassionate. If I was looking for a sound, unbiased opinion, it was going to come from Andy.

Crystal's phone lit up and she picked it up to read Andy's response, "He said he'll be right over."

Minutes after Crystal read the text, Andy appeared at her door. He had been out running an errand and didn't have to make an excuse to slip away. Upon entering, he could tell something wasn't right. Why else would he be called over to see me after I had had an unscheduled visit with the doctor?

"Hey, Andy. Thanks for coming over," I said as Andy stood in the doorway of the room.

"No problem," Andy replied. "Hey, Crystal."

"Hey, Andy," greeted Crystal.

"Crystal, could we use your office to talk privately?" I asked.

"How about you go across the hall and use the exam room?"

suggested Crystal. "I'll be in here if you need me."

"Okay," I said as I stood up and moved out of the room, Andy leading the way. We sat down across from one another in silence, with Andy trying to figure out the situation before I began. I took a breath and gathered my courage before opening with the blunt fact of the situation, "My HIV screen came back positive." I paused for several seconds to let the weight of the fact settle before I continued, "Nothing is certain yet because it was a screening test. I'll have to have another test run to confirm it."

"Okay, what are you thinking?" Andy calmly pressed.

"I don't know. I'm thinking about what to do if it is a true positive," I said with a notable quiver in my voice. "Crystal said I could have contracted HIV when I got the stitches done on my foot at the hospital in Bobo. Then, there is always…sex."

"Tyler, I think the situation is in your favor. For the region, Burkina has a low rate of HIV," offered Andy in encouragement. This was the logical Andy I was looking for. "Either way, no matter the outcome, I'm here for you."

"Thanks."

"You think it was the hospital or someone you slept with?" Andy asked.

"Either, possibly," I replied.

"Well, I think the hospital story is a bit far reaching. I don't really think it is very possible. Who have you slept with?" questioned Andy.

I agreed with Andy and had a growing fear that it wasn't because of the stitches. Contracting HIV from stitches seemed farfetched, yet anything could be possible. I told him with whom I had slept with since entering the Peace Corps. On my list, there was one name that stood out to me, an unwise, one-time act of alcohol-driven hedonism.

Andy and I continued to talk, thinking through the situation and possible other ways I could have contracted HIV.

"Andy, my problem is that I don't know if I should tell Kate," I finally said. "Crystal says that I should hold off telling my past partners until I have confirmed test results. But, Kate leaves tomorrow and I can't help but imagine her going home and sleeping with someone. If I am positive, she could also be positive. I want to be safe."

Kate and I were close friends, confided in one another, but we were never in a relationship. The intimacy we shared stemmed from loneliness and a longing for human connection. Did I think she would sleep with someone as soon as she returned from her service? No. Not in the least. Kate, however, was a good friend. I cared about Kate and I was worried. Above all, I didn't want to make this situation worse.

"What do you think you should do, Tyler?" Andy asked.

"I have to do it," I replied without hesitation.

"I think you're right. It's not easy, but you're right."

"But when? I don't want to tell her today. I want to her to have a good last night in Burkina, without this on her mind. But, I need to tell her before she leaves."

"How about tomorrow after they've had their pinning ceremony and after brunch? That way, she can enjoy those two final things. Then, in the afternoon before she leaves, you can tell her," suggested Andy.

I agreed. "That's when I'll do it," I said, trying to build up the resolve in my response.

"And Tyler, I'm here for you. I can't imagine what's going through your mind right now, but I'm here for you."

"Thanks. Is it too early to start drinking?" I asked. It was barely past 11 a.m.

"No, I think that sounds good," laughed Andy.

"Good. I'll see you over at the transit house. I'm going to talk to Crystal for a sec. Tell her what I decided to do."

"Okay, see you over there," replied Andy.

We left Crystal's exam room and Andy headed back to the transit house while I informed Crystal what I planned to do. She supported my decision and said that she was glad that I had Andy to talk to. I would be returning to her office tomorrow morning to have blood drawn, but until then I would bide my time and try not to think about the positive test results. I didn't want anyone else to know, but several volunteers knew that I had been called over to see Crystal. The others would be eager to know why.

I quickly concocted a lie that my blood results had come back and showed that I had low platelet levels, which would require additional tests. Low platelets could indicate any number of problems, but it wasn't worth worrying about until other tests were run. This was my story. This was also what I had to tell myself. It wasn't worth worrying about until the other tests were run.

Chapter 4

Why the Peace Corps?

I grew up outside Owensboro, Kentucky, surrounded by corn and soybean fields. I spent my childhood farming, playing outdoors, catching animals, fishing, and learning about far-off exotic places of the world through any means possible. I longed to travel and see the world outside Kentucky.

From the moment I heard of the Peace Corps in high school, I knew I wanted to join. Through various clubs and youth programs, I had grown to love public service and volunteering. The Peace Corps could provide a way to travel to a remote region of the world and an opportunity to help others in need.

But, what exactly is the Peace Corps?

The Peace Corps is a volunteer program run by the United States government, established by President John F. Kennedy on March 1, 1961, with the mission to promote world peace and friendship through three goals:

1. To help the people of interested countries in meeting their need for trained men and women.
2. To help promote a better understanding of Americans on the part of the peoples served.
3. To help promote a better understanding of other peoples on the part of Americans.

Peace Corps Volunteers are American citizens from all backgrounds and demographics. While the majority of volunteers are in their 20's, typically a few years removed from college, ages range from 18 to 87 years old. Volunteers commit to 27 months of service, comprised of three months of training and two years working in a host community.

If you asked a volunteer what they did during their service, they'd likely have a short and long answer. Their short answer would be the official Peace Corps volunteer sector that they served under: agriculture, environment, community economic development, health, education, or youth development. Their long answer, however, would be a mix of various short- and long-term projects, covering numerous sectors. While I was actually an agriculture volunteer, I referred to myself as an agribusiness volunteer given the mix of agriculture and community economic development projects I worked on, not counting the other environmental, health, education, and youth projects I did along the way.

Since I served as a volunteer, the application process has changed. Today, potential volunteers apply to specific posts from a list of available volunteer opportunities, as they might with any other job. Each position includes the application deadline, when to expect an answer from Peace Corps Headquarters, and when you would depart for service.

When I applied, I had no idea where I would be going, when I would be going, or what I would be doing. I completed a general volunteer application in addition to a sector-specific application for agriculture, given my background in farming. After sending off my application, I waited for several months to hear back from Peace Corps and then had an interview with a recruiter. After the interview, I waited even longer until I moved to the next stage where I completed my medical clearance paperwork. Finally, seven months after I started the process, I was tentatively accepted into service, with no indication of where I would serve, when I would leave, or what I would be doing.

Nearly a year after applying, my parents received a package from the Peace Corps. The package was mailed to my parents' house because I had begun graduate school since starting the long process.

Over the phone, my mom opened up the large envelope and read my official Peace Corps offer letter aloud. I would be serving in Burkina Faso as an agriculture volunteer.

Was Burkina Faso a city? Maybe a country in Africa? I had absolutely no idea. I had never heard of it.

Burkina Faso is a landlocked West African country bordered by Ghana, Côte d'Ivoire, Mali, Niger, Benin, and Togo. Roughly the size of Colorado, it has a population of 19 million people. The name, Burkina Faso, is a combination of two Mooré and Dioula words that translate to "land of the upright people" or "land of the honorable men." As a former French colony, French is the official language of Burkina, but with 63 distinct ethnic groups, there are an equivalent number of other local languages. Roughly 60% of Burkinabé are Muslim, 25% are Christian, and the other 15% practice an indigenous religion—although many Muslims and Christians also adhere to traditional Burkina beliefs and practices.

The vast majority of Burkinabé are subsistence farmers growing corn, sorghum, millet, rice, and cotton. Prone to extreme heat, droughts, and floods, Burkina Faso's people often face food shortages. Burkina Faso is one of the poorest countries in the world, with nearly half of its population living under the poverty line and continually ranked at the very bottom of United Nations Human Development Index.

These facts and figures, however, do not do Burkina Faso justice. Digging beyond the dry, dusty exterior of Burkina, you find a beautifully vibrant tapestry of culture. I spent countless evenings with local artisans and musicians, slowly sipping rounds of dark, syrupy tea as I watched them practice their crafts. The all but lost art of weaving thread into fabric and grass reeds into baskets lives on and is essential to life in the Burkina village. The trades of leatherworkers, blacksmiths, tailors, and potters was not vanishing but thriving in my town. I made close friends with people who not only played traditional guitars, drums, and balafons but also handcrafted the instruments on which they played. In Burkina, men could be seen walking down the street wearing sacred masks during the day, and on quiet nights you could hear the sounds of ceremonial drums in the distance.

Outside of village life, Burkina Faso takes on many important cultural roles for the region. Every two years, the capital hosts the Pan-African Film and Television Festival, the region's prominent film festival. The film festival, however, is not the only large regional gathering. While the most traditional mask ceremonies do not welcome foreigners, FESTIMA, or the Festival of Arts and Masks, features masked dance troupes from across West Africa.

In addition to the large events and festivals that draw international crowds, Burkinabé always welcome an opportunity to celebrate life. Weddings, baptisms, all religious or national holidays, and even funerals are celebrated to the utmost extent possible. Walking down the street, I was called to join in celebrations filled with food and drink, even during the most meager of times. The people of Burkina Faso were some of the kindest people I have ever met and a population deserving of the title 'honorable.'

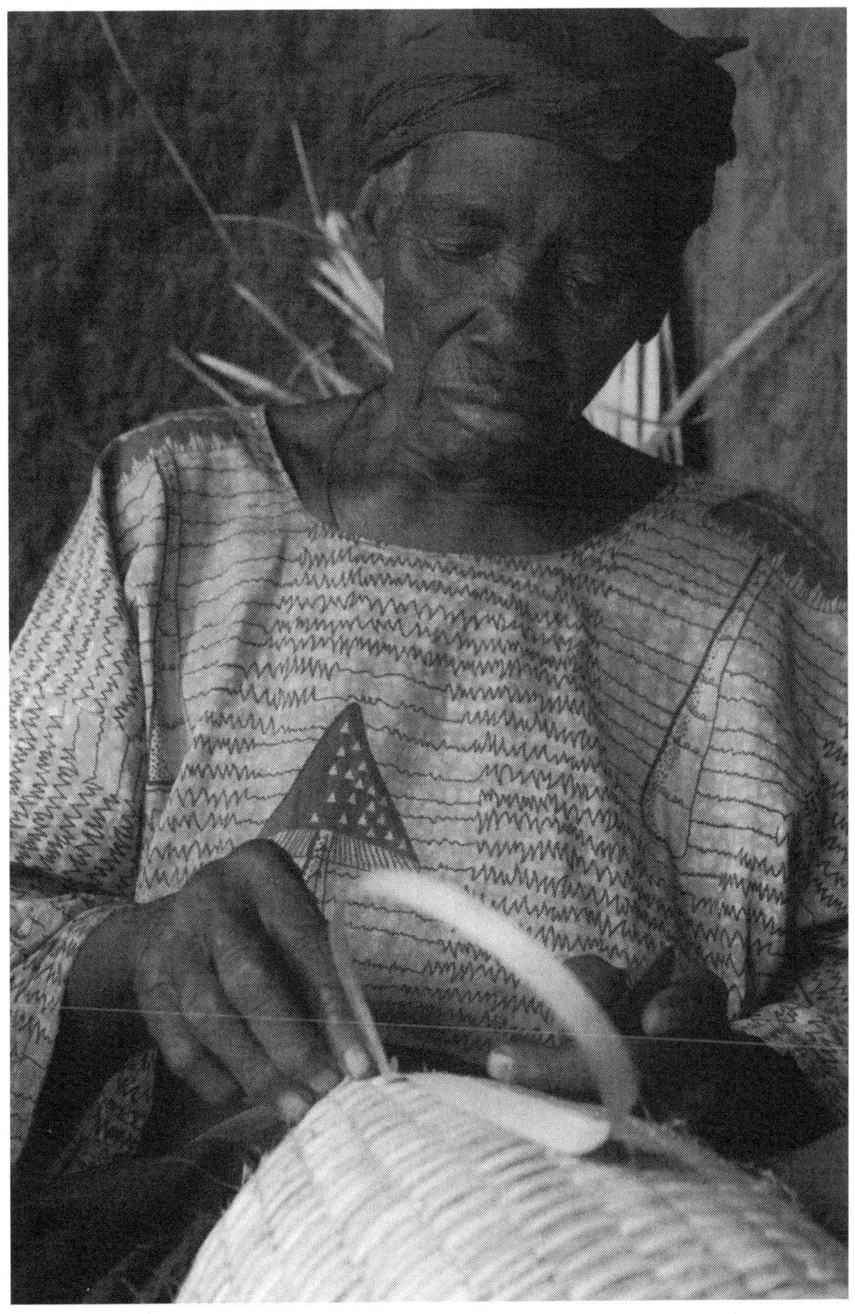

Woman weaving a basket out of dried grass.

My friend, Amedue the tailor, holding up his work. He used a foot-powered Singer sewing machine, the kind often seen in antique stores in the U.S. Amedue worked from pictures and his imagination, not sewing patterns.

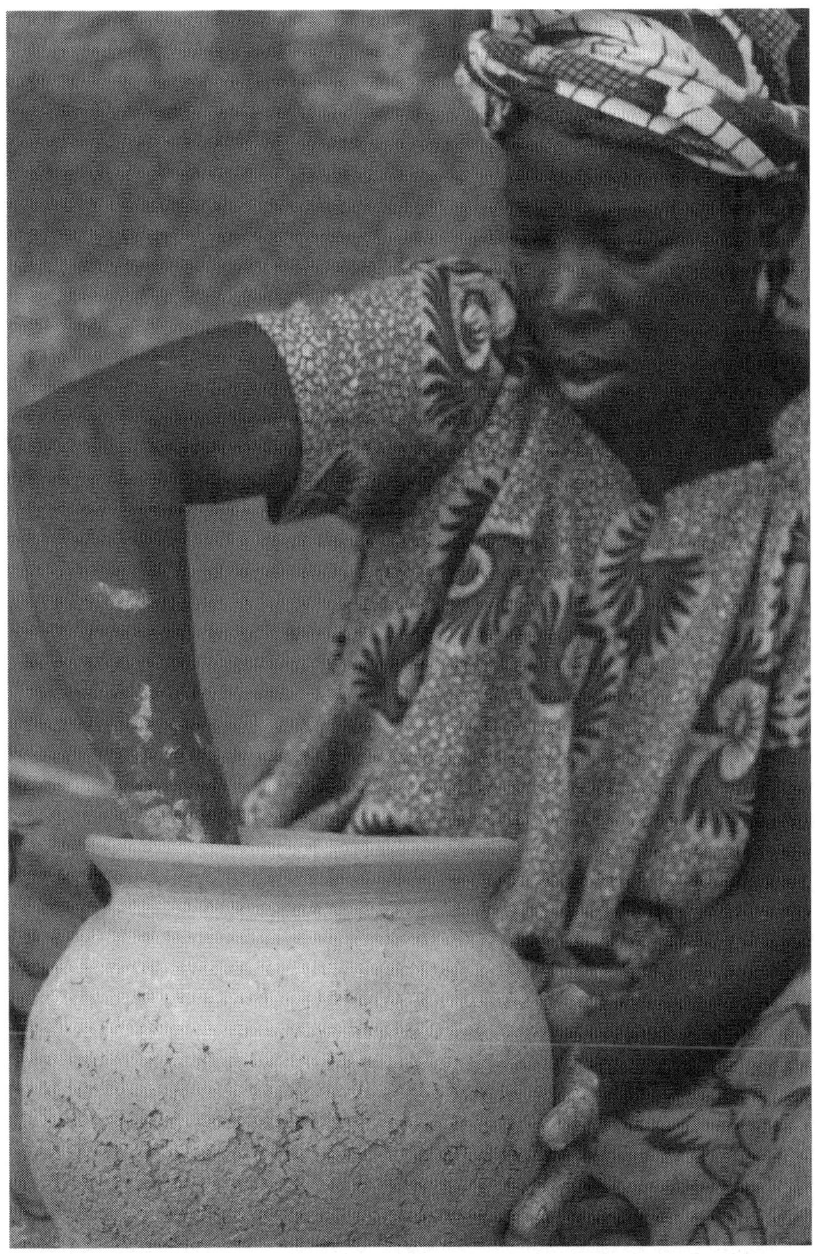

Woman throwing a clay pot on a hand-spun pottery wheel.

Chapter 5

Whiskey Sachets

I returned to a nearly deserted transit house. The group of friends going to the pool had already left, and Andy and I decided to grab a taxi rather than bike to the pool. After I packed a bag with a towel and a book, we left the house, heading for the main road.

"How about we grab some whiskey sachets?" I suggested as we neared a boutique on the side of the road.

Burkina was a country of plastic sacks and sachets. You could buy a lot of things in a sack, anything from water, yogurt, and ice cream, to hot coffee or hard alcohol. To consume, you ripped a corner off the sachet with your teeth and sucked down its contents. After you finished, the empty container was disposed of by throwing it on the ground or, at best, in a ditch, as was standard in Burkina Faso. When I first arrived in Burkina, I instinctually looked for a trashcan, but as time passed, I reluctantly gave in and began to litter like everyone else around me.

Andy and I stepped into the cramped boutique. There was enough space to shimmy sideways down the one aisle. The rest of the floor was filled with merchandise, precariously stacked to the ceiling. Similar boutiques were found on most blocks throughout the city and served as one-stop shops for everything that wasn't meat or produce. We found the bags of alcohol sacks sitting on the counter. They were out of my drink of choice, Obama Café Rhum Whiskey. Gin and bitters remained.

"Do you have any more of these?" I asked the shop owner as I held up the empty bag of Obama Whiskey.

"Yes," he replied and stepped out to rummage through a storage shed behind the boutique.

The shop owner soon returned with a new bag of whiskey sacks. Andy and I bought four whiskeys and four bitters. We'd have two of each.

As we continued to the main road, Andy and I reveled in the wonder of cheap alcohol in a bag. Soon enough, we'd both be back home in the States where drinks were more expensive, but also much higher quality. Andy and I were both whiskey people and truly appreciated aged, brown liquor served neat or poured over one big ice cube. At the same time, we had consumed our fair share of rotgut hooch from 1-liter plastic handles and unlabeled quart-sized mason jars. Each of us recounted the worst booze we had consumed. Grain alcohol distilled in the bush of Ghana. A clear spirit more closely resembling jet fuel than liquor in Greece. As we walked and talked, we simultaneously tore into the sacks of bitters.

"Nope," I said with a grimace. "This is the worst thing I've ever drank."

"Damn, I agree," replied Andy with a contorted look.

We had assumed that the bitters sacks wouldn't really be the cocktail bitters we knew back in the U.S. but rather whiskey or rum.

"I guess these really are bitters. Who the hell would put bitters in a sack?" I asked.

It was okay, even normal now, to have vodka, gin, rum, or whiskey in a sack. Bitters, however, was an abomination and an assault on one's taste buds and esophagus.

"Ghana. They were made in Ghana," answered Andy as he read the label, before taking another painful swig of bitters.

"If my second test comes back negative, I'm going to have to assume that the bitters cured me. This stuff is foul and has to be killing something inside of me," I said jokingly.

Andy replied with a laugh. That was all he could do. How, otherwise, should he respond?

I was the one who was potentially HIV positive. Joking about it to lighten the mood was acceptable for me, but dangerous territory for anyone else.

We continued toward the road, sipping the bitters rather than shooting them down in one go. We immediately followed the nauseating bitters with an Obama whiskey that had never tasted better.

When we arrived at the main road, I spotted a taxi parked on the side of the street. The driver was buying a large bundle of local greens from a woman seated on a tarp under the shade of several trees. Andy greeted the taxi driver in Moore, the major local language of central Burkina Faso, and we negotiated a price for driving us to the pool.

In the taxi, Andy and I exchanged small talk back and forth, but my mind wasn't present. My mind was elsewhere, but I couldn't tell where. It was as if my brain was working away on a problem but wouldn't allow me to be part of the process. The majority of my mental capacity was tied up and I was left with only enough to seem awake and present, all the while dull to the world.

The green taxi laced its way through traffic. *I can't believe that I have never been in an accident while taking a taxi*, I thought. The road was filled with cars, motorcycles, and bikes that weaved back and forth to their individual destinations. Lanes were a recommendation and street lights a highly encouraged suggestion. For the most part, it all worked. However, I had passed many car accidents. Motorcycles folded like tin foil. Crumpled car hoods that resembled the lids of opened sardine cans. Burgundy smears across the road. Blood-soaked sheets draped over a lifeless form.

We pulled up to the pool, quickly handed over our predetermined fare in exact change, and promptly left the taxi driver sitting in his car before he had a chance to heckle us for more money. As I passed through the gate to the pool, I paused, took a deep breath, and using what cognitive function remained, told myself, *Everything is fine.*

Our friends were enjoying a conversation while standing in the shallow end of the pool. We were the only people there, just how we liked it. Being in the capital was a chance to escape. We'd try to find pockets of peace and quiet, places without teasing banter and gawking—something nearly unavoidable in village. In village, you were always being observed. It was sometimes even hard to find solace in your house because Burkinabé would come and check on you, or bug you depending on how you viewed it. It was not an active attempt at annoying us, but rather that we were different, interesting to them, and that many people honestly were looking out for our best interest. Personal time and our culture of individualism were not easily translated.

Andy and I ordered food before we joined our friends. The pool was free if you bought food. I wasn't yet ready to jump in with the others, so I sat down on a bench in the shade, at the edge of the pool where everyone else waded. I pulled out my second whiskey to sip on. Heather saw that I was drinking a café rhum and gave a disapproving look. I returned a smile and motioned toward her with the whiskey, as an offering for her to join me. She countered with a grimace.

"What did Crystal want?" asked Heather. It hadn't taken long for someone to ask. "You're not dying are you?" she added jokingly.

Any other time that would have been an entirely suitable exchange between us. Now, it was a bit too real to be funny.

"There was a problem with my blood test that was taken yesterday," I said.

You could sense the tension my response created in the air.

"What?" asked Kelly.

"Apparently my platelet levels came back low," I offered as a lie. "It could mean any number of things though, from a minor infection to something more. I have to get additional tests run to figure out why."

I didn't think that the lie was good enough, but it seemed to work.

"Are you worried?" asked Heather, now a little worried herself.

"No. It doesn't make much sense to be worried until I know what's wrong," I said, trying not to let it show how I actually felt.

"You don't have AIDS do you?" questioned Jen with a laugh.

Son-of-a-bitch.

Damnit.

Nailed it.

We have a winner.

Who the fuck jokes about AIDS?

I couldn't blame Jen. She was trying to lighten the mood. Right? She was merely offering up a worst-case scenario that would make my current situation look fine. Little did she know...

"No," I said with a twist of my head that was possibly more of a nervous twitch than a 'no.' I couldn't look in Andy's direction. Move on. I had to move the conversation forward.

"No, but I have to get more blood drawn to figure out what's wrong," I said as I lifted the whiskey sack to my mouth.

"Sorry to hear that. I hope everything is okay," said everyone present, in one form or another.

Heather was the most sincere in offering a mix of condolences and concern. Kate, Melissa, and Chris were leaving tomorrow and their minds were elsewhere. Jen was occupied by a fight she had with her new fiancé. Kelly's concern was sincere but was overshadowed by Heather's.

Heather and I were previously in a relationship. Although rocky and short-lived, we had invested emotional and physical time that wasn't easily swept away. Heather knew me pretty well. She knew why I was drinking sacks of whiskey. I was trying to drown something out. I had done it before while in Peace Corps.

Our sandwiches arrived, and Andy and I quickly devoured them. There is something to behold in the properly balanced combination of meat, cheese, bread, and condiments. I didn't eat a lot of sandwiches in the States, but when you are without something, it becomes ever the more special when it comes back into your life. Absence makes the heart grow fonder, even for sandwiches.

If I were HIV positive, what would become absent from my life?

No. I stopped myself before following that question down the rabbit hole. Eventually, I would fall into the mental trap of rationalizing and projecting, but for now, I was with my friends. It was time to get in the pool.

I floated about in the shallow end with my fellow volunteers. I liked going to the pool well enough, but I don't like swimming. Rather, I was not a good swimmer. I spent several summers taking swim lessons at the local YMCA, rising through the ranks of minnow, pollywog, and on to shark. Yet, if I found myself capsized in the ocean, I would likely drown if not soon rescued. I'm dense, quickly become tired, and sink like a rock. The three sacks of alcohol also wouldn't do well to improve my swimming ability.

As we floated and talked, the topic of discussion turned to Kate,

Melissa, and Chris's return home. What would they do first? What would they eat?

I couldn't help but concentrate on Kate. Tomorrow, I would have to tell her that I tested positive for HIV and that she may need to be tested again.

But until then, I wanted her to have a good time. She had made it. Completed the Peace Corps.

Not all Peace Corps Volunteers finish their two years of service. Some volunteers are pulled from their country early due to disease epidemics, natural disasters, political unrest, or war. This was known as 'Interrupted Service.' Months before I left for Burkina Faso, Peace Corps Volunteers in Mali were consolidated and evacuated from the country due to a civil war.

Some volunteers break the rules or don't fit well with the program or needs of the host country. In those cases, volunteers are 'Administratively Separated.'

As a result of illness or injury, volunteers can be 'Medically Separated.' Medical separations happen for a whole host of reasons including skin infections unresponsive to medication, chronic digestive problems, or broken bones.

In the past, mental health issues were grossly misunderstood and poorly managed by the Peace Corps, a parallel to the American health system at-large, but in recent years the Peace Corps had become better at addressing these issues, sometimes requiring medical separation.

The most severe instances of medical separation are the result of assault or rape.

Peace Corps Volunteers have also died serving. Disease, illness, accident, and even murder have taken the lives of hundreds of volunteers serving abroad. While a very tiny fraction of volunteers give their life, it is not a point to be taken lightly. The Peace Corps is not without risk. It is not easy.

Peace Corps Volunteers commit to serving two years in an underdeveloped foreign country, but we weren't bound by any contract other than a contract to ourselves. If ever we were ready to go home, we simply had to call the office and tell them, "I'm done. Send me home."

Days later, our service would be over and we'd be on a plane back home. This was known as 'Early Termination,' ETing for short.

At any time, each of us could have thrown in the towel. But we didn't. The distance from our friends and family back home, heat, diarrhea, fear of malaria, or worse, hadn't stopped us. I had seen my peers demonstrate a mix of self-determination and stubbornness that drove them day in and day out to keep going, to finish their service in hopes of making the slightest difference.

I had a friend that had fly eggs laid into her skin and had the larva erupt from her flesh like aliens days later. She stayed.

I had multiple friends robbed at knifepoint. They all stayed.

I had a friend get in a bus crash that killed several passengers. After he pulled two children from the burning bus, he stayed.

I had a friend lose his father during his service. He returned home for several weeks, and he came back to Burkina to complete his stay.

From my experience, those that did leave Burkina early, if not for family or medical reasons, did so because they had something better waiting for them back home.

Twice, I nearly left the Peace Corps. Once, for a girl. The second time, for a job opportunity.

When I started the Peace Corps, I left a girlfriend back home in the United States. We tried long distance for nine months before everything fell apart. I came very close to leaving the Peace Corps in an attempt to salvage the relationship but quickly learned that there was little left to salvage.

The second time I almost ended my service, after a year of the Peace Corps, I entered into the second interview round for a well-regarded internship opportunity to work with a major company in their sustainability department. I knew that after the Peace Corps I wanted a career in environmental protection and here was a chance to start my career even sooner. I decided that taking the internship over completing my service was the right choice. But, I didn't get the job.

Both my plans to rekindle lost love and start my career had fallen through, and I stayed in Burkina. I didn't know why, but I told myself that it would always work out for the best. Thus far in my life, I had been lucky. I put in a lot of hard work and tried to make my own luck, but sometimes it felt like the universe had my back no matter what. My mother once said that I could "fall into a pile of shit and come out smelling like roses."

I was currently in the shit.

After we were sufficiently waterlogged, we gathered our things, settled our bill, Andy and I shot the remaining sack of bitters, and we headed to the road to locate a couple of taxis. We returned to the transit house and many of the girls began to get ready for the evening. I was in no hurry, so I sat on a couch amongst my group-mates, in the bedroom that we had claimed.

"Want me to go get more whiskey?" asked Andy.

Andy was a good drinking buddy. He was on a mission to keep me the right level of drunk for the night. A diluted haze that would keep me light, energetic, fun and away from a sober dwelling rationality. It would be a delicate balance though. If I overshot the target, I would find myself in a very dark, whiskey-soaked cave of depression. For the time being, I was in a good place.

"Of course," I replied and handed over two dollars. "Use it all."

Andy came back with four whiskeys each and a Coke. I had no qualms with drinking the caramel tasting whiskey straight, but it was a good idea to slow my pace by diluting my drinks with soda.

Sipping my whiskey and Coke over ice, I scanned the room. Everyone was enjoying themselves. Tonight we'd go out for a good meal, drink, dance, and celebrate the service of our three friends. The room was filled with a relaxed, positive energy. Fueled by my drinks, I was eager to talk amongst my friends, but again, my mind was working on something else.

Caroline sat on her bed copying music from another volunteer's hard drive. As I watched her, animosity started to grow inside me. She was the drunken one-night hookup.

At this point, there was no way of knowing if I was HIV positive. It could have been a false positive. For the time being though, the test results were not in my favor. I was trying to connect the dots. I was looking for a scapegoat.

I tried to tell myself that I shouldn't jump to conclusions. Caroline was my friend, but in trying to piece everything together, she made the most sense for several reasons.

First, I didn't use a condom that night. Second, my other partners in Peace Corps already had their Close of Service medical exams and tested negative; Caroline had yet to be tested. Third, I was previously tested for STDs while in the Peace Corps because of a urinary tract infection. That test followed two past sexual partners, stitches from the local hospital, and occurred months before the night in question. That test came back negative. Lastly, a final fact glowed red hot in my mind. Caroline had previously told me that she slept with another volunteer that I knew to have slept with local Burkinabé. While the prevalence of HIV in Burkina Faso was low for the region, it is much higher in sub-Saharan Africa than elsewhere in the world. This, I feared, was the cause.

I had constructed a logical argument that I couldn't shake. The facts made a lot of sense, but I still didn't know anything for sure. Crystal hadn't seemed too worried. She was, of course, concerned by the initial results, but she seemed very hopeful. I also knew that the other doctor, Dr. Patel, wasn't worried.

After my previous STD test in January, Dr. Patel told me that in all his years of serving as a Peace Corps doctor in three countries, he had never had a volunteer test positive for HIV. Merely because it had never happened, did not mean it couldn't happen. Maybe it was apathy toward this possibility that led me here. HIV was never something I had considered. Very stupid of me.

The time came when I could no longer put off getting ready for the night. I jumped into the shower and sifted through my canteen to choose between one of the three good shirts I had in Burkina. My nice clothing was reserved for the big cities, when we would go out for dinner, drinks, and dancing. In village, I dressed like my friends, rather than the affluent government officials. Well-worn pants, a clean t-shirt or old button down dress shirt, and sandals. This was my village uniform. My friends were farmers, craftsmen, and shop owners.

Could I have worn newly tailored dress slacks, pressed shirts, and shined leather dress shoes like the more affluent members of my community? Yes. And I did dress this way when I had to attend an important function. Yet, I wanted to be more like my village friends.

For tonight, I chose my default city outfit. Brown leather dress shoes, dark jeans, and a tailored dress shirt.

Once the majority was ready, we began to vacate the transit house in small groups and head toward the restaurant, which was within walking distance. The Peace Corps office and house were in a nicer area of the capital, home to many other aid and development organizations. As a result, we had several of the better restaurants nearby from which to choose.

The sun began to set as we walked. I always wondered what people thought when they saw groups of volunteers. A pack of Americans, the vast majority of us white and in our 20's, walking down the street rather than being driven by a chauffeur. We looked even more out of place when on our bicycles. You could always tell at a distance when it was a Peace Corps Volunteer biking, as signaled by the helmets we were required to wear, for good reason, as I had come to learn.

Walking counter to traffic, we watched the road filled with passing cars and motorbikes. It was starting to get dark, and those with working headlights had switched them on. The dirt shoulder of the road on which we strolled was filling with street vendors who were setting up for the evening and preparing to serve food. We passed several meat stands where roadside butchers readied grills of goat, lamb, or pork. Rice with sauce, usually peanut, was easy to find, as was some variation on fried dough.

Tonight at Chez Benoua, I wouldn't be dining roadside. We filtered into the restaurant and began to fill the long row of tables reserved for our group. The waitress arrived with the menu written on a large chalkboard, balanced on an easel. She then began to move around the table and take drink orders.

"One glass of the Four Roses," I requested.

This was the only restaurant that I knew of with bourbon in Burkina Faso, and which only had the one bottle of Four Roses. Andy, several others, and I had slowly consumed that bottle over the past two years. We would have finished it long ago if it weren't for the price; $7 a glass, compared to a large $1 beer. As a bourbon-loving Kentuckian, this was a treat, and tonight I would be treating myself.

Our drinks arrived and our food orders were taken. The restaurant had their famous duck dish this evening and, fortunately, plenty of it, as half of my end of the table ordered a plate. As I sipped my bourbon, I joined the meandering conversation. Our conversations were almost always identical. Our daily lives were simple and our problems routinely the same. We talked about our work. Drama in our villages. Recent bouts of illness. Future projects.

The conversation found its way to a Mickey Avalon song. I knew it well. The group began to sing the song.

My dick cost a late night fee
Your dick got the HIV
My dick plays on the double feature screen
Your dick went straight to DVD

The group continued to recite verses of the vulgar but catchy song. *Your dick got the HIV.*

Did HIV always come up this natural in conversation?

Son-of-a-bitch.
Damnit.
Who the fuck jokes about AIDS?
A lot of people apparently.

I smiled and took larger sips of my drink as the song died out. Thankfully, the food came out and the group became quiet as we tried to savor eating something that wasn't rice and sauce.

The duck. In front of me lay a side of roasted duck, crisped and served with a Port wine sauce. Next to it sat a mass of roasted garlic potatoes. I slowly picked up my knife and fork and steadied myself, as a surgeon would before making the first incision. Pinning down the duck with my knife, I slid the fork into the tender bird and lifted away a portion of fatty duck skin. That bite hit my mouth and I forgot everything. There was butter, herbs, and garlic; a crispness to the bite that somehow crunched and then melted slowly over my tongue.

"This is amazing," I uttered to everyone around me, followed by two friends who answered in agreeing grunts, before the table returned to sounds of silverware clinking against porcelain. No sooner than we had started, it came to an end. I looked up from my plate and scanned the table of faces glowing with a post-feast radiance. I wanted to repeat that series of bourbons and duck dishes until my body could hold no more.

The waitress returned and asked, "Anyone for dessert?"

Could I consider a second plate of duck a dessert?, I asked myself.

The long and expensive bill arrived and I handed over a wad of money, enough to pay for a week's worth of food in my village. It was worth it. Once everyone had paid, we rose sluggishly and departed the restaurant, fuller and happier than when we arrived.

I was drunk and full, but my thoughts were keeping me from enjoying the experience. I continued to replay Crystal's words in my head—*your HIV screening test came back positive*—and then thought of Kate, who I would have to tell, and Caroline, who I increasingly blamed. But I had only tested positive with a screening test. It didn't mean that I was positive. Nevertheless, I was beginning to worry. I was scared, but I wouldn't dare let anyone know what was happening behind my eyes.

Two taxis were sitting outside the restaurant and we began to pile in. A taxi has places for four passengers. A taxi carrying volunteers easily transports eight people and can carry upwards of twelve if it is a hatchback. Using a taxi like a clown car cut down the price and the number of cars we would have to take. Efficient and cheap, cornerstones of the volunteer decision model.

"To Dinario's," we told the taxi driver.

Dinario's was a local bar and the closest thing to a dive bar in Burkina. The owner, Dinario, was a gruff old Frenchman that had a love for us that he refused to show. With cheap beer on tap, pool tables, darts, and a large patio, it was our usual starting place. From here, groups would splinter off back to the transit house or to one of the few dance clubs were we felt were safe. We previously enjoyed Appaloosa and its odd Native American murals, but there were questionable signs of human trafficking as marked by the wait staff comprised entirely of Eastern European women that had been brought to Burkina Faso to 'work.' But, after a man was raped and stabbed to death at Appaloosa, we were no longer allowed to go there, for good reason.

Our taxi pulled up and we began to spill out. It was always enjoyable to catch the mildly disgusted expressions on other expats' faces as they watched foreigners seemingly endlessly tumble from a car. After giving my portion of the fare, I made a line for the bar.

"Good evening. One beer please," I ordered with Dinario.

"Two dollars," replied Dinario as he began to fill several beers in advance of our approaching group.

With a cold half-liter of light lager in hand, I moved to the adjoining room that held two pool tables. The back table sat empty and I signaled to the guy who ran them that we wanted to play. He was currently playing a game at the first table with another Burkinabé. The first table was almost always in use by local pool sharks. It was also the better of the two tables. I liked to believe that the back table to which we were relinquished was off kilter and thus explained how poorly we played.

Eight-ball was our game, and the one game we knew how to play since the balls were solid red or yellow with a black eight ball, rather than a numeric series of solids and stripes.

Caroline quickly spoke up and asked if I would be on a team with her. While she was good at pool, I understandably had reservations. She, however, did not deserve any of the contempt I was holding for her. I accepted her offer, hoping it would help me move past the unwarranted feelings.

As we played, I began to joke with Caroline and taunt the other team. For the first half of the game, we were in control of the table. Soon, however, our luck gave way and we were unable to sink the eight ball. We challenged the gloating winners to a rematch, who accepted and quickly sank the eight ball in the second shot. The third game seemed as if it would never end. With each missed shot, my introspection intensified. As I watched Caroline laugh, drink, and move around the table, I became resentful. I continued to play until I could no longer concentrate on the game. Without much cause, I handed off my stick to another volunteer and left the table to join others on the patio.

I sat down across from Andy at the end of a row of three round tables we had pushed together.

"How are you doing?" asked Andy.

"Great. What are you drinking?" I responded.

"Scotch," Andy said while motioning the drink in my direction as to say 'have a sip.'

I took Andy's offer of a drink. Andy wasn't merely offering me alcohol though. The gesture was more than that. I could see that Andy was telling me something. Telling me that even if I were HIV positive, he wouldn't regard me as an untouchable. For all we knew, I had HIV and Andy wasn't afraid to drink after me. He knew, as well as I did, that drinking after someone doesn't transmit HIV. Would others be so kind? Would I have even been so kind?

Soon after sitting down, the conversation shifted to Close of Service medical exams. I couldn't escape them. I couldn't escape the topic of HIV.

"Crystal said she wasn't going to do my HIV exam," said a volunteer. She was married and serving with her husband. She had no concern.

"I told her 'No. Do the exam.' I know I'm fine but I still want the test run. Why not?" she continued with a laugh.

Yes. Of course. Why not? It's always better to be safe.

What negative karma had I put out into the world? This was the third time today that HIV organically came up in conversation. I was overly aware of those three letters, but this rate of occurrence had to be abnormal.

"Ready to go dancing?" asked Amanda as she came to the table, raising a burning cigarette to her lips.

"Yes," I said and slid my chair back. I was ready to go. Ready to change locations. Ready to move and get my mind off things. Ready to be somewhere where they blasted music and it would be impossible talk. No more talking for tonight.

The taxi pulled up to Star Night and seven cramped volunteers emerged. Star Night was my favorite of the two dance clubs we frequented. The dance floor was slightly smaller than Fresh Bar, our other spot, but the ceiling above the dance floor was filled with lights and lasers to create a luminous concert that accosted one's senses. Fresh Bar did have mirrors along the walls of the dance floor though, which many volunteers enjoyed.

Many locals also liked the mirrors. They would dance with themselves in the mirrors, staring into their own eyes while making awkward sexual faces as they shuffled back and forth. Although sometimes entertaining to watch or briefly join, I didn't miss the mirrors.

Pushing aside the black padded leather door, I entered Star Night and bypassed the bar for the dance floor. Drinks here were too expensive, I was already drunk, and even sober I needed no excuse to dance. I love dancing.

As I danced, I briefly forgot. Dancing felt primal to me and allowed me to shut down the logical centers of my brain. I was able to react naturally and move with the music. Everything else faded away and only the present remained. One second at a time, I was able to enjoy the moment without an internal dialogue running through my head.

My gaze fell on Heather as she moved on the dance floor. I liked Heather but I was never sure to what extent. Peace Corps both amplified and skewed my emotions, and in turn led me to question them. Because I often felt unsure of my actions and place in Burkina, I regularly found myself doubting my feelings as I became entrenched deeper into every emotion. My sadness felt sadder, frustrations more frustrating, and anger angrier, yet, joys were more joyful, and I too often found myself overwhelmed by happiness nearly to the point of tears by modest actions, such as a group of children shouting my name and extending their hands for high fives as I rode past on my bike.

Given that I felt out of place every day in Burkina, some days more than others, I longed for acceptance and deeper human connection, deeper connections than what many of my village friends or family could provide, given language barriers, cultural differences, or my status as a foreign volunteer and representative of the U.S. Peace Corps who would one day leave Burkina. Heather, however, could provide the level of connection I longed for. I enjoyed spending time with her, yet I questioned if my feelings were situational infatuation rather than true affection.

My eyes then fell on Kate. I could see that she was ruminating on a thought.

Serving in the Peace Corps presents a lot of low points that make you look longingly to the end, waiting for the day when you could return home. Though when that day arrives, it is bittersweet. Even with all the hardship, living and working in your village becomes your life. You make friends and build relationships that you come to depend on. A self-identity is created that hinges on you being a volunteer, a foreigner. When the day you've been waiting for arrives, it becomes far too real. You may never see your village again. Never see your friends again. I projected and assumed that this is what Kate felt. I hated that I would have to make it even harder.

I tried to clear my mind with more dancing, but the dance floor had begun to lose people. It was getting late and those left were very drunk. I danced with my fellow volunteers and moved closer to a female volunteer. Our hips began to move back and forth together. We pressed against each other as we danced, triggering two competing reactions. She took my hands that were hovering at my side and placed them on her hips, closing any space left between us.

Any other time, our dancing would have been harmless. While it would still trigger certain feelings, they would have been answered by an internal, *you know you shouldn't.* This time, however, the message was, *you know you can't.* The weight of this difference was blunt and depressing. Was this my future?

Kate and others headed for the door. Overwhelmed with internal conflict, I needed this exit.

"Sorry, I have to go," I said as I removed my hands and left my dance partner.

In the taxi, I stared out the window at the passing lights and closed shops. The streets were dead. In a few hours, people would begin to stir. Women would fill the streets to sweep away the dirt of the previous night. The morning call to prayer would sound from the mosques and a new day would begin. I was tired and ready to go to sleep. Today was over and tomorrow would come whether I wanted it to or not.

Chapter 6

May 30th – Waiting

I woke up slowly, gradually transitioning to wakefulness. The sun had risen and was shining through the window. It was early and I could hear no other volunteers stirring. I loved mornings and the calmness they brought. For a few moments, all was right in the world. Gradually, yesterday began to lap up like waves of a dim distant night's dream. To no avail I grasped at the fleeting calm I had awoken to, trying to hold on to the sense of peace. A deep tiredness began to seep into my bones. Had I slept? The internal dialogue never stopped.

Locating my phone beside me, I checked the time. 6:05 a.m. I had gone to sleep three and a half hours ago, but as always, had woken up at my regular time. The COS ceremony was today at 8:30 a.m. For the next two hours, I would have to occupy myself, while most everyone else continued to sleep. I left the bunk-filled bedroom and moved out to the common room where I found my laptop. At least the internet would be faster with no one awake.

I moved directly to Facebook and mindlessly scrolled through the news of my friends. All my friends in Burkina were asleep and all my friends in America were asleep. I had no one to interact with and I did not need to be left alone with myself. I stood up, headed down the stairs to the first floor, and out the guarded gate. I needed to move as well as eat something. I lazily walked to the small store down the road, the same store where Andy and I had purchased bitters and whiskey.

"Good morning," I greeted the store owner.

The small shop was packed with three other people occupying the small walkway and shopping for breakfast.

"Good morning. What do you want?" replied the store owner as he looked up from a baguette he was buttering for a lady.

"Half a loaf of bread, buttered. Five eggs. Two packages of instant coffee. And, umm, three packets of those cookies, the Jingles," I answered, pointing to the chocolate cream-filled cookies in the case. The cookies were an impulse buy and the start of stress eating.

I handed over money in exchange for the black plastic bag of breakfast food and shuffled sideways out of the cramped boutique. I returned to the Peace Corps house to find that others had woken up in my absence and were milling about. I walked into the kitchen, placed my bag on the counter, and went to the refrigerator to find the butter I had purchased a few days earlier. Opening the disorganized fridge, I began moving other volunteers' leftovers, some of them spoiled, and searched for the gold foil-wrapped butter on which I had written my name. Writing your name on your food didn't guarantee someone else wouldn't eat it but rather increased the moral weight against doing so. Condiments and ingredients were almost always a lost cause over the long-term, as other volunteers would 'borrow a little,' thinking it wouldn't be missed. When repeated, your food slowly disappeared. Luckily, I found my butter intact.

I searched for a clean pan and spatula to cook my eggs, indignantly standing in front of a sink filled with others dishes. *People, wash your damn dishes*, I thought. I found a good pan and spatula, one of the few non-warped pans with a handle and non-melted spatulas, and cleaned them.

I cleaved off a hunk of butter and tossed it into the pan. On the counter sat three unattended onions with no indication of who, if anyone, laid claim to them. It was an unwritten rule that certain areas of the house were grab areas. Leaving something there meant that you were saying, 'take and use this if you want to.'

I grabbed a large onion, sliced it, and tossed it into the hot liquid butter with a sizzle and set a battered, partially filled, tin kettle on a back burner for my coffee. After the onions were limp and translucent, I added five whisked eggs to the pan, quickly folded the rapidly cooking mixture over itself with the spatula, and left them to set while I took off the boiling water for my two packages of instant coffee. I transferred my eggs to a plate with my bread, added salt and pepper, and carried my breakfast back to my laptop.

Nothing had changed on Facebook since I last checked. I finished my eggs and buttered loaf of bread and began to drink my now cold coffee. As if being handed a surprise present, I lit up with excitement when I remembered I had bought cookies.

I opened up the first package and began to dunk each cookie into my coffee before popping the sodden, chocolate-filled biscuit into my mouth. I vacantly regarded my laptop as my hands created an assembly line, opening packages and moving cookies to my mouth. Opposite to the excitement of remembering the cookies, I was saddened when my right hand reached to open another package and found I had eaten them all.

I had managed to fill an hour since waking and could no longer sit idle in front of my computer. It would soon be time to head over to the office for the Close of Service ceremony and I needed to get dressed in something nicer than gym shorts and a t-shirt. Getting ready didn't take as long as I imagined, and I found myself at 7:15 a.m., searching for a way to bide my time.

I wonder what will be said during the ceremony.

I had seen several ceremonies of volunteers ending their service. They stood at the front of the room while the Country Director comments on the great work they did over their two years. Then Peace Corps staff members take turns talking and complimenting the volunteers on their hard work. Lastly, fellow volunteers take turns in congratulating their departing friends. The honored volunteers are then pinned with a Peace Corps pin and given a certificate declaring their status as a RPCV, Returned Peace Corps Volunteer, a title held in high esteem by those who achieved it, which often meant little to those outside the Peace Corps community. And with that, it's all over.

Sometimes the ceremony becomes very emotional. The event is an attempt to capture the significance of a volunteer's accomplishment, although kind words, a pin, and a piece of paper can never come close to encapsulating the enormity of a volunteer's service. No matter the status of one's community projects, completing two years of service is a massive success in its own right.

I wonder what will be said today in honor of my three friends.

I wonder what will be said at my ceremony.

I wonder if I will even have a ceremony.

As far as I knew it, I was HIV positive. Positive had been the result of the first test. Yes, it was a screening test and I had to wait for conclusive results, but for the time being the sole indicator pointed to positive. If the second test came back to confirm the results of the first test, I could no longer stay in Burkina Faso. I would have to be medically evacuated to the United States and medically separated from the Peace Corps. This was standard procedure for medical issues. I assumed there wouldn't be a COS. I would return to the U.S., and my service would be over, but it would be because of a medical issue rather than finishing my service. Did this completely negate my past two years?

What about my years to follow if I was HIV positive? I wanted to be optimistic, yet I also wanted to make sure I had an idea of what to expect, a plan to deal with the changes.

How was my life going to change if I was HIV positive?

I knew that a lot of advances had been made in the management of HIV/AIDS. The drugs had radically improved since HIV first entered the social lexicon in the 80's. It would be possible for me to manage this disease. Who knew how medicine would continue to advance? Some things in my life, however, would be radically different.

What would HIV prevent me from doing? I asked myself.

I didn't know if I could continue to practice karate. I definitely couldn't fight. Fighting was a risk to others. Cuts were common and my blood would be hazardous. The idea of losing karate hurt. Karate provided an adrenaline rush and an escape. During a fight, time seemed to slow. I could react without thinking and disconnect my body from my mind. Fighting was euphoric.

But as much as I enjoyed karate, I was more lover than fighter. How could I love someone if I had HIV? Could I allow myself to be loved? I wanted to find someone to spend my life with. How was that going to be possible? They would have to have HIV.

What types of people have HIV? Such negative stigmas surround those three letters; I couldn't imagine that my dream girl would be HIV positive.

Were there online dating groups? There had to be.

I felt alone. Empty.

"Tyler, you ready to walk over?" asked Andy.

"Yeah. I'm ready."

At the Peace Corps office, the downstairs meeting room was filled with volunteers and staff members. Melissa, Kate, and Chris were introduced and their past two years of accomplishments were recounted. They had been amazing volunteers. They had been amazing friends.

The floor was opened to others to congratulate these three volunteers on their service. Staff member after staff member expressed different variations of 'it was a pleasure to work with you' and told personal stories.

After the staff members had finished speaking, it was customary for other volunteers to offer praise. No one moved forward to speak.

"Would any volunteers like to say something?" asked Rick, our Director of Management and Operation.

One of us needed to say something, but we were hesitant. We all had plenty to say, these were our close friends over the past two years. We, however, were sad to see them leave. Many had already teared up.

Finally, I stepped forward. "I'll speak."

One by one, I talked about Kate, Melissa, and Chris. I congratulated them on their service and spoke to the unique friendships I shared with each of them. As I searched for the right words to express the sincere respect I held for them, I avoided looking directly at Kate, Melissa, and Chris.

"I can speak for our group as a whole when I say that it was an extreme pleasure to serve alongside the three of you," I said as I began to close my brief speech, when my eyes met Kate's and I felt an upsurge of emotion. My voice quivered as I uttered, "Thank you."

No one else stepped forward to speak after me and the ceremony moved to pinning. Kate, Melissa, and Chris were each pinned with a Peace Corps Burkina Faso lapel pin, presented with their certificate of completion of Peace Corps service, and given a handshake. They had each completed the Peace Corps.

It all seemed a little lackluster. Two years of service, two years away from friends and family, and you get a few kind words, a lapel pin, piece of paper, and a handshake. Not exactly a sense of crowning achievement. Yet, since completing the Peace Corps is such a varied and personalized experience, carrying its own unique meaning for each volunteer, I don't know if there was a better way to celebrate.

I was confident that no one had the same service as me.

Chapter 7

Second Test

While my friends filed out of the room and back to the house, I slid out from the group and headed to the second floor, to Crystal's office for my second HIV test.

I left her office less than 24 hours ago, yet it felt as if weeks had passed, many sleepless weeks where I hadn't told anyone else. Weeks of faking that I was okay. How much longer would I have to wait to know for sure?

Again, I knocked on Crystal's plush padded door, before remembering that it was virtually sound proof. Opening it slightly, I called out, "Crystal?"

"Tyler, come in," she replied with nervous and startled tone.

I moved into her office and took my place. "So…" I started and faded away.

"Yes. First, how are you? Are you doing okay?" asked Crystal.

"Yes. Fine"—a fucking lie, but would it be worth unraveling the mess going through my mind? No. "Are we ready for the blood test?" I replied.

"Yes. We've confirmed with the WHO lab at the Ouaga hospital that they can run the second test. Let's go to the exam room, and we can draw a sample," she said as we both stood up in unison. I could sense that Crystal had an equally sleepless night.

I took my place on the exam table as Crystal rolled a stainless steel cart over to my side. She had already laid out the supplies. Rubber band, alcohol swab, needle, vial, gauze, and medical tape. I extended my left arm out to Crystal. I studied my arm, scanning back and forth, examining the blue veins below the surface of my skin. I looked up to see Crystal working her hands into a pair of blue nitrile gloves. The sharp pop of the glove rang in my mind, accentuating the importance of the gloves, a separation between Crystal's skin and mine. She wrapped the rubber band around my lower bicep, opened an alcohol swab, and began to prep my arm. I watched the cold, clean wipe prepare my skin for the needle.

"Ready?" asked Crystal.

"Yes," I responded. I opened and closed my fist several times and clinched hard to pump up my veins.

Crystal picked up the needle and snapped off the translucent green cap. As the needle drew close to my arm, I looked up and away, over Crystal's shoulder with an unfocused stare to the wall behind her. I felt the stick and slow glide of the thin metal rod into my arm. With one hand holding the needle in place, she reached for the purple-capped vial and in one swift motion snapped the vial to the needle while removing the rubber band from my arm.

"Okay?"

"Yes," I replied.

My unfocused gaze moved from the back wall to my arm. I fixated on the stream of dark red blood spraying into the glass tube. When it was half full, Crystal unclicked the vial and placed it back on the stainless steel cart, next to the open sterile gauze packet that she picked up to cover the small puncture wound. She folded my forearm up to hold the bandage in place as she disposed of the needle. A strip of medical tape was then smoothed down across my arm to securely hold the gauze in place. It was done.

"Okay, that's it," said Crystal. "I'm going to send the sample with a driver to the hospital. Do you have any questions? Still doing okay?"

"I'm fine."—*I was not*—"How long will the results take?" I asked. I hoped that the response would be in hours.

"I don't know exactly."—*damnit*—"It could be this afternoon or tomorrow. It is hard to say with the WHO lab. They couldn't give me a clear answer. I wish I had more to tell you, Tyler," Crystal replied. She was trying.

"Okay, and you'll call me when you have the results?" I asked.

"As soon as we know, you'll know."

I also wanted to know what would happen after the results. But, there was no point in asking. There were two very different possibilities. One would instantly throw me back into normalcy. The other would send me home on the next available flight. I would have to wait.

I left Crystal's office and headed back to the transit house. I descended the stairs, each step a slow, plodding thud, once again thinking about everything and nothing at the same time. I didn't know if I could do another day of waiting, especially surrounded by other unknowing volunteers.

I wanted to be alone, but there was no avoiding the transit house and other people. I was in the capital and had few options for privacy. If not in the transit house, I would be wandering the dusty, busy streets of Ouagadougou.

In the last hour, the house had come alive. All but a few volunteers were awake. People staring at laptops or reading American pop culture magazines received in care packages filled the couches in the living room. I could hear the clanking of pots and pans in the kitchen as people made some variation of eggs, bread, and coffee. Many volunteers couldn't get eggs in their villages, and they savored the opportunity to eat something different. If not eggs, cereal was another option. The cereal in Burkina, however, had always disappointed me.

Four dollars, which was a lot of money, bought a small box of generic cereal. Milk cost another three dollars. For seven dollars total, you could make two or three bowls of cereal. But something was always off with the cereal. Either stale or poorly made, it didn't match the overly sweet, crisp cereal of America—it fell short of Cinnamon Toast Crunch.

One dollar for three eggs, half a buttered baguette, and a packet of instant coffee was a much better deal.

Fortunately, I had eggs in my village. Each week, I would walk to a small shop and buy a flat of 30 eggs for five dollars. When getting eggs, I took a back road from my house to the shop, which passed through the rice fields and past very few other houses in village. Not only the shortest path, but the back road also helped me avoid heckling.

As Peace Corps Volunteers, we weren't paid a lot. Relative to our surroundings, however, we were rich. My diet of 30 eggs a week was one sign of my wealth.

Each month, Peace Corps deposited $240 into my bank account, and each month I traveled to Bobo and withdrew $200 for the month and left $40 to save for a future vacation. With no rent or utilities to pay, I budgeted $40 a week for all my expenses, which were mostly food. I bought fresh produce and meat every day. I spent without concern on Sundays, the main market day, when I stocked up on cashews, avocados, and sourdough bread that I could find nowhere else in the country.

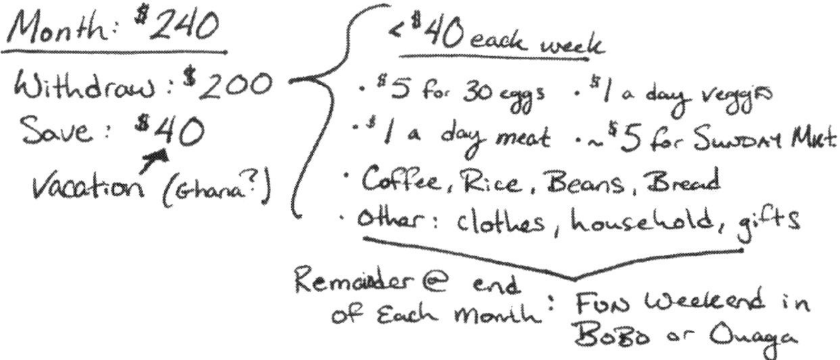

Once the week was over, I put any remaining money back into my general fund and withdrew another $40 for the next week. I never overspent or dipped into next week's funds. I had more than enough. After the month was over, I would have $60 or more left. I would then head back to Bobo with my monthly surplus and withdrawal next month's money. While in Bobo, over the course of three days, I would spend the remaining $60 on souvenirs, pizza, fries, burgers, and beer. In village, $40 a week was more than enough for me. It was excessive: $40 was enough to feed some families in Burkina Faso for a week, a country where more than 70% of the population lives on less than $2 a day. Less than two dollars a day for food, transportation, medicine, school fees, house repairs, and clothing.

Each week, after I bought my five-dollar flat of eggs, I would slowly walk back down the dirt road to my house, carefully carrying the cardboard carton. It was inevitable that I would pass someone along the way who would hassle me for an egg.

"Give me an egg."

"Are those for me?"

"Cook me some eggs."

"Where are my eggs?"

They said all of this in good humor. I would try to play along and tell them that these were my eggs or I would jokingly invite them to my house to eat eggs. This nearly weekly interaction, while veiled as a friendly jest, underlined an unavoidable truth. I had, they had not. Rather than dwell on the disparity, I had to compartmentalize it and keep it at arms' length.

I knew that I had more, that's why I was in the Peace Corps in the first place. At times I would be tempted to give out an egg to someone as I passed, but I resisted. I wasn't there to give handouts. I was there with an idealistic dream that I could teach and empower others, set a foundation for lasting change. Every day, good or bad, was an opportunity, an adventure, and a reminder of the abundant life I lived.

It was going to be a few hours until brunch. Kate, Melissa, and Chris were doing last-minute paperwork and heading to the artisan market to pick up last-minute souvenirs. Time passed slowly, making it difficult to quell the perilous internal dialogue.

I moved about the transit house, trying to kill both time and my thoughts. I sorted through the grab pile, the place where volunteers dropped off clothing and things that they brought to Burkina, had sent to them, or purchased and no longer wanted. The grab pile was the place for departing volunteers to unload everything they wouldn't be bringing back home. Things from the pile constituted half of my wardrobe and more than half of everything I owned. When I left the U.S., almost two years ago, everything I owned fit into two bags weighing a total of 72 lbs.

Peace Corps Packing List

- Hiking backpack
- Day backpack
- Duffle bag
- Quick dry polo shirts x 5
- T-shirts x 8
- Button-down shirt x 3
- Underwear x 8
- Socks x 5
- Hiking pants x 2
- Dress pants x 1
- Jeans x 1
- Shorts x 2
- Bathing suit x1
- Tie
- Hiking boots
- Teva sandals
- Leather loafers
- Dry bags x 4
- Ziploc bags
- Cash ($100)
- Rain jacket
- Hat
- Watch
- Pocketknife
- Multi-tool
- Kitchen knife
- Headlamp
- Towel
- Safety razor
- Razor blades
- Shave brush
- Shave mug
- Shave cream
- Soap
- Shampoo
- Beard trimmer
- Deodorant
- Photos
- Journals
- Bike helmet
- Toothbrush
- Toothpaste
- Floss
- Sunscreen
- Camera
- Video camera
- Laptop
- Kindle
- External hard-drive
- Unlocked smartphone
- Rechargeable batteries
- Bug Hut
- Sleeping bag
- Sleeping pad
- Camp cup
- Neck pillow
- Pens
- Sharpie
- Journals
- Passport

Searching through the pile, I found some rope, a travel power strip, and a small backpacking water filter that looked to be brand new. The thin, plastic rope was purchased in country. Volunteers, however, had brought the other two items to Burkina.

It was hard to know what you'd need for two years in the Peace Corps. You're going to be traveling for two years? Then it makes sense to bring a travel power strip. Until you remember that most of the country has no electricity and you own four electronics, which you discover will spend the majority of your service uncharged.

Traveling to Africa to live in a remote West African village? Then it makes sense to bring a small hand pump water filter. Until you arrive in country and Peace Corps gives you a large tabletop water filter, which is much more efficient that what you brought, and you find that you can purchase clean bags or bottles of water at every roadside stand. The water is likely warm and has a funny taste, but it won't make you sick.

I brought several things with me to Burkina that didn't make sense. One was a sleeping bag rated for 25 degrees Fahrenheit, to a country that regularly saw 115-degree days. Most of my nights were spent either under a thin sheet or with no sheet at all, always with my small fan running, blowing warm air over my sweating body.

But, I thought I needed the rope, power strip, and water filter. I could use the rope in village, in my garden. While not practical in country, I could take the power strip and water filter back to the U.S.

While sorting through my canteen, a collection of things kept in the capital and mostly found in the grab pile, Caroline passed by.

"Tyler, are we still good for tomorrow?" asked Caroline.

"Yes, works for me. What time?" I asked.

"11? No need to be there too early. We'll arrive around lunch."

"Perfect. I'll call ahead to remind them. I don't know if my Dad understood me the first time."

Tomorrow, Caroline and I were visiting the host families we stayed with during training. These were the families we lived with during our first three months in country. The three months filled with language barriers, confusion, loneliness, and many midnight dashes to the latrine, hoping to make it in time while not tripping over a sleeping goat on the way.

For Peace Corps training, each training group stayed in the same village with individual host families. Monday through Friday, 8:00 a.m. to 4:00 p.m., my fellow volunteers and I trained at the training center in Ipelce. Each day we had a mix of language classes, technical training, cultural lessons, safety and security sessions, and overall guidance on how to serve our future host communities as volunteers.

Given that we were to work with farmers, we spent a lot of time learning about agriculture and running a small business in Burkina. On weekends, we were free to explore and experience village life with our host families.

Over three months of training, we learned the language, came to better understand daily life in village, built friendships with other volunteers, and became accustomed to the food—or learned that some foods were never going to agree with us.

I looked forward to seeing my former host family but had reservations. I hadn't seen them since I finished training and moved to a new village. Additionally, I had done a poor job of keeping in touch. I rarely called.

I was also hesitant about going with Caroline. Had I contracted HIV from her?

I looked down to my watch. It was 15 minutes until my second doctor's visit today. While it only took five minutes to walk to the medical unit, I left early. I needed to leave the transit house and change my surroundings. Sadly, however, my thoughts would be coming with me. I grabbed my ID from the guard at the front gate of the house, slid my ID under the glass window at the office, and climbed the stairs to the second-floor medical unit.

I checked in with the receptionist and sat alone in a row of chairs outside the office. Across from the row of chairs hung a bulletin board covered in medical posters and fliers.

Have an issue with your Peace Corps medical team? Report concerns to Peace Corps HQ at 1-888-…

Don't forget to take your malaria prophylaxis. Symptoms of Malaria: headache, fever, fatigue, muscle pain, chills, sweating, dry cough, nausea, and vomiting.

Safe Sex: Condom Use. When should condoms be used? Condoms should be used EVERY time you engage in sexual intercourse. Why use a condom? … HIV/AIDS…

"Mr. Lloyd?" Dr. Patel appeared in the doorway, holding my medical file and saving me from my thoughts. "Are you ready?"

"Yes," I replied.

I assumed that I would be seeing Crystal again since I had been seeing her the past few days. But, it was Dr. Patel who performed the first part of my medical exam, reviewed my Peace Corps medical history, and conducted a head to toe physical and several blood tests.

Dr. Patel opened my file, scanned over the paperwork, and sat it down on the counter as I seated myself on the exam table, atop the crinkling paper.

"First, let's check your TB test," Dr. Patel said.

I extended my left arm, exposing my inner forearm and the tiny bump that had formed from the TB test. Dr. Patel held my arm, quickly examined the test, and said that I was all clear for tuberculosis. That was a relief. Dr. Patel moved back to my records, documented my test results and started running his finger down lines of a report.

"Tyler, we got your other results back, and everything else is fine," Dr. Patel casually stated.

"My *other* results?" I questioned. I knew he didn't mean my HIV test, given the nonchalant way he said it. He meant the other test they had run, from my first round of blood samples. *Right? That's what he meant? Right?*

"Yes, the other tests we ran," replied Dr. Patel. At this point, he was avoiding the topic of my HIV tests.

"Your white blood cell and platelet levels are good. Kidney and liver function are fine. Your cholesterol is great," reported Dr. Patel as he flipped back and forth between pages clipped into the file folder in his hand.

"That's good to hear about my cholesterol. I've been eating 30 eggs a week and a plate of goat or pork almost every day," I replied. I had a reason for concern after two years of eating 120 eggs a month and countless plates of crispy grilled fat.

"Dr. Patel, have you heard anything about my tests from this morning? My HIV test?" I finally asked.

"No, we sent the sample off this morning with a driver, but have not heard back from the lab yet. I'm not worried, Tyler. In all my 20 years of being a PCMO, I have never had an HIV positive case. I've had three false positives before, but never an HIV positive case. I'm not worried."

"Okay, thanks."

While it was meant to be comforting, his reassurance did nothing for me. Because something hasn't happened in 20 years, doesn't mean it can't happen. Even though I knew it to be wrong, I began to quickly tell myself that the probability of a positive case would increase over time, in the absence of another positive case. That's how the numbers worked, right?

Again, I began to rationalize that I was HIV positive. I reasoned that if you were flipping a coin over and over, and it landed on heads 10 times in a row, there was a much greater chance of the 11th flip landing on tails because overall it had to be 50/50. While I knew each flip was a discrete event, independent of past outcomes, I couldn't help but feel that I was the 11th flip.

People have contracted HIV in the Peace Corps, it was very possible. How many people had Dr. Patel cared for over the years? What number was I?

We finished my exam by reviewing all the medical authorization forms that I would receive at the end of my service. Those forms would entitle me to Peace Corps insured medical care back in the U.S., for medical conditions that developed over the past two years of service. I would get one form to update my glasses prescription, another form to fix several broken teeth, and a final form to see a dermatologist about several questionable moles that appeared under the hot West African sun.

The Peace Corps is supposed to care for returned volunteers who are injured or became ill during service. Would I need ongoing medical treatment? Was this a potential silver lining of possibly being HIV positive? At least the Peace Corps would take care of me. I knew I shouldn't have been thinking it, but there was no suppressing my thoughts.

I thanked Dr. Patel and slowly walked back the short distance to the transit house. He said that I shouldn't be worried, but I was.

Kate, Melissa, and Chris returned to the house, and it was finally time to start cooking brunch. We were having French toast, another variation on eggs and bread. A few volunteers held coveted bottles of real maple syrup, an extreme luxury. Since Melissa was leaving this afternoon, she offered her syrup for brunch.

Those of us who liked to cook formed an assembly line in the kitchen. We created stations whisking eggs, soaking bread, and manning the stove. I stood at the four-burner gas stove, frying the egg-soaked toast in butter, moving back and forth between the four best pans in the kitchen.

As I moved from pan to pan, flipping browning toast, I continually adjusted the flames of each burner as they fluctuated on their own. When lighting the stove at the transit house, or even my tiny stove in village, I hesitated. Given the questionable construction of the stoves, you felt there was a good chance of blowing yourself up. The old stove at the transit house even had a sign warning volunteers not to light the stove while the oven was running. It was uncertain how this was known to be a problem, but it fanned the flames of our fear that we might burn the house down.

Plates of French toast left the kitchen as fast as we could make them and were consumed equally as fast. After I had made more than half, I traded cooking duties for my turn to eat. I found an open spot at one of our two large tables and quickly devoured my plate. I was hungry. Very hungry. After everyone had eaten, I returned for a second round. I ate this plate slower, trying to savor each bite of the golden brown eggy bread.

In village, I made French toast every Sunday. Using the spongy sourdough bread that could only be found on Sundays in my market, I made one of two styles of French toast, either sweet or savory. I topped the sweet version with maple-extract, simple syrup in addition to bananas and toasted coconut, which were both plentiful in my village. I topped the savory version with sautéed onions, garlic, and spinach that were cooked down with a bit of cumin and a Maggi bouillon cube, packed with salt and MSG.

I was still hungry after finishing my second plate of food. I could not satiate my appetite. I knew why I was hungry. I was nervously eating, trying to find pleasure in food. Enough pleasure to further cover up the pain I was keeping suppressed inside. Ever since hearing the results of my first HIV test yesterday, I hadn't stopped moving. I had to keep myself occupied, try to stay one step ahead of my thoughts.

For more than 24 hours, Andy was the one other person who

knew. Everyone else, unaware, acted as they typically would, which was for the best. The sense of normalcy around me helped to ground my thoughts. If they knew, they would have treated me differently, looked at me and wondered. I would catch side-glances. They'd go out of their way to check in on me, to make sure that I was ok. I did not need that now.

For all I knew, I was fine. There was no reason to let others know. Once my blood tests came back, I could let people know. Until then, it was my burden. I would tell no one. Except Andy. Except Kate.

After my third plate of food, I had to cut myself off. I would be ill if I kept going.

I planned to talk to Kate after brunch. Realizing what I had to do, I began to panic. How would I tell her? Where would I tell her? What would I say? How would she react? Was I going to completely devastate her, ruin her last day?

I hadn't shown any emotion since I heard the news yesterday. While I felt sad, angry, and confused, I kept those feelings below the surface. Talking with Kate, however, I would have to open up and confront my feelings. Unlike Andy, she would not be a third party observer to the situation. There was, after all, a reason I had to tell her.

I found Kate packing her bags on a lower bunk bed. No one was around, but we couldn't talk in the transit house. We wouldn't be alone for long.

"Hey, Kate. How are you doing? Are you all ready?"

"Almost done packing. It feels a bit surreal."

"I bet. Do you have time to talk? Privately? I wanted a chance to talk before you left."

"Sure, we can talk now. Go for a walk?"

"Perfect."

We left the transit house and headed down the dusty, paved road. I wanted to find a place to sit, away from the house and off a side street where another volunteer would not pass by. As we walked, we talked about today, her COS ceremony, and reminisced about her service. I kept the conversation rolling with light, off-topic subjects, trying to build up my confidence. I had to make a conscious effort to take my eyes off my feet and to look at Kate. I was trying to remain calm, preparing myself for the conversation to come.

Turning onto another street, I saw two concrete blocks sitting under a tree. This would be the best place I would find. I asked Kate to sit under the tree with me. I sensed concern. Why exactly I had wanted to talk to her? Why did it need to be in private?

I assumed she thought that I only wanted time alone before she left because I was going to miss her, maybe admit my love for her.

But I told her I tested positive for HIV.

I told her about the results of my medical exam, that I had another test run, the results of which I was waiting on. I gave her the facts and avoided looking her in the eyes until I was done. I told her that Andy was the one other person who knew, besides Crystal and Dr. Patel.

Once finished, I looked up at Kate. She sat there, looking back at me concerned. Concerned, but not for herself. Concerned for me. She asked if I was doing okay, and tried to comfort me. She said she was glad that I told her, but I couldn't help feeling that she missed the point. I was telling her that I had tested positive for HIV because we had slept together. I didn't want to alarm her, but I wanted her to be aware before she flew home, so she could know and act accordingly.

As we continued to talk, I tried to indirectly express my concern. Kate told me that her HIV test came back negative. That was good to hear, but my mind could not ignore the fact that if done early enough, a screening test could be too weak to catch HIV. Or, maybe her test was a false negative. I, however, did not offer up these ideas to Kate. I was trying to keep my hopes up and believe my first test was wrong. I did not need to plant seeds of doubt into someone else's mind.

Kate and I walked back to the transit house together. I did it. I told her, and I felt emptier than before. She returned to packing, her mind likely adrift, and I withdrew back to my computer, trying desperately to find anything to keep me from thinking.

A temptation to research HIV/AIDS pulled at the back of my mind, enticing me to look up the likelihood of a false positive, or the possibility of a false negative. I resisted. I had to remain in the moment and not speculate. There would be no point in torturing myself with any more than I already knew. My second test would come back and then I would know. Then I could research.

My phone buzzed on the table and I looked down to see "Dr.

Patel, PCMO" on the black and white pixelated screen of my Nokia. The doctor was calling. I picked up my phone and answered as I quickly moved out of the room and downstairs to the first-floor volunteer lockers.

"Hello, Dr. Patel?"

"Hello, Tyler. How are you?"

"I'm good…"

"I wanted to let you know that we got the results back. Negative. Your tests were negative for HIV," said Dr. Patel. The word negative hung in the air.

"Negative?" the word seemed thick and palpable in my mouth.

"Yes. The lab called me to tell me the results, and I called you when I got off the phone with them. You're okay, Tyler."

I was more than okay. "So, no need to worry?" I asked. I wanted to be sure that this was over.

"I was never worried, Tyler. I've been a Peace Corps PCMO for more than twenty years, and I have never had a case of HIV. I have had three volunteers have false positives, but I have never had a case of HIV. I wasn't worried. I told Crystal it would be okay. You're okay, Tyler."

"Thank you."

I finished the call with Dr. Patel and found myself standing alone in the middle of the room I had been pacing in. The second test was negative. I was not HIV positive. I was okay.

At that moment, the many emotions and feelings I had compressed began to unravel. An explosion of energy and emotion surged through my veins. My hands were shaking and I wanted to cry. Negative. The word still felt heavy in my mouth.

What now? For the past day my mind had constantly been running, thinking, planning. I had scoped out two different potential realities, one where I would live a life as HIV positive and another where I would make the most of the scare. Even though I tried not to think, I had continuously been processing both what I knew to be true, plus a growing number of panicked fabrications. I was beginning to tell myself that if I was HIV positive, I had contracted it from Caroline, who contracted it from another volunteer, who had contracted it from someone in his village. I was certain that this was how I got HIV. But I was not HIV positive. I was negative.

As much as a positive test result had thrust me into a frenzy of overthinking, delusion, and a torrent of emotions that I fought to restrain, a negative test result reset me back to where I had been yesterday morning, before Anna walked into the room and told me that Crystal was trying to get in touch with me. It was as if I suddenly woke up from a dream.

My eyes opened and I found myself in the volunteer cubby room at the transit house. How did I get here? As I played back the previous day, both reality and my thoughts, they didn't seem real. I was both numb and emotional. Energized and completely drained. What now?

I had to tell Andy and Kate.

I bounded up the stairs to the second floor of the house with a newly found liveliness to my stride. Unable to find Andy, I asked another volunteer if he had seen him. Andy was out. I couldn't wait until he got back to unload the weight of the good news. I took out my phone and wrote him, *Test came back. Negative. NEGATIVE. I AM OK.*

Minutes later, Andy wrote back, *CONGRATULATIONS! Glad to hear it, buddy. See you in a bit.*

I was beaming at this point. I felt that I had overcome some significant hurdle, a physical challenge that I had labored against for days, weeks, even months, while in actuality, I had only kept myself, with the help of Andy, from outwardly falling apart for a day due to something false. But, it felt like much more.

Worrying has a way of growing, feeding off of itself in a negative feedback loop of despair and becoming something material that builds up walls that trap you inside of yourself. Those walls were gone now. I was free.

Kate. I had to tell Kate. I was ecstatic that I could tell her the good news before she left. Now, I wished I hadn't told her in the first place. Yet, I hadn't known I would get the results, good results, before she left. I did the right thing.

I found Kate in the hall and stopped her there. She could read the happiness radiating from me.

"I got the results. They were negative. I'm fine," I quickly announced.

"Tyler, that is amazing. I'm happy to hear that. I am glad that you are okay," Kate said with a brimming smile.

"Thank you, Kate," I said and paused, "Can I have a hug?"

"Yes, of course!" said Kate as she moved in to wrap her arms around my waist.

It felt good to touch someone. To have her close, feel the warmth of her body, and to know it was going to be okay. With a last tight embrace, we separated.

As we parted and walked away, my phone vibrated in my pocket. I had a text. It was from Crystal. *I heard the good news. I am so relieved and happy. I hope you are well!*

I smiled at my phone and replied, *Thank you. I am very well.*

Kate, Melissa, and Chris watched their luggage be strapped to the top of a white Peace Corps Land Cruiser, preparing to leave for the airport. Tomorrow evening, they'd each be back home, in different states, celebrating with different sets of loved ones. Two years of living in Burkina Faso was coming to a close.

I had a little more than two months left and I knew they would fly by. There was much I wanted to do. I would attempt to fit in as many last-minute adventures as possible. I would be wrapping up my projects in my village. I would savor the remaining conversations with my village friends and family. At this point, I knew I wanted to return to Burkina Faso to visit and return to my village. I, however, didn't know when that would happen and realized the truth that most volunteers never go back.

For most, American life gets in the way. Soon after landing back in the U.S., priorities begin to shift. Long lazy days in village turn to busy daily schedules, segmented into 30-minute blocks. Returned volunteers start graduate school, start jobs, and start families. Friends and family in your village, who you talked to every day for two years, are now only reachable by expensive long distance phone calls. With time, weekly calls back to village become monthly, then bimonthly, to major holidays, or cease to exist altogether, even though you think of them every day.

While a volunteer always carries with them the memories and impact of the Peace Corps, it becomes their past. Over the months and years after serving abroad, returned volunteers reunite with fellow volunteers and reminisce about their service, waxing poetically about the good times and finding humor in bad times, or neglecting to recall them all together. Kate, Melissa, and Chris would likely never come back to Burkina Faso. Tonight, their plane would take off and that would be it—their Peace Corps service, over.

Everyone in the house poured outside onto the street to say goodbye to the three returning volunteers. I said farewell to my friends, wished them luck, and moved to the outer edge of the group. I stood back, watching the smiles, tears, hugs, and promises of "when I get back, I'm coming to visit you." After the previous day, it was overwhelming to be amongst the many emotions. I still hadn't recovered from the panicked physiological state I had been thrust into, nor would I fully return to normal for many weeks, possibly months. How was I going to move forward from this point? What lessons could I learn? How, if at all, would this change me?

The Peace Corps car pulled away, as the remaining volunteers waved their final goodbyes. Each of us left standing on the side of the road would finish our service and be driven in a white Peace Corps car to the airport. For some, it would be weeks, for others, years.

Back in the transit house, I was filled with nervous energy. I had confided in Andy and Kate. No one else knew. My fellow volunteers were oblivious. My friends back home were unaware. My family, none the wiser.

Now that I had the last results and knew that I would be okay, I wanted to tell someone. More than anything, I wanted to be acknowledged for what had happened. I had never been more scared in my life. I had never been more fearful of my death.

What would typically amount to months of emotion and internal dialogue had been compressed into a day. I now needed to decompress and unburden myself from what felt like a rock, a boulder, in the pit of my stomach. The events were too fresh and I too emotional to convey in person what I felt. I needed to write it out and put words on paper or, in my case, on my computer screen. I sat down at one of the large wooden tables and began to write.

Words poured out, but immediately after I completed a sentence, I would highlight and delete the passage, unable to accurately compose my thoughts.

I focused on my screen, trying for the first time to put into words what it felt like to test positive for HIV. What it felt like to hide my fear from everyone else around me. What it felt like to get my second test results and the emotions that were triggered by the word, "negative."

A volunteer sharing the table with me noticed my deep concentration and the deliberateness with which I typed.

"Tyler, what are you working on?"

I looked up to see Justin sitting across from me and replied, "I'm working on a blog post. Actually, could you read it when I'm done?"

"Uh, sure," he replied. I wanted other volunteers to know. I felt that each additional person that knew would be another person to unload my pent-up emotions upon and help me to relieve the tension I felt inside.

I finished writing, reviewed my work, and sat back, more relieved than when I had started. Now, all I had to do was to hit the publish button. I hesitated.

Was this right?

What would people think?

It didn't matter. I had to share. With an assured click, I published the account of my scare, posted the link on Facebook, and asked my friends to read it.

Within minutes, friends began to respond.

'Great post, Tyler' – undergraduate counselor

'This one scared me for a bit' – one of my best friends

'Damn. That's surreal; glad you came out ok. I almost need a beer from reading it' – friend from karate

'Holy cow, man. That made me sick at my stomach worrying for you there. I'm glad everything is okay!' – an old roommate

'Oh, Tyler...that is one of the scariest things anyone can ever be told. It's is good that the confirmation test was negative...but I'd say still get tested once more when you get back stateside to be sure. While we are finding that it is no longer an absolute death sentence (patients have it for 30-40 yrs. now and end up dying from something completely unrelated), it is still a major life-changing problem. Scary, scary thing...' – a friend who is an E.R. nurse

'I'm glad you're alright, Tyler. Let me know when you're in town.' – a high school friend

'That was a rough read. I'm not feeling well. Super glad you're okay!' – another old roommate

'Glad you're ok! I know it was scary, but 1 in 100 HIV screening tests give a false positive.' – friend in pharmacy school

'Wow. Just...wow. Tyler. I'm so happy you're OK, but even if you weren't, I hope you know that I wouldn't love you any less. <3 I hope others can learn from your experience and continue to talk about HIV and AIDS so that it becomes less stigmatized. The disease itself deserves pariah status, not the person.' – a wise friend

'What the fuck man!' – Kyle, my brother

'Call me.' – Kyle, my brother, again

'Holy shit! Yes, call your brother!' – a fraternity brother

I didn't even think about letting my brother or parents know first. What would I have told them anyway? "I thought I was HIV positive, but I'm not." That would quickly turn into a conversation that I did not want to have. Now that I had broadcast the fact to the world, I had to contact Kyle.

Me: *Hey, are you online? My smartphone isn't charged.*

Kyle: *Yeah, I'm home. Positive you don't have HIV?*

Me: *Yes.*

Kyle: *Damn. I was scared for a minute into your blog. Have you told Mom?*

Me: *No. Can you call her and warn her and Dad before they read that?!*

Kyle: *Yeah. She's going to freak and want you home. I'll call now.*

Tyler: *Thanks. The second test was sent to a WHO lab. I'm fine. It's just that the tests sometimes have false positives.*

Friends continued to comment on my post and express how happy they were that I was okay. The comments, however, weren't helping me feel better about the situation. I still felt uneasy. Nervous. Confused.

Needing to move, I got up to get water from the kitchen, where I found Justin. Maybe if he read my post I would get more of what I was looking for, a sense of closure and acceptance.

Justin sat back down at the table in front of my laptop. I walked away, back into the kitchen to pace and wait for him to finish reading.

Yesterday, I was told I tested positive for HIV.

I was called into the doctor's office, after having blood drawn for my Peace Corps end-of-service physical, and was told I tested positive for HIV.

I sat there still, hearing the words be replayed in my head. I was told I tested positive for HIV.

How? The doctor asked if I had taken part in any potentially risky behaviors. Unprotected sex? Sex with high-risk partners? Intravenous drug use?

Then the doctor said, "Maybe it was your cut that was stitched in the local hospital…if sterile material wasn't used. It's unlikely, but I don't know. Tyler, are you okay? You're not reacting how I thought you would, how I would. What are you thinking? Do you have any questions?"

I had no questions. Then I had a million questions and was unable to process anything. I had tested positive for HIV.

Today, I was told that the first test was a false positive. A second more extensive test declared that I was negative for HIV. Some people see their life flash before their eyes, snapshots of their past when they have a near-death experience. I had this happen once, in middle school, when I stepped out in front of a bus and had the bus shoot past me, inches away. This time, however, I slowly saw my future life be projected in front of me. What was going to happen? How would I now live my life?

I spent 24 hours on edge, planning a new life. Preparing to manage a disease that would eventually claim my life. With the end more seemingly near, I began to be more aware of the present. As all this reflection was taking place behind my eyes, I was keeping this a secret from all but one person in whom I had confided for support and guidance.

You have no idea how much HIV/AIDS can come up in conversation. Three different times last night HIV/AIDS was jokingly brought up. A Mickey Avalon song. A volunteer humorously commenting that they were clean, as confirmed by their end-of-service medical exam. My exam did not yield the same results. I sat there smiling, laughed, and died inside.

I was going to die. I thought I was going to die. We all know we're going to die but one's end is normally not so present.

As I said already, today, I was told the first test was a false positive. I don't have HIV. I don't have HIV. When I heard the news, every emotion I had been keeping at bay sprang forth at once. My life had been reset. Renewed. I couldn't stand. My heart raced and I felt clean, healthy blood, life, be pumped out and back from the crown of my head to my toes.

In 24 hours, I processed more than I have in months. I discovered what was important to me and was surprised by what immediately fell off my radar once I was confronted with a life-altering challenge. I could go on about what I realized in this deeply trying experience, but I want to keep things short. I want to take this renewed energy and run with it.

And more urgently, I'm going to get a beer.

Unable to wait and pace in the kitchen any longer, I walked back into the other room as Justin looked up from my computer. His blank stare mirrored the dull reserve I had felt inside while waiting for my second test results.

"Tyler, let's go get a drink," said Justin.

As Justin and I left the house, we ran into another volunteer who we asked to join us for beers down the street. While we walked down the dusty path to the restaurant, the three of us barely talked. If I were paying attention, I would have sensed the tension created by Justin not knowing what to say, especially in front of the volunteer who was not yet aware of what had happened. I, however, walked on naïvely, electrified by the news that I was healthy.

Outside the restaurant, slightly removed from the road, we sat around an unlevel, painted metal table, on equally unlevel plastic chairs, drinking our cold beers. A little more than $1 could buy three-fourths of a liter of extremely light beer. It wasn't good, but it was beer and it was cold.

I told the new volunteer about my HIV scare. She reacted in shock, as my other friends had. I dug a little deeper into the past day but remained unable to entirely describe all that I thought, all that I felt and didn't feel. The conversation moved away from me, which it should have. More than talk about the past day, I wanted to talk with people who merely acknowledged what I had gone through but didn't dwell on it.

My phone vibrated on the metal table, against the green glass bottle of my first and now empty beer. Heather had sent me a message.

"How are you doing? Did you learn any more from the PCMOs today?" asked Heather.

I responded, telling Heather about the first HIV test and the second test that had come back negative. Immediately after I sent the message, Heather called me.

"What?" Heather demanded.

I walked away from the table and quickly retold my story. I stressed the fact that my second test came back negative. There was nothing to worry about.

"Are you sure? What if the second test was a false negative?" questioned Heather.

I hadn't considered that. For a brief second I began to feel sick and worry, but "No. I'm sure. The second test was a better test. I'm fine."

After finishing my brief call with Heather, I returned to our table to finish what remained of my second beer.

I was fine.

Chapter 8

May 31st – Ipelce

I propped myself up from my bottom bunk and scanned the room full of sleeping volunteers. Fans oscillated back and forth in an attempt to move the warm, heavy West African air. Kate, Melissa, and Chris would now be in the Brussels airport, waiting to board planes back to different U.S. cities. Their vacated beds had already been taken over by other volunteers.

The two previous days were a challenge I would never accurately capture with words. I had written a blog post that scared friends and family back home, but it didn't do the experience justice. It didn't have to though.

Today, I was visiting the family I stayed with during my first three months of Peace Corps' training. They were an amazing host family, but I hadn't done a good job of keeping in touch after I completed training and moved to the village where I served. In the beginning, my host father, Jean-Claude, would call me every couple of weeks to check in. When I remembered, I called him to run through a list of basic greetings and pleasantries. I asked how he was doing, about the family, his work, the cornfields I worked in, the weather, and then about Ipelce, their village. Everything was always 'good.' Jean-Claude would return with the same questions and we would wish each other a good day, ask for blessings from God, and hang up.

I would have talked more, but this was nearly the extent of our shared language ability. Our simple exchange was enough though and it let them know I was well and hadn't forgotten them. But as time passed the period between calls grew wider. I kept telling myself that I would visit them again. I more than owed it to them for all they did to help me transition and become comfortable in Burkina Faso. I, nevertheless, hadn't made an honest effort to return.

With two months left in my service, opportunities were quickly disappearing. I honestly would not have visited if Caroline hadn't arranged to take a taxi today to visit her previous host family. Our families lived in different villages, but only separated by a 15-minute drive. I had no excuse not to join her, though I was a little worried about seeing them. I knew they would be happy to see me and surprised that I visited, but I felt ashamed that I had done such a poor job of keeping in touch.

Days before, I called my host Dad to make sure the family would be home. I wasn't exactly sure he understood me when I said I was coming to visit, but I knew they would be there even if I showed up unannounced.

Our taxi arrived at the transit house at 9:30 a.m., thirty minutes late. Caroline and I loaded our bikes into the back of Seydou's taxi. Seydou was one of two taxi drivers volunteers primarily used when in Ouaga. When possible, rather than flagging down a random taxi, we called ahead for Seydou or Ismael, the other taxi man, to come directly to the transit house. As volunteers, there were only so many different bars, restaurants, and shops we visited and these two drivers knew exactly where to take us.

Even better than knowing where to take us, we didn't have to barter over the price. Taxis in Burkina didn't have meters to calculate the fare. Once you flagged down a taxi driver and told him where you wanted to go, he would throw out a price. Like most things, this price was up for discussion. Also like most things in Burkina, there was a price for Burkinabé and a price for foreigners. The color of your skin or accent was a factor in the calculation of a fare. I hated fighting back and forth for a reasonable price, but I couldn't fault the taxi drivers.

Most foreigners in Burkina Faso weren't Peace Corps Volunteers. A foreigner getting into a taxi was likely naïve of the fair price and seemingly eager to hand over whatever price was asked of them. As a result, many Peace Corps Volunteers developed a disdain for other foreigners. We wanted to be different. We wanted to be respected and treated the same as a local, yet we were also naïve in thinking that was possible.

In Bambara, they say, "Jirikurun men o men ji la, a te ke bama ye" or "No matter how long a log stays in the water, it doesn't become a crocodile." Volunteers would always be slightly out of place in Burkina Faso. Rather than fight it, it was much better to come to terms with and accept the fact that we were different—a lesson applicable beyond the Peace Corps.

The ride to our host villages took an hour in the taxi. As we left the capital, the scenery transitioned to a mix of scrubland and farms. Buildings became one story and turned from cement block to traditional mud bricks.

Caroline was first dropped off at her training village. This was the third time she had come back to visit. When we pulled up to her house, two very happy women came to the taxi. The two women likely thought Caroline had brought back a husband for them to meet. They'd be disappointed to learn that I was only a friend

Seydou and I left Caroline with her host family and headed toward my training village. When we first passed my village, we missed the turn to my old house. The village didn't look the same. Something was different. The small buildings that lined the road had changed. On the second pass, we turned down the dirt road toward my family's home. Luckily, I could easily spot the massive mango tree outside their courtyard.

As we pulled up to their house, I saw a white girl sitting out front.

"Is that another volunteer?" asked Seydou.

"No, I don't know who that is," I replied. *Who the hell was at my host family's house?*

During site development, Peace Corps staff members worked with the community to screen and select host families. Before hosting a volunteer, host families were trained themselves in order to learn more about the Peace Corps and the needs of volunteers living abroad in a foreign village for the first time. During training, host families in Burkina Faso had to have at least one fluent French speaker in the household and have proper housing for the volunteer. Each volunteer was to be provided a private bedroom with a secure locking door, a window, and a cement floor. The host family also provided a bed, storage for clothing, and a small table. As volunteers in training, we ate breakfast and dinner with our host families, for which Peace Corps provided a stipend. Additionally, I heard rumor that host families also received a sizable sum of money at the end of training for successfully hosting a volunteer.

The taxi stopped under the shade of the large mango tree and I stepped out of the car while children ran up beaming with smiles.

"Tyler!" they shouted. They remembered me. I couldn't believe it.

Trailing behind the group of children, I saw my host brother Victor. He smiled wide, showing his broken front tooth.

"Welcome, Tyler!" greeted Victor.

"Thanks, Victor. How are you?" I returned.

"I'm well," said Victor still with a big smile. He was happy to see me. Victor and I had spent a lot of time together. In the evening, he would join me while I ate. At first, he would sit with me while I ate, and eat later with the family. With time, I got him to join me. It was tradition and respectful for guests and special groups to eat separately. In a traditional household, meals would be eaten by separate groups of men, women, and children. In polygamous families, it was normal for the head of the household to be served individually while his wives would each eat with their own children and not together. There was no large family meal enjoyed together, even during celebrations. I didn't like this. I wanted to eat with everyone and enjoy their company.

I scanned the group of children and spotted my two host sisters among the group. They had grown but still looked the same to me. The other kids were from surrounding households. These were the kids that stood on one another to look over the wall at the strange man in the neighboring courtyard. When I would look in the direction of their whispers, they would take off running and laughing. They were all happy to see me and I was already glad that I decided to visit.

I arranged to call Seydou when finished visiting with my family and he said he'd be in the village waiting for me.

As I unloaded my bike, the group of children rushed to help me wheel it toward the house.

"You got a new bike?" asked Victor.

He remembered my bike during training. My once brand new, black Trek mountain bike had now gone through hell and back. After being crammed into bus storage compartments and tied down atop vans, many parts had been scratched, bent, or snapped off and replaced. On top of the destructive transportation, there were numerous wrecks and the general wear of riding a bike across West Africa. It was no longer the shiny new bike Victor remembered.

My bike stayed back in Bobo though. It rarely made it to Ouaga now because I tried to keep the bike in working order. When in the capital, I used a loaner bike.

"No. This is another volunteer's bike. I didn't bring my bike with me to Ouaga," I replied to Victor. "Where are your mother and father, Victor?" I asked.

"My mother is at the orphanage and my father is in town. He's coming," replied Victor.

As we continued to the house, the white woman stood up from her chair while a young white man came out from the courtyard.

"Bonjour," I greeted.

"Bonjour à vous," they greeted in return.

They were volunteers working at the orphanage that my host mother helped run. I visited the orphanage only twice while staying with the family.

A tall chain-linked fence, suitable for a prison, enclosed the grounds of the orphanage. The housing for the kids was prison-like, below what would be acceptable for American inmates. During my stay with the family, I toured one of the housing blocks and saw the paint peeling from the wall in large sheets and the ceiling collapsing in some rooms or already completely given way in other areas.

Small children, babies even, ran or roamed the enclosed area. Not a blade of grass grew inside the orphanage's fence, long ago trodden down and killed by kids kept like livestock. The children were covered in the dirt that made up their yard. The workers of the orphanage stood watch, seemingly more as wardens and peacekeepers rather than caretakers. This was a broken system and could have served as the setting for a commercial where a pledge of a dollar a day would save a child. But I don't know if a dollar would have been enough.

The two visiting volunteers were brother and sister. They were staying with my previous host family, in my old room, while they worked at the orphanage for a month. I couldn't imagine sharing my old room in Ipelce with someone else. The room, an 8x8x8 foot cube, consisted of four cinderblock walls topped with a corrugated tin roof, large enough to fit a twin bed, a small metal canteen for clothing, and a short wooden table. At 6'3", this room was not appropriately sized for me, made most apparent by the small door that barely came past my shoulders. I knocked my head on that doorframe more than once during training. And, as if the room wasn't small enough, my host family asked that I keep my bike in the room at night for fear of theft. That wasn't going to happen though, so I chained the bike to a tree in the courtyard each evening.

In addition to being small, the room became unbearably hot. The size and construction of the room, under the hot African sun, turned the structure from a bedroom into a large solar oven. My first night with my host family would be remembered as the hottest, most sleepless night of my life. For 10 hours, I lay in bed, in a pool of sweat, under a mosquito net that kept bugs away and my body heat trapped close, listening to a cacophony of unknown sounds. I missed several things about training and Ipelce, but my bedroom was not one of them.

The brother and sister duo were working through a Canadian organization for a month. Given what I saw of international development, I didn't care for short-term volunteers. I appreciated the Peace Corps model much more.

In the Peace Corps, the first three months of service were for training, where you learned enough of the local language to get started, cross-cultural skills, and techniques related to your future field of work as a volunteer, as I did in Ipelce with this host family. After training, you become an official Peace Corps Volunteer and are sent to work in a community for two years. Two years is a long time, at least it seems that way at first, but having almost completed my two years, I could say it was almost not long enough. I spent nearly my whole first year running up against walls. I would hold meetings where no one would show up and learned that farmers didn't trust my agricultural advice because I was white and presumably grew up in a large city, having never seen a farm until Burkina. Every project I attempted fell flat on its face and exploded in a blaze of self-deprecating glory, leaving me to wonder what I was doing in Africa.

Suddenly, as if on a timer, my second year began and projects fell into my lap. Everything worked as planned. I owe my success to the first year where I lived in my village making friends and gaining the respect of the community. Once integrated and considered a fixture of my community, people were eager to listen, participate, and learn.

Along with short-term projects, I also grew to dislike projects built on the back of money. I saw these projects as handouts. The Peace Corps preaches a 'teach a man to fish' model of development and favors education and capacity building rather than the building and providing of physical goods.

What these two Canadian volunteers were doing wasn't development. It was aid. Those kids needed a handout though. They needed help. It takes a different kind of person to take on the type of work needed at the orphanage. Maybe short-term was better, as to not break you down and cause you to question humanity. Those kids had done absolutely nothing wrong but were almost guaranteed to be bound to abject poverty. As a society, how are we content to let people suffer who have done nothing wrong? While I questioned humanity as a whole, I was no better. Paralyzed by a seeming inability to make a big difference, I chose to make no difference at all.

I wished them luck.

We, the three foreign people, sat surrounded by kids while I waited for my host father to come home. Victor called Jean-Claude and he said he would be right there. In Burkina time, that meant anytime between minutes later and sometime that afternoon. I was in no rush though. It felt good to be back.

"Victor, how is school?" I asked.

"It is going well," replied Victor.

"That's good. What is your favorite subject?" I inquired. I held this conversation with almost every kid in Burkina. I loved talking about school and hoped that I could make them see the importance of school. Maybe it never made a difference, but I kept asking the questions.

"French," timidly replied Victor.

French made sense. Victor spoke French well, not that I was a suitable judge. I landed in Burkina with almost zero French. I knew how to say 'good morning' and the French word for grapefruit—

pamplemousse—because a friend had told me the word days before I left for Peace Corps. I learned to speak French during training and Victor was my tutor in the afternoon, once my training sessions ended for the day. After his sister, he had the highest level of French in the family. His sister, Yvonne, was also fluent in English but this proved to be a handicap for me.

Yvonne lived with the family for my first month of training and during that time I learned little French. I couldn't force myself to stumble and struggle through a new language when I could easily communicate with Yvonne in English. After a month, however, Yvonne left for Ouaga and I began to struggle, blunder, and finally learn French.

"How is Yvonne?" I asked.

"She is good," replied Victor.

"Does she have a new phone number? I tried to call her the other day but it did not go through," I questioned as I pulled out my phone to show him what number I had for his sister. I had tried to call her after I spoke with Victor's father. I wasn't sure if he had understood that I was coming to visit and wanted her to relay the message in Moore.

"No, she has a different number," answered Victor.

"Can I see it?"

Victor handed over his phone and I copied her number down, along with making a mental note to call her. Although a crutch, she was an appreciated safety net during my first month when everything was foreign to me.

While passing the time for my host dad to arrive, I pulled out my journal and allowed the kids to take turns drawing on the back pages. My youngest host sister drew a church. Using a ruler, she constructed a structure composed of a square with a triangle perched on top and crowned with a small cross.

The use of a ruler was indicative of the way children in Burkina learned in school. Students were taught via rote memorization and instructed to follow an exact series of steps. Creative problem solving or the use of a student's imagination was not built into the Burkina curriculum. This style of teaching hampered children well beyond the classroom.

Educated Burkinabé claimed that this was the French system of teaching.

"Look at Ghana and how much more advanced they are. It is because they were an English colony. The French system has hurt us," they would say.

My other host sister drew a picture of a woman. Afterward, she moved to the female volunteer's journal and began to draw another picture. I took the opportunity to illustrate her as she drew. The children behind me giggled in delight as I sketched. I'm by no means an artist but the group of children echoed in agreement that my picture was "beautiful."

After nearly an hour had passed, my host dad arrived.

"Tyler!" called Jean-Claude as he extended his meaty hand.

Jean-Claude was short, as were most Burkinabé compared to me, but had hands like catcher's mitts attached to arms as thick as logs. Jean-Claude, a subsistence farmer, also owned a bicycle and motorcycle repair shop in the local village market. His rough, calloused hands reflected the many years of hard labor, which had provided a good life for his family.

The sun reflected off the dark black skin of his round shaved head, only to be outdone by the brightness of his wide pearly smile. Normally reserved around me, I sensed there was much more to Jean-Claude than he let on. I only ever received pure kindness from my host father but believed him capable of inflicting unmatched revenge to anyone who harmed someone he cared for.

I took his hand and excitedly returned, "Jean-Claude, how are you? It's been a long time."

"I am good. How are you? How is your work?" asked Jean-Claude.

"Everything is good. No problems," I replied.

We seated ourselves under the large mango tree. I was glad to see them, but at a loss for words. Thankfully, in Burkina Faso, there wasn't a need to fill the silence with talking. It was enough to be in one another's company.

When I first arrived in Burkina, the silence unnerved me, compounded by the fact that if I had something to say, I didn't have the words to say it. I was used to someone always talking, and if the talking slowed, people pulled out their smartphones to aimlessly click, swipe, and scroll to fill the silence with other sensory stimuli. I refused to introduce that piece of western culture to Burkina.

Now, however, I spoke French and also found myself content to sit in silence with others, merely enjoying their company.

After lounging under the mango tree, Jean-Claude asked, "Do you want to go to the bar?"

"Yes," I eagerly replied. It would be nice to visit one of the village's bars again.

Jean-Claude, Victor, and I walked down the dirt road. We passed one of the family's small plots where they grew corn. During my Peace Corps training, I regularly joined the family in the field. I remembered their hesitation and worry the first day I accompanied them to the field to help prepare the ground for planting. As far as they saw it, I was a white American that lived in a city, who had never done manual labor. Yet, I came to Burkina Faso to serve as an agricultural volunteer, to spend two years working with farmers to improve their agricultural techniques and small business practices.

In the Peace Corps, however, I found it rare that a volunteer's prior education or experience prepared them to do their job. That's what three months of Peace Corps training did; turn a group of well-intentioned generalists into sector-specific development specialists.

Fortunately, I had grown up farming, mainly with hand tools, similar to how it is still done in sub-Saharan Africa and elsewhere across the globe. From the time that I could walk, I learned from my dad how to work the ground with a hoe, sow seeds by hand, pull weeds, and harvest every single type of crop that could be grown in Kentucky.

My father was a supervisor at a factory, not a farmer, but he enjoyed spending time outside and gardening. Gardening was a hobby for him, a way for my family to cut grocery bills and eat fresh food. Growing up, I spent my summers in a field, working in my family's garden with my brother to grow produce for the farmers' market. We would work all summer and save our money for the following school year.

I did not grow up in a city, but rather surrounded by fields of corn and soybeans. I had never worked at a retail store, restaurant, or office. My work experience prior to the Peace Corps consisted of manual labor, either from farming or two summers spent working in the factory where my father worked. I was as prepared as I could be to serve as an agricultural volunteer, but it didn't make the work any easier. The calluses on my hands were formed from years of using American tools with smooth, machined handles. The rough, uneven, handmade tools in Burkina quickly tore through my hands. My back, which had spent more time bent over a desk in school rather than bent over doing manual labor, struggled to keep up with pace of Burkina farmers. While my summers spent farming in the Bluegrass State were hot, the Burkina Faso sun burned with an intensity of three Kentucky suns.

For Burkinabé, farming was not a hobby. The vast majority of Burkinabé were dependent upon subsistence agriculture. Farming was their life. There were no retail stores, restaurants, offices, or factories to work in. The field and the field alone would provide for them and their families. This realization motivated me in the field. I destroyed my hands and back, but they grew stronger. I would work myself to the point of vomiting from overheating, but I became smarter. I could never keep up with my family in the field and I regularly made mistakes, but I tried my damndest and they saw that. That's all I could do: try.

It was three in the afternoon and Jean-Claude, Victor, and I were the lone people at the bar. The absence of patrons, however, did not stop them from blasting music from their large buzzing speakers. The bar was a spacious, walled-off courtyard behind a small building that housed two large refrigerators for beer and soda. At the back of the bar, a partitioning wall hid several latrines and a stack of empty beer crates that reached to the top of the courtyard wall. One small tree stood in the courtyard, which provided some shade along with a cement gazebo, once covered in bright blue porcelain tiles but now with numerous missing tiles, cracks, and a crumbling foundation. This was one of the town's two formal bars. The other bar had food. This bar had slightly colder drinks.

We sat in the shade of the dilapidated gazebo and ordered drinks. I got a beer, Jean-Claude a Coca-Cola, and Victor an orange Fanta. It was nice to be with them both and to be back at this bar. I spent a lot of time at this bar during my Peace Corps training. After long, frustrating days of French class or hard labor in our practice fields, my fellow volunteers and I would head to the bar for a drink and to speak English, before going back to our homes to fumble through more

French, local language, and life. On weekends, we would convene at the bar to recount our newest cultural blunders and horror stories, some of which included:

- accidentally telling your family that you were very "horny" to go to the market
- missing the hole of the latrine, while having diarrhea
- telling a woman that she had a nice vagina, when you meant to compliment her scarf
- eating bat
- eating dog
- not having a clue what you were eating
- pooping in a plastic bag in your room during a torrential downpour, unwilling to go outside to the latrine

It was at the bar, sharing our common foreign experiences that the other volunteers became my close friends. No one could understand what I was going through, except for them. Friends back home couldn't relate, and I wouldn't dare let my family know half of what I experienced; the homesickness and doubting of my choice to join the Peace Corps, which would creep up on me, usually while lying awake at night, sweating in my tiny cinderblock oven.

It was also at this bar where I first felt able to speak French. One weekend evening, the first time I walked to the bar with Jean-Claude, I sat trying to keep up with the conversation. Two of my host dad's friends were drinking with us and, after more than a month of trying to get a grasp on French, I hesitated to speak. Two very large beers into the evening, my inhibitions faded and I found myself truly, albeit drunkenly, speaking French for the first time, marking a major milestone in my service: the ability to communicate.

A month later at this bar, again with Jean-Claude, was the first time I felt I belonged in Burkina Faso and the Peace Corps. Victor had joined us and I motioned to the waitress to take our order. When she arrived, she asked, "What would you like, Nasara?"

Nasara is the Moore word for foreigner and something I did not enjoy being called, even though I was unquestionably a foreigner. The word bothered me and many other volunteers.

Kids would chant, "Nasara, nasara, nasara," as you passed them on the street, while standing outside your window, or as they ran away after being caught spying on you.

Old women would call you nasara as they passed.

Vendors in the market would greet you with, "Nasara."

Reinforcing any doubt of belonging, nasara reminded us that we were foreigners. The word, however, was not intended to be malicious. Burkinabé called it how they saw it. Old women were openly called old. Fat people called fat. Crippled people called crippled. Furthermore, during everyday conversation, people were recognized by their ethnic group. In Dioula, you'd acknowledge a Bobo man or Fulani woman by calling them 'Bobo che' or 'Fulani muso,' respectfully. There was no denying what you were. I was a nasara. I still, however, didn't like the word.

When the waitress asked, "What would you like, Nasara," I tried to look past being called nasara, which I would be called for the next two years of my service, and place our drink order. Jean-Claude, however, cut me off.

"His name is Tyler, not Nasara," declared Jean-Claude.

"What?" the waitress replied.

"His name is Tyler. His name is not Nasara. Call him Tyler," reiterated Jean-Claude.

"Tyler?"

"Yes."

"What would you like, Tyler?" asked the now confused waitress.

Nothing. At that moment I wanted nothing more than the happiness I was experiencing; the feeling of being accepted, welcomed, and acknowledged by my name. This was another major milestone in my service. Yes, I would be called nasara or tubabu, the Dioula word for foreigner, my entire service. But, as time progressed, more and more people would call me Tyler or Sanou Setile, my village name. I would develop relationships with people who would become close friends, some of whom I would consider my second family.

Jean-Claude and his family had welcomed me into their home. They looked after me, fed me, and taught me skills necessary to navigate Burkina Faso and village life. I would be forever grateful to them. Now, as I sat at the bar with Jean-Claude and Victor, two years later, I became saddened that I had not been back to visit until now. I lived across the country, in a different village, yet I regularly found myself in Ouagadougou, a one-hour cab ride away.

As we talked, I returned to asking Victor about school. I couldn't relent any opportunity to impress upon him the importance of education. Victor was smart, as was his older sister. In addition to being smart, Victor was kind and I wanted to see him succeed in life. Jean-Claude echoed the importance of school. He only attended primary school but knew that an education was the best chance his children had at having a better life. Jean-Claude worked hard, in his fields and at his small shop in the market where he sold bike parts and made repairs to bicycles. The fact that each of his five children, three of whom were girls, attended school was something to be applauded.

My phone buzzed in my pocket as the conversation began to slow and we neared the end of our drinks. I took out my phone to see if it was Caroline. It was late in the afternoon and we had planned to leave before 5:00 p.m. Surprisingly, it was a message from a volunteer that I was friendly with, but never talked to except in passing.

Message: *I heard about the other day. I had no idea. You couldn't tell at all. I hope you are well.*

While I hadn't forgotten about my HIV scare, I hadn't been thinking about it. I was enjoying Ipelce, the moment, and not living under a cloud of fear.

I am doing great now. Thanks, I replied.

I was doing well, but began to reflect on the past few days. Moving forward, what was I supposed to do? No more than 24 hours after hearing the good news, it felt like a distant memory, a memory that I pushed away. This is not what I wanted. I didn't want to dwell on the event, but I wanted to remember and to do things differently, have a greater appreciation of life and my remaining time in Burkina.

I messaged Caroline to see if she was ready, and began walking back with Jean-Claude and Victor down the dirt road that I had biked nearly two years ago with all of my belongings tied to my bicycle's rear rack or clutched by Victor as he rode on the back of the motorcycle that Yvonne drove. This was after I met Victor, Yvonne, and Jean-Claude for the first time, during our official welcoming ceremony to Ipelce and Burkina Faso.

There was dancing, singing, speeches, and utter confusion on behalf of many of the volunteers. One by one our names were called and we walked to the front of the ceremony to meet our new host families. I remember Jean-Claude's big smile and the big hands I shook as we greeted each other for the first time. From that moment, I knew I was lucky to live with them and could tell that they would be invaluable to my first months in the Peace Corps.

We reached their home and I said goodbye to everyone. I found Seydou napping in his taxi parked under a tree, and loaded the bike into the trunk. I gave one final wave to everyone, got into the car, and drove away from possibly the last time I would ever see them. Rather than be saddened by that fact, I tried to focus on how good it was to see them again and how forever grateful I was to know them.

Seydou's taxi pulled up to Caroline's house and women and children poured out from the courtyard, along with Caroline, to say goodbye. From everyone's smiles, you could tell that she also had a good time visiting her host family.

While Caroline and I rode back to Ouagadougou, I began reflecting on how I blamed her when I thought I was HIV positive. Seeds of doubt, anger, and hate had started to take root in my mind, which grew and slowly started to consume me. As I attempted to make sense of testing HIV positive, I had fallen deep into a logical fallacy. I had concluded that because I slept with Caroline and then tested positive for HIV, that it was because of Caroline that I was HIV positive. But it wasn't true. The second test came back negative and uprooted those ideas from my mind. Yet, a tender hole remained where the thoughts had flourished. I felt guilty that I had quickly cast such blame based on so little certainty.

I wanted to say I was sorry for blaming her, but that was impracticable. That would be a conversation that no one would walk away from happy. She would be angered that I had blamed her. After struggling to explain myself and apologize, I would likely not end up absolved from my guilt but instead likely finding myself feeling guiltier than before. Nonetheless, I was sorry, and Caroline and I were well.

We returned to a quiet transit house. Almost everyone had left, having returned to their villages, but I would be delaying my return and taking a few days to travel the far southwest region of Burkina to see waterfalls, climb billion-year-old geological domes, explore abandoned cliff civilizations, and visit my friend Teresa's site.

Lying on my side in bed, I pulled up my email on my laptop. Kate had sent me a message:

> *Hey Tyler,*
>
> *Currently sitting in the airport. Been traveling for almost 24 hours. Said goodbye to Melissa and Chris. I'm now waiting for my last flight.*
>
> *Thank you for being a strong, courageous, and honest person. For respecting me enough to tell me what you thought was the truth at the time, for asking for a hug when you found out that everything was fine.*
>
> *I feel very lucky to be able to call you my friend...Even if you do drive me crazy from time to time.*
>
> *I miss you already. - Kate*

I missed her too. Friends like Kate made the Peace Corps easier. She provided a sympathetic ear to listen or a shoulder to cry on. I was glad Kate was heading home, safe and healthy, after two years of service. In two more months, I would be heading home. I knew those two months would fly by and I was determined to savor and make the most out of every moment.

The host family I stayed with during my first three months of training in Ipelce, Burkina Faso.

Standing in the doorway of my bedroom in Ipelce.

Chapter 9

June 1st – Futu and Orchata

Half awake, I approached the ticket counter, "Je voudrais un ticket à Bobo." I was traveling to Bobo-Dioulasso on the first bus out of Ouagadougou. I hoped to travel to Banfora today, halfway across the country. It would take most of the day, one bus, one taxi, and one van to make it to Banfora and there was always the chance of a vehicle breaking down on the side of the road.

I handed $28 in CFA, the currency in Burkina Faso, to the attendant in return for a hand written paper ticket and found a seat in the bus station. It was still dark outside and the fluorescent lights cast an eerie yellow glow in the station. To my left sat an old man, asleep and snoring. In the aisle of chairs in front of me, a large woman in a brightly colored and ornately embroidered dress stared intently at the small color TV at the front of the station. She attentively watched a Latin American telenovela, dubbed over in French. I tried to follow the story, but the thick French accent, speed of dialogue, and nonsensical storyline made it difficult.

The bus ride to Bobo would take five to six hours if all went well. I took the morning bus to avoid the typical gridlocked traffic in the capital, which added another hour to the trip. Taking the morning bus also allowed more time for other possible delays along the route. Maybe we would hit a cow. The road could be washed out from a torrential downpour. The ropes tying down luggage to the roof could break loose, sending bags flying across the road at 60 miles an hour.

An axle could break. Or, if traveling in the East, there was a growing possibility of being stopped and robbed by bandits. There wasn't much that couldn't happen.

More than once, I spent the better part of a day standing in the sparse shade of a skinny tree alongside other passengers, thirsty and out of water, while several men stared blankly at a smoking engine. Sometimes they would figure it out, but most of the time another bus would have to be sent to finish out the trip, which could mean three hours of waiting.

At 7:00 a.m., staff loaded the bus with luggage and I boarded to grab a window seat close to the front. Moments after sitting down and putting in headphones to listen to a podcast, the bus pulled out of the station and started down the road. Twenty minutes later, we pulled into another bus station on the edge of town to pick up additional passengers before leaving the city.

The *saucisson* man, pronounced 'saucy-saun'—the French word for sausage—boarded the bus to sell breakfast sandwiches made with a thin piece of lunch meat, butter, and bread. I bought two for 80 cents, and the bus departed as the saucisson man jumped off of our bus and into another. This stop would be the last for a few hours. I settled back into my seat, turned up the volume on my iPod, began eating my sandwiches, and zoned out.

Two podcasts and one playlist later, the bus pulled into the Boromo station, the midpoint between Ouaga and Bobo. Our bus was one of 12 buses pulled into the tight, bustling waypoint. The bus driver said we would be leaving in ten minutes. Ten minutes to use the restroom, to buy food or water, and to stand up and stretch our legs. I stood up and put on my backpack, which contained my camera and other valuables, and mentally prepared myself to depart the bus. The Boromo station was an intimidating place, packed with buses, passengers, food vendors, merchants, and kids begging for money. It was an attack on all your senses and incredibly overwhelming, so much so that I knew of many volunteers that never got off the bus at Boromo. I had to pee, so I would be getting off the bus.

I stepped off the bus, hit "start" on my watch's stopwatch, and began weaving my way through the crowd, in the direction of the men's restroom. I always timed myself because I was paranoid of being left by the bus, especially when the driver gave us no more than five minutes at the station. I also knew exactly where to go, having navigated this maze countless times. It was essential to keep moving and not be distracted by the women trying to sell you bread or apples, or the sketchy looking guy selling mystery medicinal cream, typically packaged in a brightly colored box picturing half naked men and women—I had no idea what it was for, nor did I have any interest in finding out.

The men's open-air restroom contained four short stalls with doors and holes in the ground for defecating and three other stalls that served as urinals, made by a small hole at the back of an open stall that drained out the back. The air around the restroom sat heavy and ripe with body fluid and excrement. I stood in line for the bathroom, waiting to take my turn. Aside from the many unpleasant things about the Boromo bus station restroom, the line was one of the few orderly lines I experienced in Burkina Faso. Most lines, like those at the bank or the bus station, were organized chaos at best.

When my turn came, I took a deep breath, held it, and entered into the open urinal stall to quickly use the restroom before needing to take another breath. Once finished, I backed out of the stall and shuffled past the next patron trying to squeeze into the tight space. Outside the bathroom, I rinsed my left hand in water from one of the plastic kettles used for washing, an item seen across sub-Saharan Africa. The attendant in charge, who kept the wash kettles full and cleaned the area, approached to collect the bathroom fee of 20 cents.

Now relieved, I again weaved my way through the maze of people, back to my bus. As I moved out of the way of a departing bus, I remembered the first several times at the Boromo station, when I feared not being able to remember which bus was mine, in addition to being left behind. Now, after two years, I could tell the buses of each company apart and didn't have to embarrassingly inquire from the bus driver if I was on the right bus. I stepped onto the bus, past women carrying trays of peanuts and fried biscuits, and other women balancing basins filled with cold drinks on their head. Once safely back in my seat, 7 minutes and 42 seconds after departing, I stuck my head out the window to order two cold bags of water and a package of sugared peanuts.

Initially, I found it bizarre to buy things out the window of the bus, but this was how everyone did it at bus stations and stops in villages along the route. I handed down money in return for my purchases, which the women held up to my extended hand while standing on their toes.

The bus departed the station, five minutes later than announced, and bounced down the short bumpy path to the main road. I quickly drank my two waters and placed the empty bags in the side pocket of my backpack, choosing to not toss the trash out the window like the other passengers. The roadside, both leaving and entering Boromo, was littered with debris from the buses that stopped at the station. The black plastic bags trapped in the short stubby trees always signaled that we had arrived at the halfway point between Ouaga and Bobo.

Resting back into my seat, I turned my iPod on again and started moving handfuls of peanuts to my mouth, until I reached down to find that I had eaten the entire bag. I closed my eyes and attempted to let my mind move beyond the hot, stuffy bus barreling down the uneven, dusty road toward Bobo. I spent most of my service either trying to live in the moment, enjoying the amazing experiences that Burkina Faso and the Peace Corps afforded, or trying to transcend the less numerous, but sharply contrasting unenjoyable experiences. At this point in my service, especially after the previous week's events, nothing could faze me.

The bus arrived in Bobo, faster than expected, due to a combination of my daydreaming and the heavy foot of the driver. No sooner than the bus reached the station, I made my way to the exit. Lining the exit to the bus station, taxi drivers called out, trying to get me to take their taxi. These were the worst taxis to take because they were quick to overcharge and utterly unreasonable if I tried to negotiate the price. I waved them away, saying that I had a ride waiting for me. Once outside the station, I moved to the road to flag down a passing taxi driver with whom I would be able to haggle. Finally, an available taxi passed, saw me waving him down, and pulled over to the side of the road, after cutting across two lanes of traffic. I lowered my head to his open passenger side window to negotiate a price.

"I would like to go to the restaurant, Trois Karite. Do you know it?"

"Where is it?"

"Across from the airport, near Independence Road."

"Yes, I know it. Get in."

"How much?"

"500 CFA – *$1*"

"No, 300 CFA. That is the right price."

"Okay, get in."

"Thank you."

I knew this dance all too well, 300 CFA was a fair price. The taxi cut back onto the road to the far left lane and immediately took advantage of a momentary break to cut across oncoming traffic and off the main road, where we began zigzagging our way through the heart of Bobo-Dioulasso.

Bobo, the second largest city in Burkina Faso, was my favorite city in Burkina and home of the Bobo and Dioula people. Taxis, market vendors, and people, in general, were nicer. Many friends back in village, who were either Bobo or Dioula, cited the city's cultural heritage as the reason why people were friendlier—as opposed to Ouaga, the traditional capital of the Mossi Empire.

In the center of the city stood the iconic 100-year-old Grand Mosque, built from mud and wood. Several blocks away, the Grand Market sold everything from traditional arts and crafts to flat screen TVs. Numerous open-air bars dotted the city, featuring local and traveling musicians, playing West African music, reggae, Latin fusion, blues, jazz, and R&B.

Bobo's Pond of Dafra contained sacred giant catfish where sacrificial offerings in the form of freshly slaughtered chickens were made to the aquatic leviathans. If led by the right guide through the forest to Dafra, they would read and interpret the signs of your future hidden in the entrails of the chicken, before tossing the innards into the pond churning with ravenous five-foot fish.

While the sights and sounds of Bobo were worth experiencing, my favorite parts were the rituals I repeated nearly every visit. After riding two hours down a bumpy dirt road from my village to Bobo, I would head to a Western-style grocery store to buy a chocolate bar. Chocolate, which I could not find in my community, was a treat reserved for Bobo. With my dark chocolate bar in hand, I walked a few blocks to a Turkish restaurant and ordered a large Turkish coffee. Good coffee, another treat not found in my village. Slowly, I would savor the rich chocolate bar alongside the equally rich Turkish coffee in shade of several trees outside the restaurant, while enjoying free internet.

After I buzzed with energy from chocolate, caffeine, and internet, I would bike to the Peace Corps office in Bobo. The office in Bobo was a house turned into a communal space for volunteers. Vincent, the Peace Corps driver who picked me up in my village when I sliced my foot open, had his office there. At the Bobo office, a smaller version of the large Ouaga transit house, volunteers were not allowed to spend the night unless admitted to the house's medical room.

The office had a shower, and even with its cold water, I heavily anticipated the opportunity to bathe standing up. A few volunteers had running water at their site. The majority of us took bucket baths, as did the majority of Burkinabé. Unlike the majority of Burkinabé, however, we had not been raised with bucket baths and lacked necessary skills gained over a childhood to properly clean our bodies. With practice, each volunteer developed their system of bathing using a bucket of water and plastic cup to slowly pour water over their soapy bodies. Bucket baths were refreshing, but only with a shower did I ever feel truly clean.

After showering, my next ritual led me to Trois Karite, the restaurant down the street from the Bobo office. Unlike many of the restaurants preferred by Peace Corps Volunteers, Trois Karite prepared simple regional African dishes, rather than pizzas, burgers, and ice cream. The food was well-made, served in large portions, cheap, and where I instructed the taxi driver to take me.

The taxi pulled up to the restaurant, and I paid the driver 300 CFA. I walked into the open-air restaurant, a large courtyard with covered tables along the sides and a long hanger filling the middle, and sat down at a small table. A server promptly arrived, carrying water and a menu, and before he turned to leave, I quickly ordered, "Plantain futu with peanut sauce, please."

Futu is a West African staple made from plantains, cassava, or yams that have been boiled and pounded until turning into the consistency of dough. You eat the big ball of dough by dipping pieces into a sauce. Plantain futu tasted slightly sweet and paired well with peanut sauce – one of two orders I placed at Trois Karite. My other order was rice and peanut sauce.

As I sat alone at the table, I slowly pulled off pieces of futu and dipped them into the peanut sauce, while alternating between daydreaming and playing Snake, the one game on my old Nokia cell phone. As I neared the end of my meal, my phone rang. An international call, my mom. I paused before answering the phone because I hadn't spoken to her since the HIV scare. She knew about it because of my blog post and my brother's advanced warning. She would be worried, possibly angry, and likely ask that I come home.

"Hello, Mom," I answered.

The conversation followed as expected. My mom said that she was worried and that she couldn't wait for me to come home. She said that the Peace Corps should send me home now. She said that my being here, in Burkina as a Peace Corps Volunteer, made her sick to her stomach and turned her hair gray. Although more extreme than usual given the past week's events, this was a conversation I had experienced before and one that I had grown to resent.

At my send-off party, days before leaving for the Peace Corps, my mom said, "As your mother, I am worried about you, but as a person, I think what you are about to do will be an amazing adventure. I'm proud of you."

Each week her son served in the Peace Corps, her worry grew.

My parents loved me and gave me every opportunity within their means. My mother had fostered my inquisitive nature with weekly trips to the library, family vacations to science and history museums, and countless projects and experiments at home. It was because of her that I wanted to travel and see the world, to explore the far-off places reserved for the pages of National Geographic. She was half the reason I was in the Peace Corps.

My father was the other half.

It was my dad who taught me how to farm, an important skill as an agricultural Peace Corps Volunteer. More than farming, he taught me how to use my hands to make things. From a young age, I stood beside my stoic father as he silently fixed things in our house, doing my job of shining a flashlight into the dark space as he worked. You name it, and he could fix it, or at least try. He could also build nearly anything. With a few supplies, his tools, and his ingenuity, there was little my father couldn't create. I learned that with my hands, I could make things, change things, and be largely self-sufficient.

I love my parents, but they did not understand the Peace Corps. During our weekly calls, they'd ask if I had seen anything new, eaten anything new. Given that they called on Sundays and I would have gone to the large market that day, they always asked what I bought and what I would cook. Rarely did they ask about my projects, the real reason I was in the Peace Corps. While an adventure, the Peace Corps was work. I was there trying to make a difference. Trying to find projects that could make people's lives better. I was proud of what I was trying to do, my several small successes, but they didn't ask about my work and that bothered me.

They weren't alone, however. From the outside, it would be hard to understand the Peace Corps. Everyone gets the idea that being in the Peace Corps was about living and working in a developing country for two years. But what did that actually mean?

It was hard enough for new volunteers to understand their role as a volunteer. As Peace Corps Volunteers, our first goal was to "help the people of interested countries in meeting their need for trained men and women." That ill-defined goal was supposed to point us in the right direction as we served our new communities. Prepared with a shallow toolbox of ideas gained during training, we had to figure it out. Some volunteers would have more defined roles as teachers in a school or healthcare workers at a medical center. Other volunteers, like me, had less defined roles as a Community Economic Development, Environment, or Agriculture volunteer. Either way, regardless of the title, all volunteers had to figure out how they were going help their new communities. We'd all ask ourselves, "What exactly am I doing here?" It would be a question some would spend their whole service trying to figure out.

Unless you'd been knee deep in the superb mess that is the Peace Corps, it was hard to define and understand. Because of this, conversations about Peace Corps defaulted to the exotic aspects of a volunteer's service: the things we saw, the things we ate, and the parasites we picked up along the way.

Even though they didn't ask, I still happily told them about all my projects. I worked with a group of volunteers to write and illustrate children's books in local languages. I collaborated with my village's local youth group to reforest the community by planting thousands of seed, fruit, and timber trees. I spent Saturdays weighing babies and vaccinating children. With a mix of French and weak local language, I attempted to teach mothers about childhood nutrition. My parents thought all the projects sounded great, but they could never overcome their worry. I was their child after all.

I told my mom that I loved her and that I would stay safe, finished my phone call with her, and paid for my meal. It was 2:00 p.m., I had already taken two cabs and a bus today to reach Bobo, and I still had more traveling to do. Trois Karite was a few blocks away from the Bobo Peace Corps office, where I left my bike.

I no longer took my bike with me to Ouaga, because I always arrived to find a part bent or broken. I learned to avoid cramming a bicycle under a bus with other bikes, motorcycles, and heavy luggage. The truck that rode between my village and Bobo, however, always took good care of my bike. They knew me by name, joked around with me, and made sure to carefully load and unload my bicycle.

The Bobo Peace Corps office was unmarked, hidden behind high walls, and secured by large metal doors. In the courtyard behind the house lay an old metal sign printed with the Peace Corps logo and "Corps de la Paix Burkina Faso." The sign had either fallen and never been reattached or had been taken down for purposes of anonymity. The transit house and office in Ouaga also lacked signs to denote Peace Corps. You had to know where they were.

I knocked on the large metal door and waited for the guard to let me in. The door cracked open and the guard peered out. Once he saw I was a volunteer, obvious to see from my appearance and hear from my accent, he swung open the door. I handed my ID card to the guard so he could sign me into the logbook. The logbook kept track of who was at the house, and therefore also not at their site. Volunteers were supposed to be at site, doing their jobs as volunteers. When we left site, we were also supposed to text a message to the Peace Corps duty phone, detailing our travel and where to find us in the case of an emergency. I remembered to text the phone about half of the time.

I immediately left the office with my bike and began to pedal in the direction of Banfora. When traveling across Burkina Faso, you could either go to the station or spot where a particular vehicle left from, or wait on the side of the road along the route you wanted to travel. The road to Banfora was close to the transit house and I had no preference for which van I would take. After quickly biking through a precarious roundabout, I pulled off to wait on the side of the road. Within minutes I flagged down a passing van. The driver confirmed that they were heading to Banfora and I squeezed into an open spot in the back, as man jumped down from the roof to take my bike and tie it to the top of the van.

The two-hour ride to Banfora was calm and uneventful. The road was one of the best maintained in Burkina, and the van didn't break down along the way. While it was a little tight in the packed van, this was to be expected. Thankfully, there was no livestock, either alive or dead, in or on top of the vehicle.

While I waited for my bike to be handed down, I called Amanda, another volunteer already in Banfora. We were spending the night with the volunteer who lived there, and spending tomorrow visiting the Karifiguela Cascades, Fabedougou Domes, and Lake Tengrela, known as "Hippo Lake."

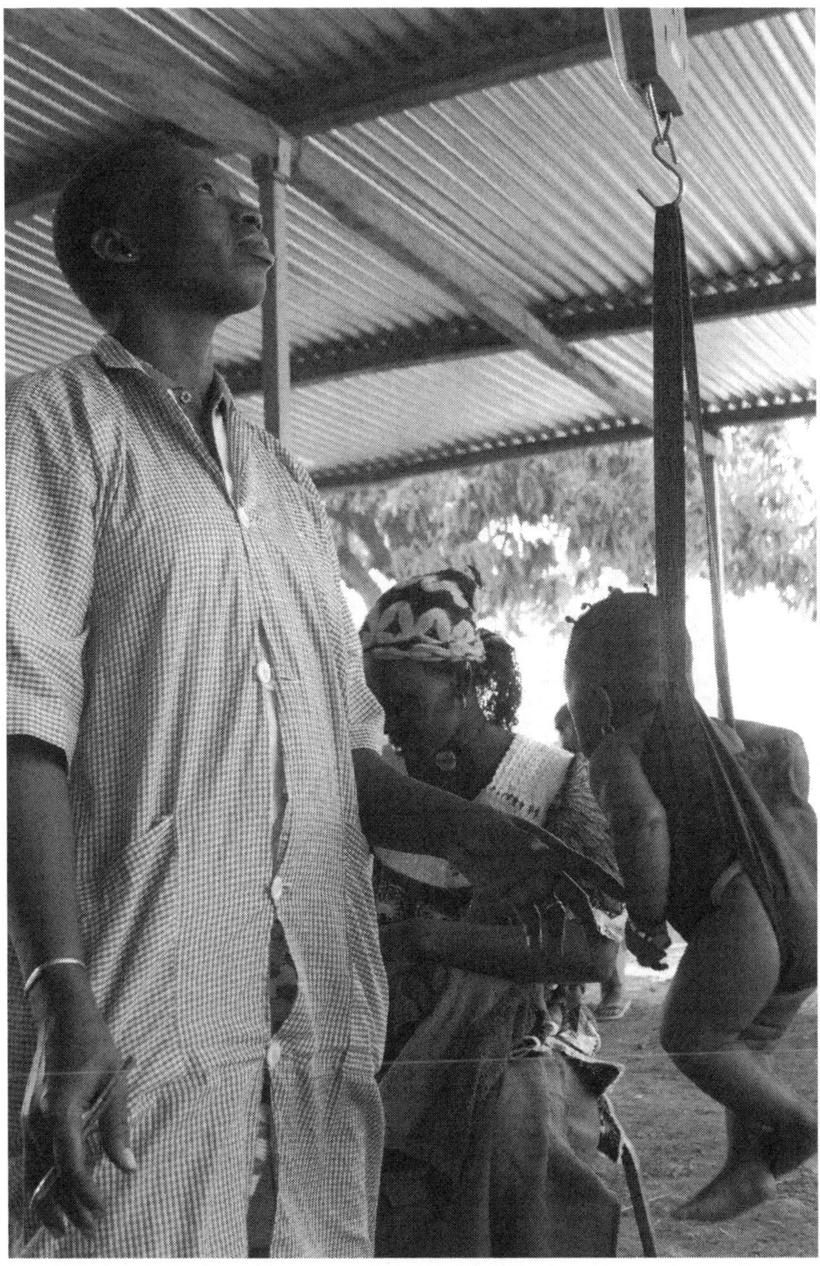

Weighing babies at local health clinic to chart their development.

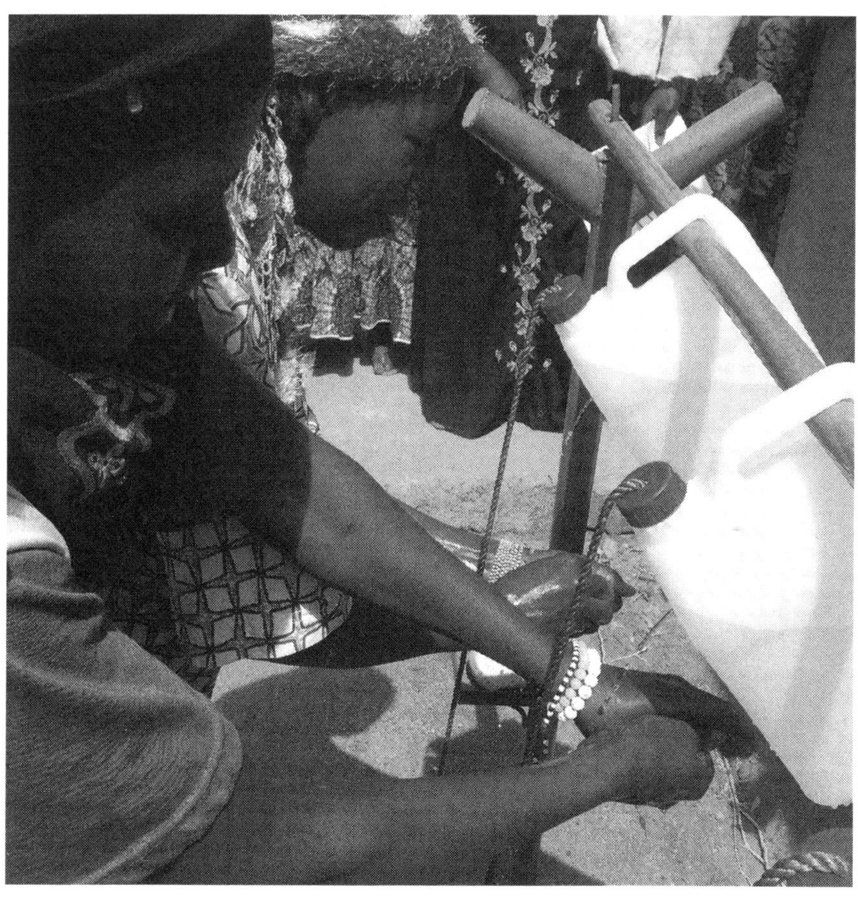

"Tippy Tap" handwashing station built at Banzon's Women's Rice Association as part of a health and sanitation project.

Chapter 10

June 2nd – Banfora

"Do we want to go to the Cascades or the Domes more?" I asked.
"Let's do the Cascades," Amanda replied.
"Sounds good to me."

Amanda and I were standing outside waiting for the driver. Because of a slow start to the morning, we had time to see two of the three sites today. I needed to catch the van to Teresa's site at 3:00 p.m. and I had already seen the Domes before, during a bike trip across Burkina Faso, so I didn't mind skipping them.

Our driver, Moussa, pulled up to the house. After going through the standard morning greetings, I asked Moussa to take us to Lake Tengrela. I hoped the hippos would be more active in the morning, before the heat of the day set in, but it was already later than planned and quickly becoming hot. Moussa was a local tour guide that the Banfora volunteer always recommended to visitors. He charged a flat rate for the day entire day, which made things easier. Moussa would chauffeur us around from site to site and even serve as a guide.

The four-wheel drive Nissan car bounced down the dirt road and turned onto another unmarked dirt road, which looked no different than the dozen other dirt roads we'd already passed. Earlier in the morning, the Banfora volunteer said we could bike to each site and unsuccessfully tried to give directions. After seeing the route, I was thankful we hired Moussa.

When we arrived at Tengrela, a guide napping under a tree quickly sprang up to offer us a boat ride to 'see the hippos up close'– $6. Amanda and I accepted and walked toward the lake with the guide, leaving Moussa to take the boat guide's place napping under the tree.

Flowering lily pads dotted the small, glassy lake. Local fisherman weaved back and forth, casting nets into Tengrela's calm waters. Regional and migratory birds glided over the lake, plucking small fish from below the surface of the water.

Large groups of hippos, often cited as the deadliest animals in Africa, called the lake home and locals revered the Lake Tengrela hippos as sacred. The idea of sacred animals was common across Burkina Faso. I had straddled a giant sacred crocodile of Sabou and offered a sacrifice to the less intimidating sacred catfish of Dafra, and lived to tell the stories. Now, it was time for sacred hippos.

I didn't know why the Tengrela hippos were considered sacred and completely forgot to ask Moussa or our boat guide. I did, however, know the stories behind the sacred crocodiles and catfish. Because of a storybook project with other volunteers, I spent several weeks collecting local folklore stories from members of my village. Fellow volunteers and I produced ten different children's books with original illustrations, written in five local languages, in addition to French and English. We started the project to create resources for preschool teachers in Burkina Faso, with the hope of improving early childhood literacy. I didn't know the impact of the books we created, but I did cherish the stories I learned from members of my community.

- - -

My best friend Issouf was a storyteller, in addition to practicing magic, making traditional medicine, and running a small restaurant. One afternoon while seated under the large mango tree behind his restaurant, Issouf told me several stories. The first was of the sacred catfish of Dafra.

Issouf stared intently, his eyes focused on me as I recorded his story. He spoke softly as if sharing a secret.

"One day, a traveler was wandering through the forest.

He came across a village and hoped he would find food and shelter for the evening.

A welcoming host, however, did not greet the traveler. The village was a village of fierce Guinean warriors.

The village of warriors grabbed their weapons and charged after the traveler that had come to their village.

The traveler ran as fast as he could, but the warriors ran as fast. The traveler was scared for his life and would not stop.

He ran through the night and ran through the day. The traveler was very tired but would not stop.

The traveler then came to a large body of water. After running day and night, he was too tired to swim across the fast-flowing river.

The traveler kneeled down and began to pray, 'Dear God, I have done no wrong. I am a traveler and only wanted to find food and shelter. Please save me from these warriors.'

As the traveler stood up to look for an escape, a giant catfish breached the surface near the shore. This catfish was large enough to ride. Without hesitation, the traveler climbed on top of the catfish, which quickly carried the travel across to the other shore.

The Guinean warriors arrived at the river to see the traveler on the other shore.

They ran into the water and began to swim. Soon, the water overcame the warriors and they were swept away.

The traveler was safe, saved by the catfish. The descendants of the traveler honored the catfish from that time forward and regarded them as sacred."

After finishing the story of the sacred catfish, Issouf stood up to greet several young men who had walked into the courtyard. Two of the men ordered tea and Issouf disappeared into his tiny restaurant. Minutes later, Issouf returned with their drinks and a coffee for me—black with no sugar. My beverage of choice gave much amusement to Issouf and others, who preferred a 50/50 blend of coffee and sweetened condensed milk.

I sat cross-legged on a tattered woven mat alongside the two men drinking tea. Two other young men shared a wood bench with Issouf, who leaned in and began to quietly tell another story, the Hunter and the Crocodile, as the young men and I listened carefully.

"Long ago, there was a hunter.

One hot day in May, he could find no animals. He searched and he searched, but all the animals had gone to find water.

He too was in need of water.

He could last for days eating leaves and roots, but he had to have water. Yesterday, he finished his water and was becoming very thirsty.

He knew of a lake near Sabou that had water all year, but it would take all day to get there.

The hunter walked in the direction of the lake. The sun was hot and there was little shade to protect the hunter. As the hunter walked, he became thirstier.

He became so thirsty that he began to fall.

Then, he saw the lake. The hunter was close. No longer able to walk, he crawled. As he neared the edge of the lake, he was so tired he collapsed.

As he lay there, a crocodile came out from the lake. The hunter closed his eyes and prepared for death.

Then he felt water splash his face. The crocodile was splashing water on the hunter. The hunter opened his mouth and drank as the crocodile continued to give him water.

After his thirst was gone and his strength returned, he stood and looked to the crocodile. 'Thank you, my brother,' said the hunter. The crocodile shook his head and ambled back into the lake.

The hunter never hurt a crocodile again and taught others to do the same.

It is said that the crocodile and Burkinabé share the same spirit. They are brothers."

- - -

Undoubtedly, the sacred Tengrela hippos had a story, but I neglected to ask. I was more interested in getting as close as I could to the large animals, taking pictures, and living to tell that story.

Amanda and I followed the lake guide to two small wooden boats floating on the lake's edge. The guide waded into the water and reached into a boat. Rather than pulling out boat oars, the guide lifted a large empty can and began to bail water from the boat. Amanda looked at me with concern. *Would we end up swimming with hippos?*

We stepped into the hull of the boat and took our seats as the guide positioned himself to push the craft off the shore. With one strong push, the vessel's hull freed itself from the muddy bank and our guide jumped into the back of the wooden craft, this time with an oar in hand. Slowly, we moved along the edge of the lake to the eastern shore. Several birds sailed across the top of the water, but no hippos were visible.

It was June and the height of the rainy season. Water was not scarce. You could see that the banks of the lake stretched to their outermost extent, filled with several months of rain. There would be hundreds of other seasonal watering holes in the area and the hippos would be spread out across the region. It would have been better to visit the lake in the dry season, either December or January, when the summer ponds had disappeared and Tengrela Lake brimmed with hippos. By that time Amanda and I would be back home in the U.S., enjoying our first Christmas after the Peace Corps.

I saw hippos several times during my service. Both hippos and crocodiles inhabited the river that bordered my village on three sides. While my village respected the animals, they were not regarded as sacred. The hippos and crocodiles in my village had killed people, and my Banzon friends and family made sure I knew.

Almost as a daily warning, I passed five mammoth hippo skulls, lined up outside my neighbor's house. My neighbor was the local forest agent and these totems were from hippos that attacked people. In Burkina, hippos were protected from hunting, but overly aggressive hippos could be killed. The warnings, however, did not deter me from visiting the river. In the evenings, I took long bike rides along the river to enjoy the setting sun and search for animals. I never saw crocodiles in my village but I did see hippos.

Standing on top of steep sections of the riverbank, I felt protected from the hippos. I knew that a hippo could outrun me on land, but figured that a 1 to 2-ton animal would have a hard time climbing the steep bank, giving me enough time to dart away on my bicycle. Thankfully, I never had to test my theory.

One evening, as I biked alongside the river, I spotted a large bobbing head of a hippo. I skidded to a stop and found a safe spot to watch. As I crouched down on the bank, intently watching the hippo, a small head broke the surface of the water, followed by another. They were two young calves with their mother. I spent half an hour hunkered down on top of the muddy riverbank, intently watching the hippo family. A head would silently submerge and reemerge, slowly cresting above the water, followed by an audible puff of air from the hippo's nostrils. My presence was no secret to the hippos. The large mother hippo's small black eyes kept a close watch on me, as her two calves ate and played.

Tengrela Lake provided no such memory. We found one hippo after the guide asked two fishermen where they had seen hippos that morning. Off in the distance, we watched a massive head quickly rise above the water and crash back down with a splash before disappearing, never coming close to the one solitary hippo. Tengrela was beautiful, but if I didn't live near hippos, I would have left disappointed.

Our guide returned us to the shore and we thanked him for the lake tour. While we hadn't seen a lot, I was merely happy that the boat stayed afloat.

"Now to the Domes?" asked Moussa.

We hadn't planned to see the Domes but we also planned to spend more time at the lake. Moussa assured me that we would have plenty of time to visit the Domes and Cascades before I needed to catch the van to Fourkoura, Teresa's site, and offered to drive me to the van. With that reassurance, we got back in the car and set off toward the Domes.

Stalks of sugarcane slowly waved in the wind, a green expanse reaching from the edge of the dirt road far off into the distance. The landscape of Southwest Burkina Faso stood in stark contrast to the central region, the edge of Sahel. Moving south beyond Northern Africa's Sahara desert, the Sahel is a transition zone of arid scrubland and grass, a wall between the dry sands of the north and iconic, lush African grasslands and jungles. Arabic for shore, Sahel is a fitting name for the metaphorical coastline to the vast sandy sea of the Sahara Desert.

Rain shaped both landscape and life of Burkina Faso. The seasonal rains dictated when and what farmers planted. The North relied on native, quick growing, drought tolerant sorghum and millet to make use of a few sporadic rainy days in June or July. Stepping down to lower latitudes, the rainy season became longer and more consistent. With more rain, corn became the staple crop, one of many crops introduced to Burkina as a result of Western civilization's exploration and conquest. Lastly, the southernmost regions of Burkina Faso experienced rainy seasons that lasted half the year, spanning from May into October. With abundant rains, the South grew profitable sugarcane and rice, an agricultural engine of the country.

Large white irrigation hoses divided the green landscape into neatly spaced parcels. The hoses hung suspended above the waving stalks of sugarcane, held up by tall metal scaffolding on wheels rolled through deep ruts in the field. Aerial photos of the farms outside Banfora reveal the scale and uniformity of the agricultural operation. From above, the landscape was a mix of neatly squared tracts of land and circular fields shaped to accommodate irrigation systems that rotated on a center pivot across the land. The area reminded me of the rolling fields of corn and soybeans surrounding my childhood home in Kentucky.

In the distance, the rocky Domes of Fabedougou jutted up from the surrounding farmland. The Domes formed hundreds of thousands of years ago when ancient seas submerged this region of Burkina Faso. Molded from the sandy ocean floor, the Domes resembled towers of deteriorating sand castles or hundred-foot stalagmites absent of a cave. The Domes seemed out of place in Burkina Faso, where the land was mostly flat and featureless. Moussa's car pulled up to the Domes and parked between two brick pavilions built for visitors to escape the sun. Amanda and I, however, were the only visitors.

Fabedougou was silent. Standing next to the towering rock formations, amid the eerie silence, I felt small. We hiked into the Domes, winding our way through the monoliths. As I walked, I ran my hand along the smooth stone surface. The natural trail ran to a dead end, blocked off by a small dome. Rather than turning around, Moussa began to climb and we followed. Easily reached handholds and ledges covered the Domes, making the climb more a ladder than a rock face. We moved to the edge of the small dome and began climbing successively taller domes, moving our way upward through the masses of rock. Finally, we reached a point where climbing was no longer easy and the risk of falling outweighed the thrill of continuing to free-climb.

From high in the Domes, the extent of the monolith maze became evident. Moussa described how the bygone tribes that inhabited Fabedougou used the Domes to their advantage when battling other tribes. Today, the abandoned Domes sat hushed, but I tried to imagine the site hundreds of years ago.

In times of war, native warriors would lure unsuspecting enemies from the flat land surrounding the Domes into the labyrinth. Weaving their way through the columns, the locals quickly disappeared before raining down arrows from above. The stone walls would have echoed their war cries. Now, only the sounds of loud tourists reverberate here.

The hot afternoon sun bore down on the rocks and signaled that it was time to move to the waterfalls. We descended from atop the

Domes, slowly and precariously down the route that proved much easier to ascend. I was glad to have Moussa with us because it was nearly impossible for me to distinguish one path from another. I couldn't speak for Amanda, but I would have certainly gotten lost.

I opened the front door of Moussa's car and reached for my water bottle, which had been sitting in direct sunlight in the sealed vehicle. The water was hot and tasted like plastic, but still satisfied my thirst.

Once in the car, I immediately rolled down my window and stuck my head out to catch the breeze as we drove. Fields of sugarcane gave way to dense woodland. Tall trees bounded both sides of the road and reached out, blocking the sun. The road was muddy, rutted, and partially flooded in sections—unmistakably rainy season in the Southwest.

Moussa didn't lessen his pace as he plowed the four-wheel drive vehicle through the waterlogged road and I pulled my head back inside the car. When we arrived at a checkpoint, Moussa slowed to a stop. For $4 we could enter the Cascades. A guide costs another $2. I pulled $4 from my pocket and Moussa handed it out his window to an attendant. We then learned that the guide was not optional and begrudgingly gave over more money.

From the moment we left the car, we could hear the sound of water. Ahead of our paid guide, Moussa took the lead and we climbed through the forest toward the waterfalls. Abruptly, forest gave way and the sky opened up to reveal the waterfalls. The rains of the past several days turned the rushing water brown with mud. As with the Domes, the waterfalls were one of a few unique features of an otherwise uniform landscape. More impressive than the Cascades themselves was the view from the top. Green trees stood out against barren soil. Even during the rainy season, freshly sprouted blades of grass were quickly consumed by roaming animals. The land looked uninhabited and unspoiled, a contrast to the busy town of Banfora and surrounding manicured fields.

We moved past a series of waterfalls until reaching a natural pool. Many visitors swam in the falls but we hadn't brought bathing suits, nor did we find the murky water inviting. After 20 minutes at the falls, Amanda and I exchanged tired glances. We'd seen three different sites today and we're done playing tourist.

When we pulled up to the van that was going to take me to Teresa's site, one of the wheels lay on the ground, with no one seeming all too eager to replace it. I unloaded my bike, thanked Moussa for the day, said goodbye to Amanda, and was left to wait with the three-wheeled van. A man assured me that this was the van to Fourkoura and that we would be leaving on time, in an hour according to him.

As various groups of men came by to stand around the barren axel and unattached wheel, one hour became two, which soon became three, and I feared would turn to four. I sent a message to Teresa updating her that I would be arriving late. She was not surprised. Teresa had told me numerous stories of breakdowns—both of the van and her emotions—when traveling to and from her site.

After three and a half hours of waiting, they reattached the wheel. The entire time, they were waiting for a wrench, which begged the question, "How did they take the wheel off in the first place if they didn't have a wrench?" Perplexed, I boarded the van.

I was tired after a day of sightseeing and instantly fell asleep in the van before we left Banfora. Awoken by a large bump, I opened my eyes to nightfall. Peace Corps HQ advised against traveling at night. I didn't care for it either, but at times it was unavoidable. I simply hoped that the van wouldn't break down on the road. I would then have to finish the trip on my bike, which would not have been the first time.

After one month in Burkina Faso, my training group divided up and travelled with a language instructor to visit a current volunteer's site. There, we gained our first glimpse into volunteer life. On this first trip, it was fitting that we rode a death trap of a bus that I'm half certain our language instructor purposefully picked, which broke down several times along the way. When the bus stopped for the fourth time in the middle of nowhere, I assumed we'd broken down again. Rachel, the volunteer we were visiting, however, had flagged the bus down. This was our stop. Rachel's small village was a few miles off the main road.

Our bikes and the language instructor's motorcycle were unloaded from the bus's undercarriage. The road to Rachel's site was more of a goat path than a road and required us to ride single-file down the trail. Sooner than planned, as a result of delays, the sun dipped below the horizon.

The idea of riding in the dark through the bush to Rachel's site excited me. Again, this was my first time traveling in Burkina Faso since I arrived, my first adventure. Until this point, my time had been spent fumbling over French or learning about agribusiness.

Justin got a flat tire and we stopped to wait while he found the puncture and patched the hole. Each of us carried a set of bike tools, tire patches, and a pump. In training, we learned basic bike maintenance and were expected to know how to fix a flat tire. At this point, our language instructor was becoming noticeably anxious. The sun had completely set and he was responsible for us for the next several days. As volunteers in training, we loved this.

We got back on the trail and picked up speed. Without electricity and lights for miles, the night sky shown dark black, filled with stars. Our headlamps illuminated barely more than the path several feet in front of us. Riding my bike through the African bush at night exhilarated me. This was the experience I was looking for in the Peace Corps. *What was out there, beyond the dim light of my headlamp?* I wondered. I imagined biking with elephants, monkeys, and even lions in the distance—the latter causing me to peddle a little faster. More likely, however, a few lizards and a stray goat watched us roll through the night.

Two years later, I still loved being in Burkina. I loved the sense of adventure and the romanticized, picturesque moments that appeared out of nowhere. But I had experienced late-night bike rides through the bush more than once. The only adventure I wanted tonight involved unrolling my sleep pad on Teresa's cement floor and going to bed.

The van pulled into its final stop, Teresa's village, at 8:30 p.m. I stretched my cramped legs, gathered my belongings, and sent a message to Teresa. She hopefully had a cell signal or knew that the van had arrived. I could find my way to her house by asking where the American girl lived but hoped to avoid an evening scavenger hunt.

Within minutes of sending my message, Teresa arrived on her bike. Today's adventure was over.

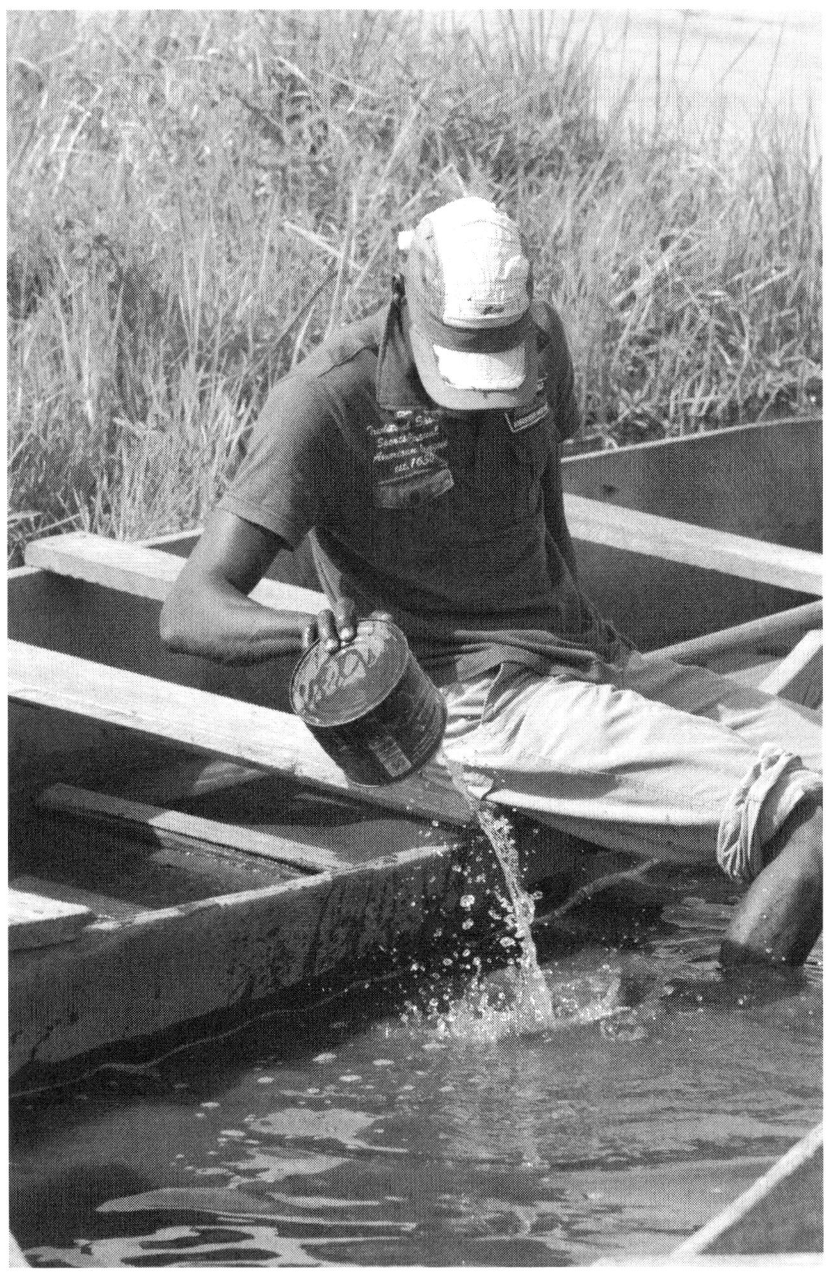

Boatman bailing out water from the boat, before our trip across Tengrela Lake.

Illustration from *The Hunter and the Crocodile*. Artwork by Fynn M'Llyr.

Chapter 11

June 3rd – Teresa's Site

A Peace Corps Volunteer's site could span a range of possibilities and define their experience. Before joining the Peace Corps, I read stories of volunteers living in yurts, mud huts, island bungalows, and urban apartments. In Burkina Faso, some volunteers lived in large towns with access to running water, electricity, and other modern conveniences—mustard, beer, toilet paper, etc. Other volunteers lived in remote villages, far from common Western amenities. Teresa's village was the latter.

Her village was small and remote, much closer to towns in both Mali and Côte d'Ivoire than to other villages in Burkina Faso. While French was the official language of Burkina Faso, its reach did not fully extend to her remote village. The handful of teachers, nurses, and gold miners who were camped on the edge of her village, and a select few other villagers spoke French in Fourkoura. Here, Dioula was the common tongue and Teresa had nearly mastered it, or so it appeared to those of us who could barely get past basic greetings or buy food in the market.

Teresa was thin, sported a short choppy haircut that suited her, and was not afraid to speak her mind, usually with the help of expletives. While her village, and especially the drivers of the van I took the evening before, didn't know the meaning of *shit, fuck,* and *damn*, it was safe to assume they'd heard Teresa use them in between French and Dioula phrases while voicing her frustration. She could come off as abrasive, but she had a big heart full of passion and was a great volunteer.

Teresa and I started the day with a simple breakfast of bread and tea, followed by a tour of her small community. As far and remote as her village was, I expected to see more traditional round houses with thatched roofs. Most of the houses, however, were plastered cinderblock or mud brick with corrugated tin roofs. Several wide roads crisscrossed the village, filled with motorbikes, bicycles, donkey carts, and people on foot. The village was small but busy and full of life.

Teresa's tante lived across from her house. The French word for aunt, a *tante* is a strong matriarch of both her household and community in Burkina Faso. In addition to having a big personality, a tante was usually big in size. Years of hard labor, carrying water, childbearing, cooking, and cleaning culminated to a point where they could spend the day seated in the comfort of a chair, delivering orders to children, grandchildren, and extended or adopted family. It was important to have at least one tante in your life. A tante was a second mother. She would teach you, feed you, send her kids to help you, and look out for your well-being.

We found Teresa's tante seated in a plastic chair, under the shade of a metal awning. She wore a colorful scarf around her head, a t-shirt, and many colorful wraps around her waist. Her tante sat with a large metal bowl on her lap, filled with shelled peanuts. At her feet lay empty peanut shells and a pile of recently harvested peanut plants. Generations of children played outside the house, ready to accept orders to run and buy ingredients in the market for the day's meal. As we approached, Teresa's tante looked up from the bowl of peanuts she sifted through and listened as Teresa introduced me in Dioula. She said that I was the Peace Corps Volunteer from Banzon and that I had come to visit the village. After this introduction, I greeted her.

"Aw ni Sogoma" (*Good morning, how are you?*)

"Herre." (*I am good.*)

"Somogodo?" (*How is your family*?)

"Herre." (*They are good.*)

"Baara da?" (*How is your work*?)

"Herre." (*It is good.*)

"Ala ka tile herre." (*May God give you a good day.*)

"Amina." (*Amen.*)

That was the extent of what I could confidently say in Dioula. I had a large Dioula vocabulary and followed along with conversations, but relied on French in my village. If I wanted to say anything further, Teresa would have to translate. Her tante, however, wasn't looking for a drawn out conversation and my customary greeting sufficed. Before parting, Teresa told her tante that another volunteer would be coming tonight and we would be biking to Niansogoni the next day. She would be back in three days. If you were going to leave village, you always let your tante know.

The tour of the small village didn't take long to complete. Teresa showed me the market in the center of village where she shopped for vegetables, the local medical center, and a small school. After checking off the few notable landmarks, there wasn't much more to see unless we biked to the fields surrounding the village or down to the Leraba River, the southwestern border between Burkina Faso and Côte d'Ivoire. We were left to find a way to pass the time, which I was all too familiar with. While in my village, I would regularly write out a long list of chores and to-do's for the day, only to find myself finishing the list before noon.

We returned to Teresa's house to relax before lunch. I read my Kindle and Teresa journaled. Over the past two years, I had grown accustomed to this pace and, as my service came to a close, I feared jumping back into the stride of everyday American life. In less than three months I would be back at Indiana University to finish grad school. After graduating, I would find a job and start a career, beginning the progression from one of life's milestones to the next. All of that sounded horribly tedious, even when compared to the long afternoon village days spent staring at my ceiling.

After two years of day dreaming, journaling, and thinking about my future, I didn't have a clearer sense of what I want I wanted to do. I was passionate about the environment, good at science, and a halfway decent communicator. The most important question, however, remained unanswered. What would make me happy? When I thought back to my favorite memories of the Peace Corps and in life, I was happiest when experiencing or learning something new. I loved adventure but also quickly defaulted to a routine-driven homebody.

I figured most people felt at odds with themselves, and while I found comfort in that, I had an unrelenting desire to find my next journey in life. The Peace Corps had helped me to savor the moment more, yet I accepted that I would always be an incessant planner. What was next?

Teresa offered two suggestions for lunch. She could make pasta with margarine and garlic powder, or we could buy rice and beans from a woman in the market. Rice and beans, the choice was easy. I never grew tired of rice; in addition to goat meat and eggs, rice was a main staple of my Burkina diet. For no good reason, I spent a month eating nothing but rice. Rice porridge in the morning, rice with peanut sauce for lunch, and stir-fried rice for dinner. It was the single thing I wanted to eat. The white, starchy grains of rice were consistent and comforting.

As much as I loved rice, I ate anything and everything during my service. From snout to tail, beak to bottom, I ate every edible cut of meat from goats, pigs, cows, sheep, rabbits, ducks, chickens, guinea fowl, and fish. A point made more amusing given that I was a vegetarian for seven years before the Peace Corps. In addition to your standard sources of animal protein, I ate antelope, donkey, bat, rat, dog, lizard, snake, petrified hippo fat, termites, and caterpillars. Yes, I ate dog. The most interesting meat of all, however, was the smoked bush cat I made into a soup. How did I find myself making soup out of smoked bush cat? Patrice.

Patrice's mother sold bushmeat and locally made millet beer. One afternoon, I followed Patrice to his house after running into him in the market. He said that he had some meat that he wanted to give me. Almost everything I did with Patrice made for a good story, which was why I kept hanging out with him. I wondered what I would be eating today.

Previously, his mother had served me boa constrictor in chili sauce, stewed monitor lizard, and roasted rat. I told them that I would try anything, other than monkey. When asked why I wouldn't eat monkey, I explained how you could contract diseases from eating monkeys and that HIV/AIDs originated in West African primates, very likely from bushmeat hunters.

We walked into his home's courtyard and he opened a meat smoker made from a 55-gallon drum. From the smoldering metal box, Patrice lifted an entire smoked animal by the tail. The creature was splayed open, with limbs reaching outward in every direction. The dehydrated skin was brown, leathery, and pulled tight across the carcass. From head to tail, the stiff body was about two feet long. Other than being a mammal, I had no idea what dried, desiccated animal Patrice extended toward me.

"What is that?" I asked.

"It's a bush cat," replied Patrice.

"Oh, yes. That does look like a cat," I returned. "Where was it killed?"

"A hunter killed it," answered Patrice.

A lot of what I ate at Patrice's house was illegal to some degree. On more than one occasion, he told me, "don't tell the forest agent."

From my neighbor, the forest agent, I learned that there were strict hunting laws in Burkina to preserve threatened native animal populations. But from the lack of exotic fauna in the bush outside my village, signs indicated the hunting laws were not well enforced, as with most laws in Burkina.

What exactly was a bush cat? Possibly an endangered species. My guesses ranged from feral house cat to an actual wild feline, likely a serval, of which I had seen pictures posted outside my neighbor's door, alongside photos of lions, elephants, and other megafauna.

Oh, what the hell. I'll try it, I thought. If it was an endangered species, it was already too late for this particular cat.

Patrice pulled out a cleaver, chopped the smoked cat in half, and handed me the hindquarters. "Clean it and make a soup," directed Patrice.

I thanked Patrice and his mother for the meat and set off to the market to buy vegetables for the cat soup I apparently would be making for lunch. I purchased onions, garlic, tomatoes, cabbage, and tomato paste. I would combine these with salt, pepper, a bay leaf, dried chili peppers, and a little cumin to make what I hoped would be an 'okay' soup. I hoped that chili powder and cumin would be able to overpower what I imagined to be the gamey taste of a smoked cat.

Once home, I prepared the soup base without the cat meat. I then began to chop up the meat but abruptly stopped, looking down in horror at the anatomy lab taking place on my kitchen counter. Inside, at both hip joints, I found maggots. Yes, maggots.

An average American would have vomited at this point. Actually, an average American would never find him/herself dismembering a smoked cat.

My reaction: slight depression at the fact that I would be missing out on free protein.

I took the meat out to my courtyard family and asked what to do with the meat (read: "Where should I throw this maggot-filled smoked cat?").

They replied, "You want to eat it? Give it to us and we'll clean it for you. Hot water will make them leave."

I handed over the cat.

As they cleaned the smoked maggot cat, I reflected on what I was about to do. Not only was I going to make soup from bush cat, I was going to make a soup from meat that had maggots feasting upon it. In the end, I reasoned that 1.) My family's nonchalant reaction meant that I had probably eaten something like this before, and 2.) maggots had soft bodies that would be destroyed by a rolling boil or quickly killed by my stomach acid.

After they cleaned and returned the meat to me, I meticulously dissected the cat—my biology degree and anatomy labs put to good use. I added the meat to the soup and cooked it on high heat for twenty-five minutes. The result was a gamey, but pleasant cat soup.

Rice and beans were a boring but safer option, although you did run the risk of breaking a tooth on a rock in a poorly cleaned batch of beans. We biked to the market and each bought a serving of rice and beans to go, placed piping hot into a thin black plastic bag, with hearty servings of peanut oil, MSG, and chili powder poured on top.

Back at Teresa's house, we ate. Teresa graciously offered a bottle of Sriracha, which she had received in a care package, to go with the rice and beans. Sriracha, or hipster ketchup as she called it, was a coveted item requested in care packages. Teresa also had real coffee sent from home. She promised to make the coffee tomorrow morning before we left for the cliff village with Jorgen.

Teresa and I regularly lamented the lack of good coffee in Burkina Faso, made more frustrating by the fact that Côte d'Ivoire, one of the largest producers of coffee, was a couple of miles from her house.

Overall, the day was a lazy and uneventful day. We passed the time with reading, talking, journaling, and napping. There wasn't much else to do. If I hadn't been there, Teresa would have been working with her local women's group or planning a project. A visitor, however, was a good reason to shirk responsibility without feeling guilty.

Late into the afternoon, Teresa and I returned to the market to buy vegetables and eggs for the morning. First, we bought onions from an old woman seated behind a worn wooden table in the shade of a black tarp held up by thick tree branches driven into the ground. She only sold onions, which were small and placed in piles on the table.

"Jàba ye jòli ye?" *(How much are the onions?)* asked Teresa.

"Duuru a duuru," (*25 CFA each)* replied the old woman.

"Aw bi tan fe," (*We want 50 CFA worth*) returned Teresa.

The old women reached under her chair and pulled out a thin plastic bag, which she filled with two piles of onions. I handed over a 50 CFA coin and asked Allah to give her a good evening.

One table over, a younger woman sold bell peppers, which were also arranged in small piles but atop a cloth spread on the ground. We bought 100 CFA of peppers. When the women picked up the peppers to place them in another bag, I stopped her.

"Saki bi N fe," (*I have a bag*) I said as I held open the bag of onions. She looked confused as to why I didn't want another bag but placed the peppers in the bag, alongside the onions.

Lastly, we bought eggs. One row over, a woman sat with two large cartons of eggs, chili peppers, and small bags of spices. I purchased a dozen eggs, an extreme luxury, to make a 12-egg omelet before our bike ride tomorrow. Jorgen, who would be arriving soon, and I could both eat a lot.

I hung our two bags of ingredients on my handlebars and followed Teresa back to her home. As we biked back, the bags swung back and forth, and I intently monitored the eggs. If I had been paying attention to the people on the side of the road, I would have seen Teresa's community intently watching me as I biked. *Who is the man with Teresa?*

Chapter 12

June 4th – Biking to Niansogoni

Villages wake up in stages. Before the first rays of sunshine are visible, animals preemptively begin to stir. It is not the iconic crow of a rooster that announces the coming of a new day, but rather the deep, throaty and seemingly uncontrollable, manic hee-haw of a donkey—a true ass among animals. Following the donkey's bugle, the chattering of guinea fowl fills the air. The footsteps of the guinea, West Africa's native chicken, are more rousing than the chattering as they run back and forth across the thin metal roof above your head.

After the animals, the women of the village rose. From the moment their eyes cracked open at dawn until finally closing at night, the women of Burkina Faso worked. They began by stoking the faint embers of yesterday's fire, coaxing them back to life with fresh tinder.

Metal pots and pans clanked and reverberated against one another as they were put in place for a day of cooking. Water glugged out from large plastic jugs and into a pot to be heated for breakfast. Drops of water that missed or escaped the pot hissed with an evaporative puff as they landed on the red-hot coals below. For a brief moment, before the rest of the house awoke, women could be seen seated next to the hearth, pausing silently in a meditative trance, reveling in the solitude of the morning.

Solitude, however, was short-lived. Children and men soon rose to start their day. Small children would linger impatiently at their mother's side, waiting for something to eat. Many families would start their day with a porridge of corn or sorghum. Less fortunate families would reheat remnants of their evening meal or nothing at all during the peak of the hunger season. More fortunate families would eat bread, dipped in Lipton tea or Nescafe coffee, heavily laden with sweetened condensed milk. Any scraps of a well-to-do family's morning meal would be tossed into the courtyard for their animals.

We awoke to the sounds of the village having already come to life. Motorcycles weaved through the dirt paths and crossed in front of Teresa's house. You could hear her neighbors shuffling about, the clanking of a large metal pot, and the exchange of morning greetings.

"How did you sleep?"

"With peace. How did you sleep?"

"With peace. How is your family?"

"They are well. How is your family?"

"They are well. May God give you a peaceful day."

"Amen. May God give you a peaceful day."

"Amen."

I began to roll my sleeping pad and shove my belongings into waterproof bags. I was the first to rise, but Jorgen and Teresa soon followed and began to prepare for the day. Amid packing, we waited in line for Teresa's latrine, passing the roll of toilet paper off to each successive person as if a relay baton.

Teresa started water for coffee and I began to cut vegetables for our pre-ride, twelve-egg omelet. I sautéed the vegetables and added salt, pepper, cumin, and red chili flakes. With a glass bowl in front of me, I reached for the first of the dozen eggs. The first egg crashed down into the side of the bowl with a dull thud. I attempted to crack the egg again, yet with the same resulting thud. Still partially asleep, I looked down with confusion at the egg to discover that we had purchased twelve hard-boiled eggs.

Discovering you bought hard-boiled eggs was much better than finding yourself covered in egg yolk after purchasing what you assumed to be a hard-boiled egg. We laughed at the absurdity of the situation but were not surprised. Thankfully, we had bread left over from the day before and our morning menu shifted to hard-boiled egg sandwiches with fajita style veggies.

Caffeinated and satiated, we began to tie down our bags and slather on last minute sunscreen. One by one we exited Teresa's courtyard, a bizarre looking bike gang of Americans on the way out of village. As we waved goodbye to villagers, they would ask where we were going. When we said we were biking to Niansogoni, each person made the same high-pitched exclamation of disbelief—*crazy to bike 20 miles.*

The ride was peaceful. Teresa and Jorgen listened to music as they peddled. I preferred to be left to my thoughts, basking in the lush green landscape as we biked. Rainy season had revived the previously desiccated plants that sprung back to life in full fervor.

In no time at all, we were more than halfway. We stopped for water and collectively remarked how great of a ride we were having.

"The next half," said Teresa, "is going to be a bit worse. The road is pretty bad and there is a portion that we'll have to walk."

She was right. It was worse, but the rocky path added excitement and required more attention. We were out in the middle of nowhere at this point. It would take several hours until anyone could reach us if something happened.

More than an hour passed until we came upon a larger village.

"This is Begwera," said Teresa as we pulled off to the side of the road outside a small shop. It was a simple town but large enough to host basic comforts, such as ice.

"It's only four more miles to Niansogoni," said Teresa.

"That's not bad at all," I replied. "Want to take a break here though?"

"Sure. I'm going to find out when the van to Banfora leaves tomorrow," replied Teresa.

"Good idea. I'm going to find food," I returned. I was hungry.

"I'll join you," said Jorgen.

Teresa set off to find someone who knew when the van would leave tomorrow and Jorgen and I looked for rice and sauce. Not far from where we stopped, we found two young boys grilling meat. We sat down and each ordered a plate of goat meat.

"Is there somewhere where we can get rice and sauce?" I asked the oldest boy, as he turned the grilling meat with the side of a machete.

"Yes. You want rice and sauce? Two plates? $1," replied the boy.

Jorgen pulled a large $1 coin from his wallet and handed it to the smallest boy who took off running down the street. Fifteen minutes later, he returned carrying two plates.

We finished our early lunch as Teresa appeared with bananas in hand.

"Banana?" offered Teresa.

"Sure," Jorgen and I replied. We had endless appetites.

"Good news," said Teresa. "I talked with the driver of the van and he'll drive to Niansogoni and pick us up in the morning, so we don't have to bike back here. It will be a little extra, but it's better than biking at 5:30 in the morning. He'll be there at 6:00 a.m."

That was good news. I knew we'd be rushing otherwise and worried that we'd miss the van. We would still rush to pack last-minute tomorrow morning, but this way we'd have the driver annoyed with us rather than leaving us behind.

With our plans set for the next morning, we remounted our bikes that had become surrounded by inquisitive village children. We gave high-fives and fist bumps to the kids who laughed and watched the group of dirty, goofy strangers take off on their bikes.

The last four miles passed quickly and we soon reached the Niansogoni campground. The camp consisted of four large circular huts with thatched roofs. The interior of each building was empty and without electricity. In the back, a partitioning wall formed an indoor shower room, with a small window to let in light.

After paying to stay for the night, we ordered a bucket of cold beers. It was slightly past noon and we were waiting until 4:00 p.m. to hike up the mountain when it would be cooler. Until our hike, we planned to rest and enjoy our cold drinks.

While we sat, the owners of the campground brought over buckets of water for us to bathe. We were each covered in a fine layer of crusting dirt but held off on bucket baths until after hiking up and down the mountain. You could tell that we were judged for not jumping at the opportunity to bathe.

Sitting in the shade to escape the afternoon sun, I took out my journal. I developed the habit of journaling in the Peace Corps, but over the past week had neglected to write. A lot had happened. I clicked open my pen and started to dump thoughts onto the page.

04 June 2014

So many days passed. So many things have happened.

-Kate, Melissa, and Chris left
-Tested positive for HIV, then it came back negative for the 2nd test
-Went dancing
-Visited my host family in Ipelce
-Saw hippos, domes, and cascades in Banfora
-Went to Teresa's site. Spent the day lounging.
-Biked to Niansogoni to see the cliff village. Waiting now to hike up.

Very sad to say goodbye to Kate. The last week was odd. We didn't spend a lot of time together. Went out for their final celebration meal at Benoua Lounge. Had the duck. It was Amazing.

Kate seems to be doing well. I hope we're able to keep in touch.

I already wrote about the HIV test on my blog. I may sit down and rewrite the post down in my journal. I also need to expand on the experience.

Things I Want To Do After The Scare
-Eat extremely well (not doing well so far)
-Start training karate and fighting again
-Start a new blog and write more
-Spend lots of time in nature

Visiting Ipelce and my host family was good. I didn't know what to expect after not doing well to keep in touch with them.

I sat with my journal open on my lap, watching clouds slowly move across the deep-blue sky, my mind floating in company with the white tufts above. Teresa carried her bags into our room and Jorgen played music on his phone.

Shortly after 4:00 p.m., I peeled myself from the chair and prepared a small bag for the hike.

The peak looked out of place. A sole towering monument jutting out of what was an otherwise flat, sparsely forested plain. At the base of the small mountain, we began to wind our way upwards along a narrow rocky path.

It quickly became apparent that I was not as fit as I thought. My fellow American hikers showed similar signs of strain. Our guide, who effortlessly bounded up the mountainside in flip-flops, stopped at each flat, shaded ledge to allow us to catch our breaths.

At our third stop, I sat down to rest on a large rock. I reached down to pick up a dried Baobab seedpod beside my foot, cracked open the pod and plucked seeds from the spongy interior, placing a small handful of seeds in my pocket. I would either plant them in my tree nursery back in village, attempt to smuggle them home to the U.S. in a few months, or forget them in my pocket until I did laundry.

As we advanced up the trail, the remnants of the abandoned civilization began to appear. Rock lines delineated past walls and hilltop fields. Scrapes in the stones formed abandoned mortars used to grind grain. The regrowth forest gave way as the mountain curled back creating a roof and we found ourselves standing in the middle of an ancient village nestled in the alcove of the cliff. Only mud grain silos and roofless dwellings remained, providing a glimpse of what once was. The village of the Wa, the Panther People.

The village was tucked away high in the cliffs, which provided protection to the tiny settlement. The Wa gained additional protection from the large stone walls they built on the ridges of the mountain. Our guide told us that those walls not only blocked the numerous routes up to the village but when warring tribes approached, the Wa would band together and push over the stone walls, sending an avalanche of boulders careening down the mountainside. If rocks raining down didn't stop the enemy, the Wa would begin firing poison-tipped arrows. Our guide pointed to an ornately decorated earthen container, which held the poison, built into the small alcove hovering above the medicine man's hut.

The Wa lived in the cliffs for protection, but the security they gained from the cliffs was not without a cost. For the majority of the year, water was unavailable on the mountain. Each day, the Wa women would climb down the cliff, walk several miles to a nearby stream, collect water, and hike water back to their cliff-nestled dwellings.

"Typical," Teresa remarked.

From our point of view, women in Burkina carried a disproportionate workload. The traditional division of labor separated duties between those in and around the house and those outside the home. Women cooked, cleaned, collected water, gathered firewood, and raised children while men were responsible for hunting and farming.

Since the protective cliffs provided little land suitable for crop production, the men of the village worked the plains below the cliff and carried their harvest up the mountain for storage in clay grain silos, or so we were told. If my observations of present day Burkina held any clues to the past, the head of the household owned the field, but everyone was responsible for farming.

In Burkina, I saw more women working in the fields surrounding my village than men, who were usually seen turning over the ground with an ox-drawn plow or spraying pesticide. The more tedious task of planting and weeding by hand was primarily relegated to women and children.

The cliff village of Niansogoni dated back to the 14th century. I felt like an explorer stumbling upon long lost ruins, but the village was abandoned in 1980.

"People were living up here in modern times. When there were Peace Corps Volunteers serving in Burkina Faso," reflected Jorgen.

After a war with a neighboring tribe, the Wa decided to leave their traditional cliff village and move down to the plains. They felt that their old way of living was no longer practical, and relocated to Niansogoni.

In my short lifetime, a lot had changed in Burkina Faso. Eight years ago, the first Peace Corps Volunteer in my village didn't have a cell phone during her service. To talk to another volunteer on the phone, you had to use one of the few landlines outside the cities and plan ahead in order for the other person to be waiting at the phone when you called. Calls back to the U.S. were rare and infrequent. News from home came in the form of letters, which could arrive months after they were mailed.

Daily, I texted or called fellow volunteers. I regularly chatted over the internet with my friends back home and posted pictures from my smartphone, all while enjoying the shade of a mango tree. My parents called me every Sunday like clockwork.

In the short two years I lived in my village, a lot changed. A new strip of buildings, small shops built by a local investor, lined the main road. Electric lines from Bobo stretched out to my village and began to electrify homes. Even small signs of my projects could be seen around town in the form of newly planted trees, vegetable gardens, and locally made soaps sold by women in the market.

Even with all the change, Burkina had one foot deeply planted in the past as the other foot strained toward progress. The intersect of modern and ancient equally a blessing as a curse. Modern conveniences provided opportunity for solutions to age-old issues but also brought with them contemporary concerns, while not completely wiping away past problems.

It was odd to realize that more than 80% of the population had a cell phone, but less than 40% were literate. In my local market I could buy Harry Potter movies on DVD, but women walked a mile for clean water. The Kindle in my backpack held more books than the local school.

The cliff village was the old way. Niansogoni the new.

After hundreds of photos and crawling into abandoned birthing houses, we descended from the peak and returned to the camp. After the others had showered, I took my bucket of water into the small dark shower room. The sun had set, so I hung my headlamp from the metal bars across the small window to provide light to wash by. I crouched down and slowly poured cool water over my entire body. Using a bar of soap, I lathered and loosened the day's grime. I rinsed each body part and worked my way down.

Crouched in the shower room, I paused. Something wasn't right. I thought that I felt something. After standing naked in the shower room and studying myself with my headlamp, I saw nothing.

It's only my imagination, I told myself.

I was thinking about the HIV test. It was perfectly understandable to be still thinking about it. I was okay though. The second test came back negative.

I finished my bath, but a thought began to replay in my mind. I couldn't shake what Heather said. Could my second test have been a false negative?

Niansogoni cliff village. Ornately decorated earthen container built into small alcove hovering above the medicine man's hut that held poison for arrows.

Chapter 13

June 5th – Call

We had overslept and were late. The van sat running outside our hotel room, and the driver was not happy. We quickly finished packing, gathered our bikes, and headed to the car. Our bikes were thrown on top, hastily tied down, and the van quickly pulled away from the hotel toward Begwera. In Begwera the car was loaded down with other passengers, goats, and mysterious packages. The drive from Niansogoni to Begwera was much faster than the previous day when we biked. The scenery looked different going fast, bumping up and down in the van.

Once in Banfora, the driver dropped us off outside a sandwich shop well-known amongst volunteers in the area. One dollar bought an egg sandwich filled with avocado, onions, tomatoes, mayo, and mustard. We all recognized that from an outsider's point of view, these sandwiches were nothing special—possibly disgusting—but for a Peace Corps Volunteer, these greasy sandwiches were a treat. Teresa ordered one sandwich. Jorgen and I ordered two each, which were followed by a round of sweetened Nescafe coffees.

As we sat at the vinyl wrapped table, looking out to the road, we talked and watched motorcycles and cars pass by. Each of us was nearing the end of our service. We took turns reminiscing about the past two years, the ups and downs we had shared together.

I distinctly remember the first time I met Jorgen and Teresa. Before leaving for Burkina Faso, the 11 people that made up my training group convened in Philadelphia. We arrived in Philly from different states, backgrounds, and experiences, for a day of staging—a long afternoon filled with bureaucratic paperwork and informational sessions.

Teresa and Jorgen could not have been more different. That first day, Teresa wore a long flowy skirt with Chacos, her unshaved legs exposed to the air. Jorgen wore a green Nike polo shirt, neatly tucked into his khaki pants. Teresa was a quick-tempered, liberal feminist, ready to take on the world. She was the living embodiment of what I had imagined all Peace Corps Volunteers to be. Jorgen, on the other hand, was conservative in both his temperate and ideological leaning. At the first meeting, I thought his big heart better-suited for a mission trip building houses or a church in South America, rather than the slow-paced, unstructured nature of the Peace Corps—he'd prove me wrong.

During three months of training, each of us grew close, and our differences held us together. When one of us would begin to second-guess our decision to join the Peace Corps, we had each other to lean on. When I was angry, Teresa was there to help me vent my frustration and made it okay to say when things were 'fucking shitty.' Sometimes, they were really fucking shitty. When I was sad, Jorgen was there to listen and help me understand, accept, and begin to move beyond the sadness.

My phone rang, breaking me away from the nostalgic reminiscing. It was one of the Medical Officers. Why were they calling? What did they want? I answered and found Crystal on the other end of the call.

"Hello Crystal, how are you?"

"I'm doing well, Tyler, how are you?"

"I'm fine, what's up?"

"I hear you are with other volunteers. Can you call me back when you are alone?"

She heard English being spoken in the background. Peace Corps Volunteers were often the only other people who openly spoke English in Burkina Faso.

"No, you can tell me now," I replied as I walked away from the table.

Given the past week's events, I didn't want to wait. If Crystal was calling me, something was wrong.

"Tyler, we got the paper results of your test back from the lab. The wrong test was run, and we need you to come to Ouaga. The hospital's lab repeated a screening test, not the test that we requested. You're going to be medevaced. We have to send you to get the correct test."

I explained to Crystal that I was in Banfora with Jorgen and Teresa and would need to head back to my village to grab a few things before I left. She said that was okay because the earliest flight would be at the beginning of next week, but she wanted me to come in as soon as possible. I didn't want to ask further about the test. I didn't want Teresa and Jorgen to overhear me. I tried to stay calm, to hide the upwelling emotions.

Everything that I experienced days ago returned. I had feared something was wrong. Was I HIV positive?

I hung up the phone with Crystal and began to sheepishly explain to Jorgen and Teresa that I needed to go to Bobo and that I couldn't spend the day hanging out with them. They knew something was wrong and had a good idea what. Yet, neither of them would dare say it.

I said goodbye and made my way up the road alone, to where Teresa said I could catch a van to Bobo. As I walked away, I resisted the urge to look back. I stood on the side of the road on the verge of tears, unsure of what to do.

Go to Bobo. I had to go to Bobo.

I flagged down a passing van and asked if they were going to Bobo. They said they were. I asked how much and the driver replied, "Don't worry about it, get in."

One of the van's attendants quickly jumped down from the top of the van, grabbed my bike, and began tying it down on top of the car. I asked again, "How much?"

"$10."

There was no way in hell that I was going to pay $10. That was too much.

"I'll give you $2," I quickly returned.

"No, $10 is the price. Get in."

I was furious, emotional, and did not have the temper to deal with the driver. It was evident to me that this wasn't bartering. He was trying to rip me off.

"I'm not paying that. Give me my bike back. I'll bike to Bobo before I'll give you my money," I yelled at the driver.

"Okay, $8. Get in."

"Fuck you. Give me my bike."

The driver, attendant, and passengers looked back at me blankly. We were in a standoff and they weren't going to give me my bike back. I had had it. I was done. I wanted to scream. This was really fucking shitty.

If they weren't going to give me my bike back, I was going to take it back. To the driver's disbelieve, I climbed on top of the van and started untying my bike.

"Get down. Get down. $2. $2. Get in."

I wasn't having it. The emotions that I had suppressed returned. I was angry. I was sad. I was pissed off. After I untied my bike, I wanted to beat the driver to death with it.

I knew the price; the price was $2, maybe even less than that. I wasn't going to be gouged. At that moment, I wanted to be anywhere else. But, I was on top of a van, fighting with a guy as I untied my bike, blinded by anger.

I handed my bike down to a man who had left the van to either watch or help the deranged foreigner. I quickly flagged down a second van, informed them that the price was two dollars, and took my seat while I waited for someone to tie my bike down to the roof.

The second van pulled away as the first van still sat on the side of the road. I was on my way back to Bobo, unsure if I would ever see Teresa and Jorgen again, unsure if I would be back in the United States this time next week. At that moment, I both hated Burkina Faso and wasn't ready to leave. I cried uncontrollably but didn't care what the other passengers thought.

When I arrived in Bobo, I immediately headed to the Peace Corps Office. No one else was there. I was happy to be alone and called Crystal again. She picked up, "Hello, Tyler."

"What do you know? What's the plan now?" I started.

"We're still trying to figure that out. We want to send you back to the United States to have the correct test run. We're still getting everything arranged," Crystal replied.

As I spoke with Crystal, I paced back and forth through the Peace

Corps office. It was good that I was alone. She provided me with further details about the situation and explained that the second test was another screening test. The U.S. Embassy lab had run an HIV antibody test, while the lab at the hospital ran a combination HIV antibody/antigen test. The second test was considered to be a better test, but still a screening test. The test that they wanted and requested, a Western Blot, would confirm the results of a screening test. The hospital in Ouagadougou, however, would not run a Western Blot unless I had tested positive for HIV in their lab. My previous positive test results were not enough.

When Dr. Patel called me last week to tell me that my HIV test came back negative, he had been told the results of the test over the phone. Peace Corps had requested a Western Blot test and assumed that the hospital ran the requested test. Today, when they received the paper results from the hospital, they were shocked to see that the negative test result was from another screening test. Without the right test, they didn't know if I was HIV positive or not.

No lab in Burkina Faso would run the test I needed. I had to be medevaced out of the country.

"When would I leave?" I asked Crystal.

"The earliest flight would be Monday," replied Crystal. "You should come to Ouaga as soon as possible."

"Okay, I will go to my village tomorrow to pack and then leave for Ouaga the next day. Once I go back to the United States and have this test run, if everything is fine, will I just get back on a plane and come back to Burkina?"

"No, because you're within three months of leaving, you won't be allowed to come back. You'll be early COSed," Crystal answered.

The conversation stopped. I would be medevaced and end my service early. That meant my Peace Corps service was over. Within a matter of days, I would suddenly be back home.

"Wait, you're telling me that you're going to send me back to the U.S. and that my Peace Corps Service is over?" I asked. I couldn't believe it.

"Possibly," Crystal cautiously responded.

"No, I don't want to do that. I'm not going to the U.S. if I can't come back. I've made it this far and I want to finish. Isn't there anywhere else I can go?" I begged.

The uncertainty surrounding my HIV test was overshadowed by the seeming certainty that my Peace Corps service was quickly coming to an end. I had a month and a half left in Burkina Faso. After numerous low points, I was proud to have made it to the end. I wanted to COS with my fellow volunteers. I wanted to stand with them as we were pinned and applauded for our accomplishment. I refused to believe I was HIV positive. I was going to come back to Burkina.

Crystal was surprised by my pushback. She hadn't considered that I would want to stay. After two years, many volunteers would have jumped at the possibility to leave early. But I did not want my service to end abruptly. I wanted the opportunity to say goodbye to my friends and family in village. I hoped to have many more lazy afternoons, chatting under the shade of a mango tree. If I could avoid it, I was not going to suddenly leave my village without warning. I owed them so much. They deserved better.

Ripe with uncertainty, I finished my call with Crystal. Was I HIV positive? Was my Peace Corps service over?

Peace Corps was going to see what they could do. My blood could be drawn in Ouaga and flown to a lab in France. Or, I could be medevaced to Senegal and have the test run there. Crystal said she would be on the phone with the Peace Corps medical team until she found an answer. She made no promises but hoped that she could find a way for me to come back to Burkina Faso to COS. Of course, that would also require that I was not HIV positive.

The Bobo Peace Corps office remained empty. I continued to pace the house, my mind racing. I needed a distraction but was in no state to leave the office. I would have watched a movie on my computer, but my laptop was back in Ouagadougou. The office, however, had two desktop computers for volunteers. I sat down at one of the Peace Corps computers and logged into Facebook.

Scrolling down my news feed, I read posts from my friends back home. Cute animal videos, recipes, and statuses filled with either complaints or self-praise weren't enough to distract me. My mind continued to run.

Heather had asked if my second test could have been a false negative. I had outwardly denied any possibility of a false negative, but for the past several days, a subtle granule of doubt rested in the back of my mind. Now, the doubt was no longer subtle. Screening tests are imperfect. 1 in 100 tests would give a false positive. What was the probability of a false negative?

Kate. What about Kate? What if I was HIV positive and she was too. She had her COS medical exam before leaving the country, after we slept together. But, her HIV test was done much earlier than mine. What if her body wasn't yet producing enough detectable antibodies? If infected, there would be a window of several weeks, possibly months, where HIV would not be measurable by a screening test. This was a possibility, right? This made sense.

Still seated at the computer, I opened a new browser window and typed *'time before HIV can be detected'* and hit enter.

> Rapid antibody test – gives a positive result based on antibodies to HIV, not the virus itself. It takes your body up to **3 months** to produce these antibodies at levels that can be detected by this test. **4-6 weeks** (up to **3 months**) after infection, most people will have enough antibodies to test positive.
>
> HIV Test Window Periods - San Francisco AIDS Foundation
> www.sfaf.org/hiv-info/testing/hiv-test-window-periods.html

I was right.

I had to let Kate know. I took out my phone and dialed her. I needed to say this over the phone. The phone rang with no response. She didn't pick up.

Seconds later Kate sent back a message: *You called?*

Rather than respond, I called her again. This time she picked up and I told her everything I knew: my second test wasn't the right test; I might be medevaced to the U.S.; I still might have HIV. The conversation was short and direct. I didn't have much else to say, other than the few facts I knew. I told her I would keep her updated and that I was sorry for all of this. She thanked me for letting her know and we ended the call.

Kate quickly wrote back with a follow-up message: *I'm confused. You tested positive again and that's why you're going to America? Or are they sending you back as a precaution?*

I replied. *No, the second test was negative, but not the exact test they wanted. The second test was better than the first, but Crystal and Headquarters want the best test to be run (which the lab in Burkina won't do unless I have two positive tests first).*

Kate: *Ok, good. That's what I thought.*

She was back home, enjoying life in the U.S., and I dropped this on her for the second time. I didn't want to frighten her, but I wanted Kate to know everything that I knew. If I was HIV positive, she could be too. I didn't want this to harm any more people than it had to.

I repeated that there was a chance the first test was right and the second test was a false negative, but there was no way of knowing right now. I would know next week.

She said she was going to get tested again and I agreed that it was a smart idea—it was more than three months after possible infection.

Kate had to go and we said goodbye. From her messages, I sensed she was worried. But telling her now, as I had done the first time, was the right thing to do.

It was 2:00 p.m. and I sat alone in the office. I wished that Jorgen or Teresa were here with me. Or Andy, who I had solely confided in the first time my test results came back. While I didn't want everyone to know, I longed for someone else to confide in.

Then there were Heather and Caroline. Given the timeline of events, I didn't think that I needed to let either of them know with such little information. I believed that Heather was safe. I, however, began to revisit the possibility that I contracted HIV from Caroline. It was a borderline irrational idea, but I was quickly losing my grip on reality. How had I managed to find myself in the same messed up place twice in one week?

Maybe no one would be in town today and I would have the office to myself. I had to do something, talk to someone. Teresa and Jorgen already knew something was wrong. I would call them. I first called Jorgen, but his wife Julie answered. She had heard about the first scare. I broke down and began to cry as I unloaded the little information I knew. She did her best to comfort me, but the greatest comfort was in telling someone. I felt good to let it out rather than hiding what I was feeling. Previously, I carried the fear of being HIV positive for little more than a day. Now, I would have to wait at least six.

Today was Thursday. My earliest flight would be Monday. If was sent back to the U.S., I wouldn't arrive until Tuesday evening. I assumed they would fly me to Washington, D.C., to Peace Corps Headquarters. In D.C., I would have my blood drawn first thing in the morning on Wednesday and would have an answer that afternoon.

If I were going to be sent back to the U.S., I would have to let my parents know. HIV positive or not, I could be back in Kentucky in a week. But until I knew my plans for sure, I wouldn't tell them anything. It would be better that way. If I was flown to Senegal and tested negative for HIV, they would likely never know.

I ended my call with Julie and thanked her for talking. I told her that she could tell Jorgen, but asked that she not tell anyone else. Gossip traveled fast in the Peace Corps. I wasn't ready for the whole country to know.

Next, I called Teresa. As I neurotically paced the still empty office, I let her know why I had suddenly left Banfora. With Teresa, I was more composed and managed to not cry on the phone. She wished me well and tried to comfort me the best she could. I thanked her, said good-bye, and repeated my request for confidentiality.

Maybe all my worry and panic was for nothing. This could merely be an unfortunate series of events. Perhaps my first test was a false positive. The second screening test, while not the test that was ordered, was right. From the sound of it, the second test was a better test. But, why was Peace Corps quick to put me on the first flight out of Burkina? It did not seem that my medevac was a precaution. Their urgency was cause for concern.

I sat back down at the computer to talk to one of my best friends,

Medrena, with the hope that someone back home, not in the Peace Corps, could calm my nerves. I opened a chat window and typed *Hey there.* I sat motionless, focused on the screen, waiting for a reply. After several minutes had passed, Medrena responded back with *Hi.* Knowing no better way to start the conversation, I told her exactly how I felt: *I'm very alone right now.*

Medrena wrote back: *I miss you. I'm glad you're ok.*

Me: *I may not be. I'm being medically evacuated Monday for further testing*

Medrena: *Holy fuck, Tyler! Where are they taking you?*

Me: *Maybe DC, maybe Senegal. Details aren't fully set.*

Medrena: *I wish there was something I could do. How are you handling it?*

Me: *Really well until about 5 minutes ago.*

I told Medrena everything—the many various thoughts that I was unable to shake. There was a real possibility that I was not okay. With every passing minute, it seemed as if the chances of me being HIV positive were growing, though the situation remained the same. The only thing to change was the web of facts I continued to weave in my mind.

After unloading on Medrena, she responded: *Everything is going to be fine. You have to be fine, I refuse any other options.*

Me: *Hope so. You're the first one back home who knows.*

Medrena: *Tyler!!! Jesus Christ.*

Me: *I found all this out hours ago. Awaiting further details before I let people know more.*

Medrena: *I'm always here if you need to talk, you know that.*

Me: *Thanks. I'll let you know when I find out something. Don't tell anyone.*

Medrena: *Good. I won't.*

It was now well into the afternoon and I hadn't eaten since breakfast in Banfora. I walked down the street to Trois Karite and ordered rice and peanut sauce to go. I wasn't in the mood to sit in public. I was afraid I would start crying again. I was handed my hot food, placed in plastic bags, and walked back to the office. I located a small tin pot in the kitchen that I poured my meal into. I found an unclaimed bottle of hot sauce in the refrigerator and smothered my food.

I sat on the couch and began to eat while thumbing through an Oregon travel magazine found on the coffee table. The smiles of happy campers hiking through the Pacific Northwest were a stark contrast to me, sitting alone, eating rice out of a pot, under the intermittent breeze of an oscillating fan.

After finishing my meal, I continued to sit on the couch, vacantly gazing into the kitchen. My hands rested together in my lap as my thumbs slowly encircled one another. A dull sense of hopelessness gradually inched its way from the base of my skull, down my spine, and outwardly through my extremities. My joints were stiff and immobile, locking my body into an apathetic torpor. At this point, even crying required too much energy.

I slowly licked my lips, which were both spicy and salty—remnants of hot sauce, sweat, and tears. My chest slowly rose and sank as I breathed. In. Out. In. Out. I repeated to myself. I felt that if I stopped actively telling myself to breathe, I would die sitting there on the couch. I could hear the beat of my heart in my ears, which formed a rhythmic pattern with the whirring of the oscillating fan.

A new sound filled the room and abruptly broke my trance. My phone was ringing. It was Peace Corps.

"Hello," I answered.

"Hello, Tyler," responded Crystal. "I have new information for you. We have you on a flight to Senegal Wednesday morning. Your blood will be drawn by the regional PCMO and then sent to France for testing. You'll then fly back here on Friday. The good news is that you'll be able to come back to Burkina Faso. The bad news is that it could take two weeks to get your test results back. How does that sound? Do you have any questions?"

"That sounds good. I'm glad that I will be coming back to Burkina. Can I stay the night in the med room in Bobo?" I asked.

"Yes, of course. I will call the guard and have him unlock the med room. You should plan to be in Ouaga no later than Tuesday at noon so we can finalize some paperwork and other details before you leave. Rick has already started your visa paperwork. Go back to your village tomorrow and pack whatever you need for a few days. Keep your head up and call me if you need anything."

"Thank you. See you Tuesday," I responded and ended the call with Crystal.

Minutes later, the guard came into the office and unlocked the med room. I brought my bags into the room and turned on the room's air conditioner as low as it would go. After taking a hot shower in the private bathroom, I turned off the lights and crawled under the thick covers of the twin bed. I slowly drifted into a restless sleep. It was barely after 6:00 p.m.

Chapter 14

June 6th – Back to Village

06 June 2014

I feel my life is an utter mess. I fly to Senegal Wednesday (today is Friday) for yet another HIV test. The second test that was run (that came back negative) was a more specific and specialized test, but it was not the test they wanted. This was discovered when the hard copy results were sent to the Peace Corps office.

The Burkina government won't run the test I need unless the patient has two positive test results first. No getting around it. It's the law or something.

I was told all of this yesterday, after returning from Niansogoni and the cliff village there. Peace Corps wants the other test run. I want it run too, but I thought I was in the clear. To think you're HIV positive twice in the same week.

I'm optimistic and have a solid logical resolve but I can only do so much and be so strong.

I was first given the option of early COS, to go home and have the test run. I want to finish with the others.

I said that I'd want to be medevaced, have the test run, and return if all was well. They couldn't believe that I'd want to return with so little time left.

With that in mind, they changed my medevac from the U.S. to Senegal.

I fly out Wednesday. Have blood drawn Thursday. Fly back Friday. Results will take two weeks. They have to be sent to Paris to be processed. So it's possible that I'll know nothing for the next three weeks.

I'll be stuck in this pending status for three weeks. A day was hell. This is going to take a lot out of me.

Fate is in my favor though, with the more specific test being negative. The fear still exists. If I hadn't slept with Caroline, I wouldn't be so worried (nothing against her, just the situation). Such a hollow act now may be very significant.

I need to become a monk.

Maybe this second scare is a good thing (if it comes back negative). All that I thought about and reflected on really didn't stick the first time.

The truck rolled to a stop outside my village's market. People handed down items that had been stuffed under their seat or held in their lap during the two-hour, bumpy ride from Bobo to Banzon. Men and women squeezed their way out the back and front exits, stepping down to the compacted ground below. For several minutes, a seemingly endless stream of people poured from the truck that had been loaded to capacity with passengers, animals, and cargo.

Members of the village gathered around the truck within moments of its arrival. They were shop owners waiting on deliveries from the city, men and women picking up recently arrived family members, children sent on an errand to retrieve a package, and others who merely wanted to see who or what had come to town that evening.

If not the first person off the truck, I was the last. I preferred to wait patiently in the uncomfortable seat for a few more minutes rather than jostle my way toward the crowded exits. This time, I was in the passenger's seat and the first to depart. I stepped down from the truck's cabin, instantly greeted by a group of children. Long gone were the days when they asked me for candy and shouted tubabu, the Dioula word for foreigner. Now, they greeted me by name, offered to carry my bag, and asked me to make the sound of water droplets with my mouth or do another of the various tricks they had grown to expect from me.

Idrissa, one of the truck's crewmembers, rounded the front of the truck, walking with a smile and my bicycle as he approached. He passed my bike to me and I thanked him. Two of the children held my bike steady as I tied down my bags to the back rack. Next, they checked to make sure the bag was properly lashed down by rocking the bag back and forth and popping the thick, black rubber strap used to secure my bag. I was only going a short distance, but it was important that I passed their inspection.

I quickly biked down the main road to Issouf's. His roadside restaurant was where I started and ended each trip away from village. In the morning, after placing a bag in a seat of the truck to reserve my spot, I would wait with Issouf. He would be in the process of opening up his shop and setting out coffee, tea, and fried doughnuts. Without asking, he prepared coffee for me, which he rarely accepted payment for and for which I would swiftly drop money into the jar behind the counter when he wasn't looking. In the evening, upon my return to village, I would stop by to let him know that I had safely returned home.

"TYYY-LURRR," Issouf shouted as I pulled into the courtyard behind his restaurant.

"EEEE-SOUFFF," I returned.

"E dance – *welcome*," replied Issouf, followed by the customary back and forth exchange of greetings. This time, the call and response of salutations was done in Dioula. Issouf, however, enjoyed challenging me to learn Bobo, Tusian, Fufulde, or Moore—the other native languages that he spoke.

Gilbert the Rastafarian and three young Fulani men were seated in Issouf's courtyard, a large barren dirt lot behind the restaurant. His small, one room, mud brick house sat in the eastern corner of the lot, the latrine in the northern corner, and his large mango tree in the western corner, which shaded his deep well and a collection of wooden benches. One of the Fulani men rose to give me his seat. I protested, saying that I was only stopping to say hello, but he insisted that I sit and relax after traveling from Bobo. Reluctantly, I took his place as he knelt down to sit on a colorful woven mat, shared by one of the other Fulani men. Issouf emerged from his restaurant, bobbing a tea bag in and out of a small glass, filled with hot steaming water. Issouf handed me the glass and with a smile said, "Lipton, no sugar.

I'm out of coffee."

I allowed the tea to steep before taking my first slow sip. I was happy to be back in village, but I was emotionally and physically drained. I wanted to tell Issouf everything. I wanted to tell him that I had tested positive for HIV, and tested negative, but now had to go to Senegal for further testing. But I didn't think that my crude explanation in French would be enough for Issouf to understand the situation. He was my best friend. I told him everything and confided in him in ways that I wouldn't dare do with other people in my village. He had helped me through other hard times. I wanted to tell him what was going on, but I knew I couldn't.

During my first week in village, I biked into town, hoping to find my way to and from the market to buy food. I had already gotten lost several times since arriving at my site. To find my way home, I would ask small children for directions to the Banzon Rice Association, which I lived behind. My second day in village, I became so lost that I had to swallow my pride and asked a kid to take me back home. "Do you know where I live? Can you take me there? I'm lost." That kid probably thought I was weird, stupid, or both.

As I turned left onto the main road, in the direction I believed was the market, a man yelled out, "Tubabu-che, nia – *White man, come here!*" Unenthused, I changed course and biked toward the man who had yelled at me. I was less than a week into my actual Peace Corps service and already growing tired of constantly being called "white man or foreigner."

The man stood up from the worn wooden bench outside a roadside shop. He was wearing all black: heavy black combat boots, thick black cargo pants, a black sleeveless undershirt, and a black cowboy hat. He had a thick matted beard and his eyes were darkened with black eyeliner. Around his neck was a thin leather strap from which a silver circle pendant hung. He was short, coming barely past my shoulder, but extremely muscular. He was unlike any other person I had met in Burkina Faso.

Standing under the rusted metal awning of the shop, the pirate-looking man extended his callused hand and I did the same, locking his hand into a firm, deliberate handshake. "E dance, Tubabu-che. N togo ko Issouf. E togo bi di? – *Welcome, foreigner. My name is Issouf. What is your name?*'

From day one, Issouf made up his mind that we were going to be friends. Every day in village since meeting Issouf, I spent part of my day either seated in front of his shop on the worn, wooden bench or in his courtyard under the shade of his large mango tree. While I was hesitant to trust others in my village, there was never a doubt in my mind that he would always look out for me.

Issouf spent his teenage years living outside the military base in Bobo because his father was in the Burkina army. As a result of his father's status, Issouf attended a well-funded high school where he learned to speak French very well, in addition to learning martial arts, and about other cultures of the world. He continually surprised me with what he knew.

Issouf Ouattara Sanou was from royal Bobo ancestry. His forefathers were the traditional mask makers of the Bobo people. Known as the Chief Costumier, his elders were entrusted with the responsibility of carving the Bobo masks, which were a connection to the spiritual world. Issouf's forefathers sat on the Bobo council alongside the Village Chief, Land Chief, Chief Blacksmith, and other Bobo nobles. For hundreds of years, his family helped to guide the Bobo people.

When Issouf's grandfather passed, his father assumed the role of Chief Costumier. As a member of religious nobility, Issouf's upbringing was deeply steeped in ritual and mysticism. He practiced traditional medicine and magic, most of which was good and performed to bring health, wealth, and prosperity to himself and others. Issouf was also known to practice dark magic, which he closely guarded and reserved for countering the dark magic of more nefarious practitioners.

With Issouf's father's passing, Issouf was next in the line of succession to become Chief Costumier of the Bobo. Being Chief Costumier, however, bound you to a traditional lifestyle and required you to live in Logofuruso, the village of Issouf's ancestors. While Issouf loved magic, he wanted to have a modern life.

On the night of his father's funeral, when he was to assume his rightful title, Issouf ran away from the village. In his absence, his brother was forced to take the role of Chief Costumier. For the next ten years, Issouf dared not return to his traditional home due to fear of imprisonment, torture, or death. He told me stories of how dark spirits and genies were sent after him to bring him back to the village, but his magic was strong and they could not catch him.

With time, tensions in his village eased and he was allowed to return to visit. He, however, never dared to spend the night in village again. For it was then that he believed they would finally force him to assume the role of mask maker.

One weekend, I traveled with Issouf to visit his family's village. He wanted to show me a true traditional village; a place where magic still lived and genies spoke to you. Issouf said that I could not leave Burkina Faso without visiting Logofuruso, because it was my home too. Issouf had given me my village name, Sanou Setile. I was a Sanou, part of his family and a member of the Bobo. My Bobo family name, Sanou, meant 'gold.' My given name, Setile, translated to 'third son.' Not only was I the third male volunteer to serve in Banzon, I was Issouf's younger brother and the third son of the Sanou, the Chief Costumier of the Bobo.

Issouf and I took a van from Banzon to Bobo-Dioulasso together and journeyed another 25 miles to his family's village. He slowly rode a motorcycle; I hastily peddled my mountain bike.

Logofuruso was inaccessible by car, far removed from the main road, or any road. Each minute, as we made our way down a thin winding dirt path, the landscape changed. Small, spindly trees and scrub brush slowly turned to dense, mature forest. Every mile put between us and the power lines along the paved road sent us 20 years into the past.

The first thing I noticed in Logofuruso was the lack of trash. Bits and pieces of plastic bags and wrappers were absent from the dirt paths. Logofuruso was largely unspoiled by the modern world. While the men and women wore secondhand Western clothing, many still donned traditional woven fabric garments.

We made our way through the network of mud huts to Issouf's family home to meet his brother, the Chief Costumier. Although the younger brother, David looked older than Issouf. He was tall, thin, and his beard was filled with gray. David lived in a small one-room house adjacent their family's original home, the mask maker's sacred workshop.

Their traditional house was dilapidated, as were many of the homes in the village—if not already reduced to ruins. Issouf and David described the plight of Logofuruso. Over the past 40 years, many of the villagers had moved to Bobo for work. When children grew up, they left for larger towns and cities with the hopes of a modern life and more opportunity, much as Issouf had done. This small village and their traditional way of life were dying.

Many of the homes in Logofuruso were a unique style of architecture that I had not seen before in Burkina Faso. The houses were two stories tall and made entirely from mud bricks and logs. The homes had staircases leading up to a roof terrace used to dry grain. Standing atop Issouf's family home, I could see all of Logofuruso. Few of the houses had roofs or signs of inhabitants. Scattered across the village were sacrificial altars and earthen magic amulets positioned atop wooden posts. The village looked like an archeological ruin.

Descending the stairs, I asked if I could see inside the house. Issouf paused at my request. The house of the Chief Costumier was a sacred place. Someone outside the noble bloodline had never entered the house. People who lived their whole life in Logofuruso would not have seen inside this house. If they had entered, they would have found a maze of rooms leading to a back room where the Chief Costumier alone was allowed to enter. It was in that room that the mask maker talked to the spirits and transformed wood and fiber into the physical embodiment of the spiritual world. For generations, the masks of the Bobo tribe were brought to life in a small back room, in a two-story mud house, 25 miles outside of Bobo-Dioulasso.

"Yes, you can see it," Issouf finally responded.

I crouched down as I passed under the small door. I was the first outsider to step inside this house. Light from a large hole in the ceiling filled the first room. It was evident that no one had lived in this home for many years. Issouf's mother and sisters would have had the dirt floor neatly swept and compacted down to resemble stone. Now, shards of pottery littered the loose dirt floor.

Bent over, I made my way to the back of the house, to the sacred room. As I approached the doorway, Issouf placed his hand on my shoulder. I turned to see his grave expression and slow head shake. While I had been allowed to enter the house, this room was off limits. I silently raised my camera to indicate that I wanted to take a picture.

Issouf paused again, then nodded yes. Positioning myself in front of the mask maker's private chamber, I quickly took several photos of the room, which was again illuminated by light from holes in the crumbling roof. A long fibrous scrap, which would have made the body of a mask's costume, lay in front of a broken wooden totem of a headdress.

In Burkina Faso, I had seen masked dancers perform and witnessed secret rituals, but kneeling outside the Chief Costumier's workshop was an unparalleled moment. I truly felt that I was in a sacred place, a place that I did not deserve to be. After taking my photos, I was overcome with an odd sense of urgency and quickly left the house.

Days following my visit, I became very ill. I was tired, nauseous, and slightly feverish. I thought that I had malaria, but my blood tested negative. Issouf, however, was certain of what caused my illness. He said that the spirits of Logofuruso made me sick. My body and magic weren't strong enough to fight their magic.

My best friend in village, Issouf Ouattara Sanou.

Long fibrous scrap of the body of a traditional Bobo mask's costume, lying in front of a broken wooden totem of a mask.

Chapter 15

June 7th – Village Family

Each morning in village, I awoke with the sunrise. Before opening the large metal door to my house, I spent two hours going through my morning routine. The first hours of the day were mine—a period of structured calm, before I pushed myself out the door to spend the day finding ways to be a good Peace Corps Volunteer. I would bathe, stretch, make breakfast, journal, meditate, and turn on my smartphone to check the news of the day.

While there existed no shortage of time to myself in the Peace Corps, I wanted to make sure my days were spent out in my village, meeting people, learning about their lives, understanding their needs, and searching for potential projects. If left to my introverted nature, I could have easily spent the majority of two years in Burkina Faso in my house reading, exercising, and taking naps. My house was a safe space. Inside those concrete walls, I didn't fumble over two or three different languages. I didn't have to introduce myself to strangers, nor was I subjected to the seemingly arbitrary quirks of village life. Inside my house, my introspective, type-A personality ran free and unchallenged. I, however, had signed up for a challenge.

I awoke after sunrise from a hot, sweaty, restless sleep. The last time I left village, I disconnected the large battery that powered my house to prevent overcharging from the solar panels I installed on my roof. As a result, the battery was weak and my fan stopped running during the night. In the absence of air movement, the thick, green mosquito net that encapsulated my foam mattress trapped my body heat and slowly transformed my bed into a musky sauna.

I lifted up the net and stepped onto the cold concrete floor of my bedroom. With my hands resting on my knees, I stared blankly at the pale blue wall across the room. What was I going to do today? My routines were not going to get me through the day. I wanted to crawl back into bed and sleep until I left for Senegal.

I stood up from my bed and turned on my phone. Kate had sent me a message.

Kate: *Tyler, I tested negative and they were pretty sure that I could trust my results. Hope you're doing ok.*

That was great news. I was glad to hear that she was safe. Now, I had to hope that I would test negative as well. I wrote back and told Kate that I would be flying to Senegal on Wednesday and back to Burkina on Friday. Unlike her quick test results, I wouldn't know the results of my HIV test for up to two weeks.

I got ready for the day as best I could and unlocked the large metal door to my house. I winced as I stepped out from my dark house into the bright morning sun. My house sat in a line of buildings, built in the early 80's by the Chinese government as part of a large-scale development project that resulted in my village's rice fields and the irrigation channels fed by a lock and dam system that diverted the nearby river. Across from my house sat another line of buildings. Collectively, these buildings once served as the living quarters for the Chinese construction workers and teachers that taught rice cultivation.

When originally built, an industrial generator supplied power to each of the buildings. Now, the generator was a seized pile of rusted metal and the buildings' electrical outlets stood as plastic relics, lying flush against peeling painted walls. Near the old generator stood a water tower that had befallen a similar fate—previously, each of the living quarters had bathrooms with running water. Behind my house, a crushed water heater sat as a reminder of the past.

A dense row of trees surrounded my home. While a few courtyards in my village had trees, none were as well forested as the collection of houses where I lived. Directly outside my door grew three large mango trees, with dozens more shading the area behind my house. Adjacent the mango trees, banana and papaya trees were propped upright with wooden posts to keep the heavily fruiting tropical plants from toppling over.

My house rested in the center of one row of buildings. Behind my large metal front door was the bathroom positioned between two long rooms resembling barracks, which would have been filled with bunk beds when the Chinese originally occupied my home. Below a small porcelain vanity, an exposed pipe indicated where a sink once existed. Going deeper into the room, a functionless shower head hung behind a brick wall partition. While the shower no longer worked, the drain still flowed to the outside. Here, I took my daily bucket baths. Behind a second partition was an old toilet. As with the shower, water no longer flowed into the toilet but the drain still flowed into a septic tank outside my home. By pouring a half-bucket of water into the toilet, I avoided two years of squatting in a latrine.

I made my home in the long room to the left of the shower room. A floral curtain divided the space into my kitchen and my bedroom. A two-burner gas stove sat atop a tall wooden table next to a smaller table with a spice rack. The majority of my meals were prepared on these two tables. Each morning, by the light of my headlamp, I sautéed onions for an omelet and heated water for my bath. In the evenings, I made a cabbage stir-fry or a thick, rich tomato sauce filled with vegetables.

My bedroom was simple. Behind the floral curtain, to the right, sat my full-sized bed, canopied by a thick green mosquito net. To the left sat a colorful cot or *lit picot*—pronounced lee-pea-co—made from a foldable metal frame and woven colorful nylon cord. Behind the cot towered my library, a pile of French textbooks, dictionaries, training manuals, and novels.

To the right of front door sat another long room that mirrored the room I made into my home. In this other long room, I made a gym. Using cement and metal pipes that were custom made by a welder in my village, I constructed a series of dumbbells. I built other weights from various oil and water canisters that I filled with water or sand. Many early afternoons were spent cycling between the weight lifting stations in my home gym. While working out, neighbors or passersby would pause outside my window, trying to make sense of the loud music, banging, and grunting of the weird American.

On Saturdays, I would carry the weights out onto my porch and teach a general fitness class to my karate students. As part of a youth development project, I taught karate to a group of young girls and boys, ages 12 to 18 years old. The karate club came about after villagers learned that I was a black belt.

Watching dubbed-over Chinese and American martial arts movies was a favorite past time in Burkina Faso. People crowded into dark movie clubs to watch Bruce Lee, Jackie Chan, and Jean-Claude Van Damme classics on a 28-inch projection TV run on a diesel generator. They loved martial arts and wanted to learn, but karate dojos were in big cities and typically reserved for the wealthy.

After being repeatedly asked to teach karate, I started a formal club. On Tuesday and Thursday evenings, in the last hour of daylight, I taught a line of boys and girls how to kick and punch. More than karate, I tried to instill a sense of responsibility and an understanding that fighting was always a last resort. To be a student, you had to show up on time and never use karate outside of class, other than practicing at home—and practicing did not include using younger brothers or sisters as punching bags.

Through push-ups and sidekicks, I gained the trust of the young girls and boys I taught. I ended each class with a time to ask questions. They could ask me anything they wanted. Initially, students asked questions like, "How would you defend against a machete" or "I saw this happen in a film. Is it real and can you teach us?" With time, however, the questions shifted. The end of each class became a time when they could ask a trusted adult, their teacher, questions.

Tuesday and Thursday evenings, as the sun was setting, I found myself seated in a circle of inquisitive young adults, guiding discussions on sexual health, family planning, sexuality, and religion. Many of these topics were taboo, yet they were on their minds. Someone would ask a question and I would provide facts whenever possible and remind them of the ground rules for discussion: all opinions are welcome and you only question ideas, not people. It was amazing to see them think through their opinions together and develop a means of healthy discourse.

Leaving my house, I walked a short distance to the neighboring home of my village family. The mother of the family, Salimata, was my Peace Corps counterpart. Peace Corps entrusted her to work with me as a volunteer and to look out for me. During my service, I worked closely with Salimata at the Banzon Women's Rice Association where she served as the secretary. More than my colleague, Sali was my village mother, a duty that she did not take lightly. She regularly and proudly declared that she was my second mother, my African mother.

Sali was seated outside the family's home on a large wooden chair. I greeted her and pulled up another wooden chair to sit next to her. As she always did, she offered me warm porridge and tea. Typically, I politely declined her offer, but today I accepted. Since I had been traveling, I did not have food in my house. And given recent events, eating warm porridge, seated next to my second mother, was exactly what I needed.

She handed me a warm bowl of millet and corn porridge, flavored with sugar, tamarind, and ginger. Warm, calming steam rolled up from the bowl as I held it below my head and began to eat. I tried to focus on eating, the taste and feel of the porridge. I looked out to the courtyard to chickens pecking at the dirt, searching for bugs. I slipped off my sandals and walked my toes across the cold polished pavement to a wide crack that I begin to pick at with my big toe. I eased back into the deep wooden chair, took a deep breath, and studied every detail of my surroundings. Yet, HIV remained on my mind.

"How was your trip?" asked Sali.

"It was good," I replied, followed by details of my time in Ouagadougou, Bobo, Banfora, and Fourkoura. I told her about the hippos, waterfalls, and village ruins. I did not tell her about my first HIV scare.

"Actually, I have to go to Ouaga again in a few days. I have a meeting with the Peace Corps. I will leave on Monday and should be back Sunday," I added. As with Issouf, there was no point in telling Sali what was going on. Nothing was for sure, and I hoped that I would fly to Senegal and then be back in my village with a clean bill of health.

I asked about Michael, Salimata's husband, and learned that he was in Bobo for work. The rest of the family milled about the courtyard, doing various morning chores or eating breakfast. Michael and Sali had two children, a 17-year-old son, Fabrice, and a 14-year-old daughter, Taibatu. Three of Sali's younger sisters also lived with the family because their parents had passed away and they were unmarried.

At two different times during my service, two of Salimata's nephews had come from Bobo to live with the family. While in Banzon, they helped in the family's fields and at the women's rice association. As with the rest of the family, I tried to get to know her nephews, but they never seemed interested in me beyond cordial acknowledgment. They were more interested in spending time in the village, chasing girls, driving a motorcycle when they could, and going dancing at the local bar, which is why they had been sent from the city to live in rural Banzon.

The family was very progressive for Burkina Faso. Sali and Michael had made the conscious decision to have only two children and to space them out in age. Both kids attended school, spent evenings doing homework after their chores were done, and planned to attend college. The family's progressiveness was afforded by their wealth. While not rich, the family was well-off. Michael had attended university and was a local school board director. Sali was also well educated, having completed high school, and now made considerable money at the Banzon Women's Rice Association, where she managed fourteen groups of women who processed rice into a commercial product.

The family owned two motorcycles, several goats, countless chickens that roamed the courtyard, and a television powered by three solar panels on the roof. Sali and Michael even owned a laptop computer with access to the internet through a USB modem, which I helped them learn how to use as part of computer trainings I taught in the village.

Salimata was Muslim and Michael was Catholic, yet mixed religion families were not uncommon in Burkina Faso, a country that had no discernable religious tensions, unlike other neighboring West African nations. The family celebrated both Muslim and Christian holidays, in addition to numerous national holidays. For Christmas, New Year's, Easter, Ramadan, and Tabaski (Eid al-Adha), the family would prepare large, multi-course, mid-afternoon meals of salads, meats, and rice dishes, completed by hibiscus wine, beer, and mogoji—literally meaning flour (*mogo*) water (*ji*), *mogoji* is a drink made from millet flour, water, ginger, tamarind, lemon, and sometimes a dash of chili pepper.

On many holidays, the family bought new matching outfits, tailored from vibrantly colored wax fabric adorned with metallic embroidery. For my contribution during each of the celebrations, I purchased chickens for the meal and attempted to help cook, although I was regularly shooed away from the hearth by Sali or one of her sisters and told to sit down with the men.

My second birthday in Burkina Faso fell on Tabaski; a holiday celebrated with feasts and sacrificial offerings of sheep. I was also born on the day Burkina Faso's revolutionary and widely beloved past president, Thomas Sankara, was assassinated. This made that particular Tabaski celebration all the more special and was cause for village-wide fanfare and an excellent birthday. I purchased a large ram for the family, which was sacrificed early in the morning by a local imam. As is tradition for Tabaski, the meat was divided into thirds. We kept one portion for the family, another was given to friends and neighbors, and the last third was given to the poor.

After finishing my porridge, tea, and talk with Sali, I excused myself to finish getting ready for the day. I walked back to my house, to the large green metal door that I left wide open. I felt safe in Banzon. I often left my door open and would later be chastised by Sali, but the worst that ever happened was returning to find a confused goat trapped in my house, stuck behind a screen door that swung inward but not outward.

I slowly bathed, dressed, and then sat on my bed, lost in thought. I had today and tomorrow to pass in village. Other than packing for Senegal and buying food for my next few meals, there was nothing I had to get done, little to occupy my time. I took out a piece of paper and made a list of things to do: buy vegetables, buy eggs, pack, clean house, exercise. I could finish the list by early afternoon, yet I wanted nothing more than to close my windows, lock my front door, and lie down on my cool cement floor in the dark.

After 20 minutes of sitting on the edge of my bed, devoid of motivation, I forced myself to stand, leave my house, and bike to the market. As I walked my bike through the market's narrow paths, I paid close attention to the low-hanging wooden beams and plastic tarps of the sprawling lean-tos that made up the vendor's stalls. Tomorrow was Sunday, the day of the big market, and only a few vendors were out today. The women that sold me vegetables were happy to see me and thanked Allah for my safe and healthy return to Banzon. I returned blessings to them and hoped that Allah would provide them with a good day.

I purchased cabbage and onions from Mamou, my favorite market woman, and played along with the lighthearted banter of the other women who told me to buy from them rather than Mamou. During my time in Banzon, I worked closely with Mamou to conduct market demonstrations on malaria prevention, lotion making, prenatal nutrition, and hygiene. She spoke excellent French, was one of the leaders of the community, and always made sure I knew when the weekday market had spinach or avocados.

After leaving the market, I stopped by a roadside kiosk and purchased five eggs, which were carefully placed in a plastic bag and hung on a handlebar of my bike. While I had managed to leave my home and go shopping, I hadn't escaped the thoughts in my head. I continued to think about my first and second HIV test results, all the possible ways that I could have contracted HIV, and what my life would look like if I were HIV positive.

Slowly biking with my bag of eggs swaying back and forth, I took the long way to my house to avoid people. As I rounded a corner of the dirt path, I saw a group of young children. They shouted, "Tubabu, tubabu, tubabu!" as they waved and jumped up and down. To their amusement, I yelled back, "Farafin, farafin, farafin!" which meant 'African.'

Back at my house, I unpacked my groceries, slowly cleaned my house, and prepared salt and pepper cabbage for lunch. It was 11:30 a.m. and my to-do list was nearly complete. After eating, I closed my metal shutters and front door and laid out a mat on my floor for a nap. While it was not uncommon for me to take an afternoon nap, I usually set an alarm. But what was the point today? I wanted to sleep away as many hours as I could.

As I lay on the floor, my mind turned like a whirlpool of thoughts, circling around the same set of facts and inevitably down into cold, silent darkness. To stay afloat, I attempted to cling to any shred of positivity that I could find in this situation. This could be a good thing, a chance for a better life. After the first scare, I easily shed the sense of urgency and my plans for a better future that began to formulate. The second that Dr. Patel prematurely called to give me the good news, everything washed away and my life was reset. I wasn't on course to make any lasting changes. I had only encountered an unfortunate bump in the road, which while jarring, passed as quickly as it came.

Maybe now, however, things would be different. Was there a cosmic force throwing me back into this hell for a second opportunity to make it right? Once was not enough. The first time didn't stick but had to happen to set me up to succeed now. Everything would be okay. I wasn't HIV positive. I was healthy and given a gift of deep introspection. I had to use this time for good. This is why I was here, now, sprawled on a plastic woven mat on a cement floor in the dark, alone in the middle of Africa. Or, I was HIV positive.

After minutes exploring one course of irrationality, I reeled my mind back in and tried to calm myself and go to sleep, but not before my thoughts darted down a different avenue of possibilities. This ebb and flow of internal tumult and stillness continued for over an hour until I finally drifted into unconsciousness.

Forty-five minutes later, I awoke in a cold sweat and promptly lifted myself off my mat. I sat cross-legged with my head in my hands and took slow, deep breaths. Maybe I needed to write and get some of the thoughts out of my head and onto paper. I reached for my journal and opened up to where I had left off.

The blank cream-colored page of my journal rested before me. The ridged lines that neatly divided paper welcomed my words, but I did not know where to start. I gently rolled a pen back and forth between my thumb and index finger, until I finally dated the top right corner of the page and began to record my thoughts.

07 June 2014

My head is very much in the clouds. Kate got tested again. Negative. These next few weeks are really going to suck. Or, they will suck if I allow them to suck. There is no reason to wallow. Think and rethink. Stop living. Put it all on pause in the meantime. Fate is in my favor.

Please, please, please be negative. Things are in my favor. The more specific test came back negative. It does, however, worry me that it was run by Burkinabé in a Burkina lab.

I began to call into question the second test. Who had run the test at the hospital in Ouagadougou? While unfounded and prejudicial, I had more faith in the first test from the U.S. Embassy Lab. What exactly did the test require? Was it simply some kind of rapid test where a drop of my blood was placed on a plastic test strip, or a more calculated, multistep, analytical screening procedure?

I believed that my village's health clinic could test for HIV with a simple test. Maybe I could have another test run today. But how would I even go about asking for an HIV test? Doctor-patient confidentiality was not a thing in village. Before the results of any screening test were complete, half the village would know I was at the clinic having an HIV test run.

Michael had a friend who ran a small private clinic in village. I visited his practice once to pick up antibiotics after Dr. Patel diagnosed me over the phone with an intestinal bacterial infection. I could go see Michael's friend, fake sick, and ask to be tested for malaria. Then, I could casually ask if they had other blood tests available and request an HIV screening test. You know, to be safe and make sure it wasn't something else.

As my mind worked on an elaborate plan to get tested for HIV in my village, I remembered that I had very little money left after my last cash withdrawal in Bobo—money that would be needed to travel to Ouagadougou. I couldn't afford to have any tests run in village, and my plans were ill-conceived either way. In a few days, I would be in Senegal to have additional blood tests. I could wait. I had to wait.

I placed my journal in my backpack and biked up the main road to Issouf's shop. I found Issouf in his courtyard, asleep in a chair under the mango tree. Quietly, I dismounted my bike and leaned it against a wall. I took a seat on an empty bench, swung my leg around to straddle the wooden plank, and relaxed back onto the smooth, worn wood. As Issouf napped, I gazed up into the canopy of the mango tree. My interlaced fingers rested across my chest and rose and fell with the expansion and contraction of my lungs as I breathed long, deep breaths. The wind gently shifted the leaves back and forth. Dappled sunlight danced through the crown of the mango tree and my thoughts began to melt away, one by one.

The rumble of a motorcycle pulling into the courtyard broke the meditative state and Issouf woke up. His eyes opened suddenly to find me reclined next to him on a bench and Gilbert balancing his now silent motorcycle atop its kickstand. I lifted myself up to make a place for Gilbert and slid my backpack toward me, which I had been using as a pillow. Issouf greeted us both as he sprang from his chair and disappeared into his shop where he began to shuffle pots and pans back and forth.

Gilbert the Rasta took a seat next to me and extended his thin calloused hand to shake. He was a regular at Issouf's, one of my friends, and a source of village adventure. Gilbert had thin dreadlocks that extended down to his shoulders. He spoke slowly with an easygoing tone, typically aided by the fact that he was high. To make money, Gilbert worked odd jobs in the village, peddled pirated DVDs and other knock-off Chinese merchandise, and was a photographer. During holidays and village celebrations, Gilbert walked from courtyard to courtyard looking for patrons wanting photos of their new outfits and hairdos. The Rasta used an old Sony digital camera to take photos, printed the photos in Bobo, and sold the copies for a small profit.

Of the various odd jobs Gilbert performed, collecting honey from wild beehives provided me with some of the best stories, and free honey.

One day, I discovered a large hive in the hollow of a mango tree near my home, drawn to the tree by the loud buzzing made by the swarming bees. When Gilbert learned of the hive, he immediately made plans to gather the honey.

Shortly after nightfall, Gilbert arrived at my house with a bucket, flashlight, and a large bundle of dried millet stalks. I guided him through the woods to the steadily humming beehive. He quickly inspected the hive and then took off his shirt. I, on the other hand, made sure to wear long sleeves and pants to protect my skin from the African bees.

The Rasta cleared away the leaves at the base of the tree and lit the bundle of millet stalks on fire. He waved the smoking stalks back and forth in front of the hive, an attempt to mask the bees' alarm pheromones, which would be released when Gilbert stuck his hand into the tree.

Quickly, Gilbert began to pull dripping honeycomb from the hollow of the tree. As he worked, the bees stung him. First, they stung his hands, but his entire body was exposed and open to attack. I stayed close in case he needed help and received several stings. As we worked, I kept track of each bee sting—fourteen in total for me and countless others for Gilbert.

Other than a sharp pick felt from the bee's stinger breaking my flesh, I had no reaction to the tiny attacking insects. Gilbert could not say the same. He was stung once in the lip, which quickly swelled and dulled his speech, and so many times in the hands that they came to resemble inflated surgical gloves. When we were all done, we divided two buckets of honey and I insisted that he take two Benadryl from my first aid kit. He warily accepted the paper packet of medicine, said he would take them at home—I didn't believe him—and peddled into the night on his bicycle.

In addition to getting me stung by bees, Gilbert enjoyed recording music on my laptop. Both Patrice and he dreamed of becoming music stars and were always asking me to record videos or audio tracks of them singing. Because I enjoyed their company and owed them for the many great stories they gave me, I conceded and began to set up recording sessions at my house.

Using a microphone that I brought to Burkina, Patrice, Gilbert and I huddled in my shower to record their lyrics over stock music tracks I downloaded from the internet. The walls of the shower blocked most of the outside noise, but roosters' crows and donkeys' brays made their way onto the tracks.

The music we produced wasn't great, but it made both Patrice and Gilbert happy.

With time, I grew tired of recording. Patrice and Gilbert would ask to record and I would make excuses and avoid them. Gilbert soon became incessant in nagging me for a recording session and I finally set aside time for him.

When the day came to record, Gilbert didn't show up. I called his phone several times but he never picked up. I was angry that after finally agreeing to record, he blew me off without the courtesy of an excuse. I spent the day being angry, pissed that after all his badgering he chose not to show.

The next day, however, I found out why he had missed our recording, and I was so powerfully overcome by guilt that I became physically ill. While I fumed over Gilbert's tardiness, he was driving his young daughter to Bobo on his motorcycle. She had malaria, which had progressed quickly and was beyond caring for in our village. She needed a doctor in Bobo.

Sadly, the disease had advanced too far. Shortly after arriving at the hospital, his daughter passed away. Gilbert then turned around and carried his daughter's lifeless body, wrapped in a blanket, back to Banzon, forty miles down a bumpy dirt road, to be buried in the village.

I was angry over a missed meeting, while someone I considered to be a friend had lost his child. I didn't even know Gilbert had a daughter. Many times during my service, I became detached from my community and the realities of village life. My life was easy. Their life was not. As a Peace Corps Volunteer, I had access to modern healthcare and a dedicated phone number that I could call at any hour for help. There were even plans for where a helicopter would land in my village if I needed to be quickly evacuated. My friends in village relied on an understaffed and ill-equipped medical center, knock-off expired Chinese medicine bought in the local market, and traditional cures.

I had money deposited into my bank account each month, more than enough to buy everything I needed. Many times, I consumed as much meat or vegetables in a single day as an entire family would in a week. They worked hard for every bit of their money, fed themselves from their fields, and leaned heavily on the social safety net of friends and family.

The village was not a collection of people, families, and homes. They were interdependent and connected to one another. While they consistently looked out for my well-being, I could not say that I always did the same. I was me, they were they. Over two years, I grew close to my village, but I would never be fully integrated or understand their life.

When I saw Gilbert after his daughter's passing, I gave my deepest condolences for his loss. I was ashamed of how I reacted. He thanked me and carried on as if nothing happened. He was his normal, laid-back, and good-humored self.

It was not that the death of his daughter hadn't bothered him, but that the death of a child was commonplace in sub-Saharan Africa. Burkinabé lived life in the moment and were grateful for every additional day given to them. Tomorrow was not a guarantee, a blunt truth that guided many of their actions. They kept friends and family close, valued community and tradition, and left much to God's will.

Issouf emerged from his shop singing a song in Bobo and carrying a plate of food for Gilbert and a coffee for me.

"Tyler, I have one piece of chicken left. 600 CFA. Do you want it?" asked Issouf.

"No thank you, but here's 50 CFA for the coffee and another 100 CFA for the previous two coffees," I replied as I held out three worn silver coins.

Issouf shook his head with a smile and accepted my money. He pulled his chair over to us and we began to talk. The conversation was nothing special, another in a long list of afternoon chats. As a Peace Corps Volunteer, large portions of my days were spent talking to people in my village. People regularly came over to my house for no other purpose than to say 'hello' and make sure everything was well. It was not foreign to spend long hours seated, talking face-to-face. Sometimes, those hours weren't even spent talking, but rather merely *being* alongside others.

Burkinabé valued conversations and greetings. They were not locked away in their private lives. While smartphones, social media, and a culture of individualism were taking hold in Burkina cities, villages still clung to earnest human connection.

At first, the innumerable greetings, salutations, and customary conversations annoyed me. As an American, I didn't understand why I needed to ask how a person was doing, how their work was going, how their health was, their family, their husband and their kids, before buying tomatoes. The first time I found myself trapped sitting in silence with another person for an hour, simply *being*, I mentally reviewed the long list of 'better things' I could be doing instead. Soon, I learned to love these conversations. Love the silence. Love the *being*.

The conversation between Issouf, Gilbert, and me began to slow.

Rather than sit in silence, alone with my thoughts and my pending HIV tests, I pulled out my journal and began thumbing through the dirt-stained pages. More than the food I ate or things I saw in West Africa, my most valuable memories were the conversations. It was through the many long hours of conversations that I built friendships and began to see into another culture.

In my journals, I recorded one-liners that stood out during the day. To me, these single sentences underscored how my new friends, family, and acquaintances viewed themselves, the world, and me. As we sat in silence, I flipped through my journal and re-read the quotes I had recorded.

"When you came here, you were a fat American. Now you are a beautiful, beautiful boy." – Michael

"I am a friend of the genies. I know magic. It will protect you. You'll be okay." – Issouf

"God made leaves and fruits for people. The blood of an animal is the same as ours. It does not make sense to eat them. They speak to us." – Issouf, he thought a lot about vegetarianism

"France is bad. Look at all their former colonies, all backward. The French education system teaches you only to memorize, not think for yourself. We don't innovate." – Issouf

(At 7:00 a.m., handing me a sack of whiskey) "Drink?" – Patrice

"America needs to stop letting people in. You can't become American. You have to be raised in it. They'll become terrorists."
– Michael

"What type of meat is this?" – Me "Rat." – Patrice

"China is ruining Burkina. Every kid has a cheap cell phone. On those cell phones, there is porn. They think nothing of sex, then have kids when they are 15 years old and get STDs." – Felix, 16-year-old karate student

"I have gone to church, I have gone to mosque, but I don't believe in God. It doesn't make sense to me, but I'm still a good person." – Noufou, 17-year-old karate student

"Africans have too many kids. It's not good for development. I want two, spaced out by three years. It will be easier to send them to school that way." – Ali, 17-year-old karate student

"The Peace Corps is hard, but you are strong like a Marine. Like an American." – Michael

"I had the imam write this prayer for you. Have it sewn into an amulet and hang it in your bedroom. God will see to it that your prayer is answered." – Mamadou, boutique owner

"I don't think girls should go to school. If they get jobs, they won't respect their husbands because they won't need money."
– English teacher at my village's school

"Are you going to work today?" – Alima, host sister/aunt, after I spent all morning on my computer writing a grant

"Grandson! Come here and buy something from your grandmother. No…not that. You won't like that." – Old woman that sells spices in my village market

"Those pants are too tight. Change your pants." – Salimata, upon seeing my new pair of pants from the tailor

Reading those memories briefly filled me with happiness. I did not regret my service. The previous two years were an amazing time. Nevertheless, it was hard to feel good about the past with my future this uncertain. Were every adventure, every conversation, and every experience to be overshadowed by HIV?

As we quietly sat with one another, my friend Amedue the tailor rolled into the courtyard on his bicycle and injected liveliness back into the languishing conversation. Amedue exchanged village gossip with us and began talking about a radio program he heard that afternoon. I tried to remain engaged in the discussion, but my mind was elsewhere. As they talked back and forth, I nodded in acknowledgment. When possible, I added an open-ended question to their conversation and retreated back into my head as they disagreed with one another.

I stayed as long as I could but was soon overcome with the need to be alone again. I said goodbye to them and began to walk my bike out of Issouf's courtyard, before he stopped me.

"Let me walk you out, Tyler," Issouf said.

Issouf took hold of my bike's handlebars and rolled it down the street, in between us as we walked toward my house.

"Tyler, you've been through a lot. These past two years have been hard on you, but it is almost over," said Issouf. He could tell that something was wrong. He was my best friend and spent hundreds of hours getting to know me. I would have loved to tell him what was wrong, but I knew I couldn't. Not yet.

"Yes, Issouf. I have been through a lot. It may have been hard, but it has made me stronger. I've learned a lot," I replied, and faintly smiled back.

We paused in the middle of the road and Issouf handed my bike to me. He wished me well and waited for me to bike away before turning around and walking back to his house and restaurant. As I rode home, Issouf's words resonated in my mind.

Tyler, you've been through a lot.

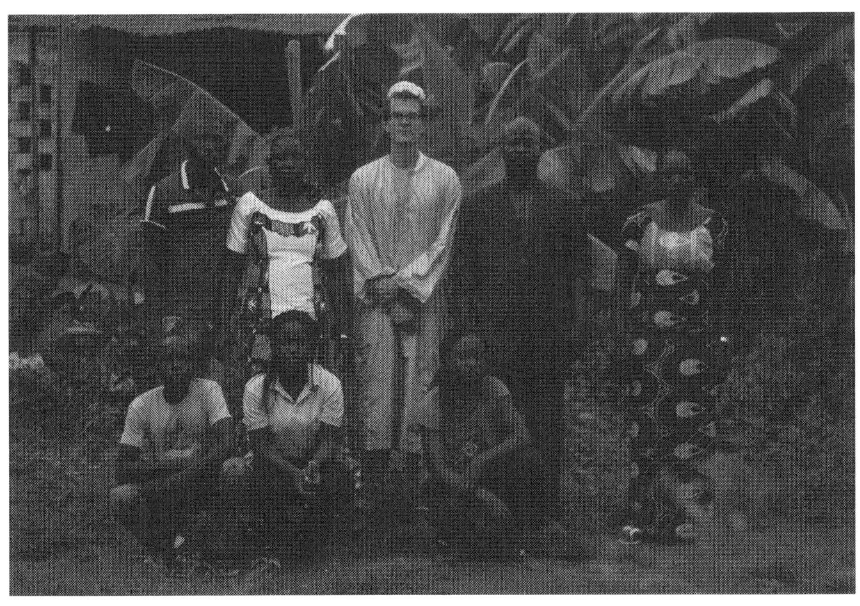

My Banzon village family. Without their love, kindness, and guidance, I would not have completed the Peace Corps.

Gilbert the Rasta, taking photos at Banzon village celebration.

Chapter 16

June 8th – Please ship to U.S.

08 June 2014

I'm hella broke. I have $46 to my name, $40 of which I'll need to head to Ouaga. If my U.S. Bank card doesn't work, I'm sorta screwed. Having to be medevaced doesn't help. My U.S. Card has previously worked, but I was sent a new card. I do have the new card with me, but I don't know if I can activate the card from here.

Also, my bike tire exploded yesterday.

The money situation is more pressing though. I hope my card works. 100,000 CFA would do it. $200. I also hope I am given some money for medevac.

Today:

- *Pack*
- *Laundry*
- *Workout*
- *Market*
- *Sell bed*

Good Daily Rituals / Habits

- *Journaling*
- *Stretch or Yoga*
- *Meditation*
- *Walking*

- *No electronics 2 hours before bed*
- *8 hours sleep*
- *Evening weight training*
- *Intermittent fasting*
- *Fatty coffee/tea*
- *Bathing before bed*
- *Fiction reading before bed*
- *Academic or inspirational work in the morning*
- *Set time for emails (batch processing)*
- *Cold sleeping environment*
- *Dark sleep environment*
- *Clutterless sleep environment*
- *Gratitude journaling*
- *Floss*
- *Cold baths*
- *Set time each day to write or be creative*
- *Learn languages*

Right now I'm very hypersensitive about every tinge of pain in my body. Every twinge. Tweak. Heat rash is back. I think its heat rash. I hope its heat rash.

I was manically writing lists. With lists, I planned my way out of problems and provided myself with a false sense of accomplishment. My journal entries were often a mix of updates and lists. I was constantly planning and collecting ideas on how I could improve my life. I toed the line of self-help addict, if such a thing exists. When faced with a difficult task, I spent hours avoiding the problem by planning. My internal dialogue would tell me I was wasting time thinking about doing something rather than taking action. Yet, I remained frozen in thought or pacing back and forth, carrying on a multifaceted conversation with myself. I searched for comfort in a measured, rational decision…rational to me at least. Likely irrational to others.

To calm myself, I thought of all the things I wanted to change in my life. Positive or negative, this was an invitation for making substantive changes. Given all the free time over the past two years, I listened to hours upon hours of health and self-improvement podcasts and read no less than forty motivational or how-to books. I had enough New Year's resolutions to last the next 50 years, in addition to an absurd and growing bucket list of projects and adventures.

I held tightly to the idea that in this moment of despair, I could turn this into something good. I was either HIV positive or negative and I could do nothing to change the outcome now. I could, however, control my reaction to the situation. That was the one thing in my control.

I was leaving for Bobo tomorrow and needed to pack and do laundry. It was also Sunday and I expected a phone call from my parents between noon and 1:00 p.m. I would try to keep the conversation short. I wasn't in the mood to talk and I would not tell them about Senegal. Hopefully, they'd never have to know. I would leave village and be back in time for next Sunday's call.

Because I was leaving for the week and running low on money, I wouldn't spend my Sunday morning leisurely shopping for groceries, souvenirs, or sifting through piles of secondhand clothing in the market. I would buy a loaf of sourdough bread and visit my butcher for grilled fatty goat meat. I was depressed and the only foods that sounded good were full of carbs and fat.

As long as everything went well with my tests in Senegal, I would finish my Peace Corps service at the end of next month and move back to the U.S. In preparation, I started clearing out my house, selling off things I didn't need or carting loads of free stuff to Bobo and Ouaga for other volunteers to take. I rarely used my second bed, a woven cot, during my two years because my host family provided me with a full-sized mattress and bed frame. I hoped to sell the cot and have extra money for buying last-minute souvenirs.

Issouf said that he could sell the bed for me and since it was a market day I figured today would be the best day to find someone looking for a bed. I cleared the piles of stuff off the cot and folded it in half. With the cot poorly strapped down to the back of my bike, I slowly made my way up the road to Issouf's place.

Two vans sat parked out in front of his restaurant. Men and women were unloading things to sell at the market. Issouf was busy switching back and forth between cooking a large pot of sauce for lunch and making coffee for the people huddled around the kiosk window.

I unstrapped the bed and sat it against a wall in Issouf's courtyard. I stuck my head into Issouf's tiny, sweltering restaurant and told him that I dropped off my bed. Full of energy, Issouf told me to come around to the other side to sit with the men drinking coffee. I declined, saying that I needed to go to the market and be back home for my parents' weekly phone call.

"Okay, I will see you later!" Issouf responded as he vigorously frothed a coffee. Turning around, I found two men curiously examining my bike. They were from a surrounding village, in Banzon for the market.

"Tubabu-che, nice bike. Did you bring it from Europe?" asked one of the men.

"No, I'm not European," I replied and continued to explain in Dioula that I was American, which completely confused them. I could assume that it wasn't often that they met white foreigners who spoke a local Burkina language or even saw an expat looking so unkempt, wearing thin rubber sandals bought in the market, and not driving a motorcycle or car. While a big village, Banzon was off the beaten path and not regularly visited by foreigners.

I told them that I was a Peace Corps Volunteer from America and that I lived here in the village. They couldn't believe it. Normally, I would have entertained them with a longer conversation explaining the Peace Corps and my work, but I did need to go to the market and be home for my parents' call. Speaking Dioula again, I wished them well, asked Allah to give them a good market day, and headed down the busy main road toward the market.

The main road was filled with donkey carts and lined with market vendors. An old pickup truck loaded down with cassavas slowly tried to make it to the other end of the market where agricultural goods were sold. On the right side of the street were several groups of merchants selling metal housewares, across the path from another group selling plastic goods. On down the road and throughout the market, the types of goods they sold grouped vendors. There were the men that sold rope, next to the men who sold new rice sacks, followed by the large group of women who sold rice. I stopped to greet many of the women selling rice, because they worked at the women's rice association where I primarily spent my time. They fretted back and forth with me and playfully yelled at me for not buying their rice.

Next to the women sat the singular person known to sell sourdough bread in the entire country. When he saw me approaching, he beamed with a wide smile. The fact that there was a tall goofy white guy who spoke a little Dioula and liked his bread never ceased to amuse him. As was done every Sunday, we exchanged greetings and I asked to buy one loaf of bread, "N be buru kele fe."

After buying my bread, I quickly ducked into the market to buy onions and spinach for dinner. Vendors' goods spilled from their booths into the walkway, which was further filled by men, women, and children. Cautiously walking my bike through the crowd, I found the first person selling what I needed and promptly left the bustling marketplace.

I had an hour before my mom and dad would call; time enough to go to my friend's butcher stand. A skinned goat hung from the front of Alu's thatch hut. He busily filled butcher paper pouches with chunks of fresh goat, sliced white onions, and a homemade spicy blend that relied heavily on salt, ground peanut flour, and MSG. Two men sat across from each other, straddling a wooden bench and sharing a large plate of steaming goat meat. I sat down across from the men and ordered a plate of goat meat, extra fatty, after which the two men customarily invited me to join their meal.

One of Alu's sons brought me a plastic cup filled with water to rinse my hand before eating. Off to the side of the bench, I slowly poured the water over the fingertips of my right hand as I worked them back in forth to remove the dirt. I quickly shook my hand dry and handed the cup back to the small boy who quickly retreated to his father's side.

Alu sat down beside me and placed my plate of warm goat meat in front of me. He cooked his goat meat in paper pouches, on top of a grill made from a perforated piece of scrap metal. Three sides of the grill were made of mud brick, with an open front for firewood. Today, a thick five-foot tree trunk stuck out from the front of the grill. Over the course of the day, the tree would slowly burn and be fed into the fire.

I began to eat, but not before customarily inviting Alu and the two men to join me. I lightly dabbed each piece of meat into a pile of chili powder on the side of the plate and tossed them into my mouth. Alu, unlike many other Burkina butchers, was meticulous when butchering meat. Rather than crudely hacking away at a piece of goat, leaving a scattered trail of bone shards to eschew, Alu carved meat and cleanly chopped through bone with a machete that he sharpened multiple times each day. Given his attention to detail and his pleasant company, I regularly patronized Alu's roadside butcher stall.

As Alu and I talked, his youngest son hung close to his father, inquisitively watching me as I ate. I tried to engage in a meaningful conversation, but my head was elsewhere. Whenever I stopped moving, my thoughts caught up to me. Small talk about the market was the most I could muster; all the while my mind nervously rehashed the series of events that led me to this point. Could Alu, like Issouf, tell that I was despondent?

I finished my meal, rinsed my hand again, and handed a large brass and silver $1 coin to Alu. I biked home quickly, using the exhilaration of weaving in and out of traffic to still my mind. I sped down the road, forced to concentrate on the immediate path before me, not the pending HIV test.

A rooster darted out of my way as I rounded the corner to my house. In front of my door, I wrenched down on my brakes and slid the back tire around, spraying gravel into the air. I wanted to keep biking until my legs gave out. Anything to avoid the circuitous track my mind raced along. I could feel my heart thumping heavily in my chest, a pulsating calm radiating out from my breast and through my limbs.

The thick metal bolt lock of my door slid open with a metallic screech and thud as I unlocked my house. Immediately after crossing the threshold, my phone that I left charging on the windowsill began to ring. My parents.

I quickly laid my bag down and answered, "Bonjour Mama et Papa. Comment allez-vous?"

"Bonjour. Je vais bien. Et toi?" replied my mother. She studied French in high school, and as is such, this was the extent of what she remembered, along with a handful of vocabulary words and provocative phrases.

From there, our conversation continued in English and followed its normal pattern of questions.

"What have you been doing?" -- "Not much."

"What did you buy at the market?" -- "Spinach, onions, and bread today. Nothing exciting."

"Eaten anything interesting?" -- "Sadly, no."

"Have you talked to your brother lately?" -- "Yes. Over Facebook last week."

"Are you ready to come home?" -- "Not yet."

My mother proceeded to update me on life back home. Nothing changed. It rarely does. She then handed the phone off to my father. It was his turn to talk. The trouble, however, was that my father was not a talker. He was a gruff, stoic man whose silence and demeanor had made more than one friend nervous. If coaxed, he could carry on very insightful conversations but today was not going to be one of those times. I wasn't up for it. The only thing on my mind was my HIV status, which would not be a topic of conversation. I didn't need to worry them.

My dad was as uneager to talk as I was. He remarked that I was quiet today and I told him that I hadn't slept well the night before—true. He said that he'd let me go to take a nap, and we each said, "I love you," and ended the call.

I stood in my shower room. When I started the call, I was in my kitchen. I had been restlessly pacing my house the entire conversation. I stood motionless in the stall, eyes slowly scanning the peeling painted walls that bound me on three sides. My body began to gradually sway as I shifted my weight back and forth. I ran my fingers over the buttons of the phone that hung in my hand at my side. Slowly, I squatted down, rested my head on my knees, and wrapped my arms tightly around my body.

The sway turned into a rocking motion. As I teetered, I began to softly hum. With each back and forth motion I held my body tighter. Maybe if I squeezed hard enough, the thoughts and feelings would be forced out.

No.

Get up.

Stop it.

Stand.

Just stop it.

Now.

In a burst of energy, I stood up and quickly walked out of the stall and back into the main room of my house. I had to do things. Things to do. Something, but what? Laundry.

You need clothing for your trip to Senegal, I reminded myself.

"Yes, and I need to do it now so they can dry by tonight," I replied aloud.

I grabbed my bag of dirty clothes and two buckets and headed outside to start my laundry. Rather than pay someone, I tried to wash my clothes. Doing my laundry showed my family and others who saw me that I, both an American and a man, could do my own laundry. It also gave me something to do for a few hours during long, slow village days. I had to admit, however, that my clothes were much cleaner when someone else washed them.

I took my family's two large metal washbasins off the porch, along with the hard, brown plastic washboard, and positioned them in the shade of the mango trees in front of my house. Riffling through my bag of dirty clothing, I sorted out what I would need for the next week, except for underwear, which would be washed and dried inside my house. It is not appropriate to have your underwear hanging outside your house.

I opened a small packet of detergent and sprinkled it on top of my dirty clothes in the first basin. The second basin would be my rinse cycle. I began to make trips to the well in our courtyard. Hand over hand, I pulled up pails of cold, clear water. It took three pails of water to fill two buckets with water, and eight buckets of water to wash and rinse my clothing. I was privileged to have a source of water in my courtyard.

Each day in my village, hundreds of women and girls took long repeated trips, sometimes more than a mile each way, to fill up 20-liter jugs of water. If fortunate, they owned a cart or bicycle to transport the water. If not, they would carry the 40-pound container of water back to their homes, only to repeat the trip several more times.

Weekly, I came out of my house to see a woman or young girl filling up a jug of water. Our eyes would lock and I sensed their alarm, as if I caught them stealing my water. But the water wasn't mine or anybody else's—it was for everyone. I would smile and wave, trying to signal that they were okay and not doing anything wrong. They would quickly finish filling up their container and depart. I felt bad for making them feel as if they had done something wrong and even worse for not knowing how to fix the problem.

I filled both basins with water and began to agitate the dirty clothes to dissolve the detergent. One by one, I began to knead each item of clothing against itself, before moving to the hard washboard to scrub my clothing clean. Once satisfactory, I rang out the dirty water, tossed the item into the basin of clean water, and started again on the next piece of clothing.

Doing laundry by hand was meditative. Usually, I listened to music or allowed myself to become lost in my thoughts. Today, however, I did not want to unwind into deep reflection. As I washed my clothes, I tried to concentrate on each little action. I tried to make each movement thoughtful and deliberate. I counted, "One, two, three, four," as I pushed a portion of fabric down the hard ridges of the washboard. I then moved inches up the garment to another section to repeat my one, two, three, four cadence. Methodically, I scrubbed each quadrant of the garment in hand before ringing it out, placed it in the now murky rinse tub, and starting the process over again. One, two, three, four.

Lost in the process, I escaped my thoughts until I split open a knuckle on the washboard. The soapy water burned as it entered the bleeding cut, and the pain broke my methodic trance. I tried to return my focus to measuring each action, but it was lost.

As I began to deliberate with myself, I questioned if I needed to call Heather or Caroline to let them know I was going to Senegal. While I didn't have much information to tell them and did not want to subject them to unnecessary mental anguish, I did not want them hearing about any of this secondhand. If I were going to call them, I needed to do it soon. Not today though. I wasn't ready. I needed more time to think about what I would say, how I would say it, and more time to gain the courage to call them.

Because I began to believe I contracted HIV from Caroline, I didn't feel much of an obligation to call her. At the same time, it would be the easiest call to make. My resentment toward her mounted. I didn't care what she thought. As much as I tried to take responsibility for my actions, I couldn't help but think that this was her fault.

Calling Heather would be harder. Heather and I were much closer. She was a good friend and I confided a lot in her. While I believed it to be impossible that I contracted HIV from Heather, and as unlikely that I would have given her HIV, she would not take it well. Her reaction was so strong the first time, after the second test prematurely determined that I did not have HIV. I had to call her though. I owed it to her.

I began thinking through what I would say when I called Caroline and Heather. Short and direct, or have a full conversation? It might be dangerous to have an open-ended dialogue. I was unsure how I would handle it.

Slowly, a script began to form in my mind. Tomorrow, once in Bobo, I would call them. First Caroline, then Heather.

I finished washing my clothes and hung them to dry. In the hot afternoon sun, they'd be dry in a couple of hours. I then washed my underwear and hung them on a rope strung across my gym room.

I laid out my mat and spread out across my floor to take a nap. When I told my dad I slept poorly the night before, I hadn't lied. All night, I tossed and turned. I was tired to the point where it hurt, but I had little hope that I would be able to sleep for any decent measure of time but longed to catch a few minutes of stillness.

I passed out instantly.

I awoke confused and disoriented. I had slept for more than an hour but needed a full night's rest. Sluggishly, I stood up. There were more hours in the day to fill before I could try and sleep again. I began to clean my house and sort through everything I owned. I made a pile of items I no longer needed and began to make a mental note of what I would give away when finally done with Peace Corps.

Still half asleep, my mind was stagnant. There was also little more to think about. I finished sorting through everything I owned and stared at the large sack I filled with stuff to give away to other volunteers.

Outside, my laundry hung dry and stiff. I pulled each item off the line and gave it a quick pop to break the rigid shape it had formed when drying. Inside my house, I neatly folded my clothes and started packing my bag for Senegal. My underwear was still wet and wouldn't be dry tonight so I wrote myself a note as a reminder to pack my underwear in the morning and sat it on top of my backpack.

It was now late enough to justify cooking dinner. I cut the round of sourdough bread down the middle and sliced one of the halves to open it up. I cracked two eggs, whisked them with a fork, and sat the two slices of bread face down in the eggs. While the sliced bread soaked up the eggs, I wrapped the other half of bread in a bandana and placed it in my backpack for breakfast tomorrow.

I heated oil in a pan and chopped three small onions. When hot, I dropped the onions in the pan. Once the onions were soft, I added spinach, salt, pepper, cumin, and paprika, and cooked the mixture until the spinach leaves wilted. I moved the spinach and onions to the side of the pan and placed the soggy bread faced down on the hot metal with a sizzle. After two minutes, the eggy bread became my version of French toast. I lifted the bread from the pan with a spatula, laid it egg-side up on a plate and topped the golden bread with the cooked spinach and onions.

I made this meal often and more than one Peace Corps Volunteer who visited my village fondly remembered it. I sat on the floor with my plate in my lap and back against my bed. The sun now began to set and it turned dark in my house. As I ate by the light of my headlamp, I thought through my packing list again. Did I have everything?

How many days would I be gone?

Six.

Did I have enough clothing for six days?

Yes.

But what if I was gone for longer? You never knew what could happen. What if Peace Corps wanted to hold me in Senegal or have me stay in Ouagadougou until my tests came back? That currently wasn't the plan, but plans changed.

What if that happened and my test came back positive? They would have me on the next flight to the U.S. I would be medically separated from the Peace Corps and not allowed to come back to my village to say goodbye.

What if I was leaving tomorrow for good?

Hastily, I stood up, emptied the clothing from my canteen and began to fill it with meaningful keepsakes and souvenirs. I continued to add items until I filled the canteen. I latched the lid and drug the metal box into the center of my floor. I then wrote a note to Peace Corps on a piece of paper and taped it to the top of the canteen:

If I do not come back, please ship to my address in the U.S.

Cooking in my house by the light of a battery operated lamp.

Chapter 17

June 9th – Storm

My alarm blared at 5:30 a.m. and I quickly silenced it. I didn't want to move, but it was time to get up and start moving. Moving toward Senegal. Moving toward an answer.

I switched off my fan, left my bed, washed my face, brushed my teeth, got dressed, quickly folded my dry underwear, placed the stack of underwear into my packed bag, and locked my front door, twenty minutes after my alarm sounded. I tied my small bag to the back of my bike and was on my way.

Before exiting the courtyard, I saw my host mother and stopped to greet her.

"Good morning. How did you sleep?" I asked

"I slept well. How did you sleep?" Salimata replied.

"I also slept well. I'm going now," I said, readying myself to push off on my bike.

"May God give you a safe return," Salimata called as I moved away.

"Amen," I shouted back.

I peddled slowly and deliberately, glad to leave village where my thoughts were getting the best of me. I had a feeling I couldn't shake. A gray dread about leaving hung heavy in my chest. Why was I worried? Maybe it was 'why' I was leaving. What I would discover.

I passed Issouf's boutique. He was awake and heating water for coffee. I would drop off my bags, secure a place in the van, and go back to sit outside and drink coffee at Issouf's before departing. This was my ritual when leaving village.

I arrived at the van and found it already being loaded. Looking inside, it didn't look good. Today would be a packed ride. I walked around to the back doors and saw that there was one spot left, at the very back in the center. I placed my bike helmet on the open seat and stepped away from the van.

"We're about to go!" yelled one of the chauffeur's assistants.

As with all local transport to and from a village, you never knew if what they said was true. Yet, he did look to be telling the truth, as my bike was already up on top of the van and tied down.

I hadn't seen Issouf to say goodbye though.

I decided to call Issouf and tell him that the van was going to leave soon and I couldn't come to his shop. I hoped he would walk down to say goodbye. I wanted to see him before I left.

"Good morning, Issouf," I greeted over the phone.

"Tyler! Good morning!" Issouf yelled back into the phone.

"The van is ready to go, so I can't come to your boutique."

"Okay. Bon voyage! Safe return!" replied Issouf.

"Thanks. See you soon," I said and ended the call.

Issouf wasn't going to walk down. What if I wasn't going to see him soon? Everything was set for me to fly to Senegal to have my blood drawn and return to Burkina Faso and my village. Yet, what if I never came back? What if I never came back to properly say goodbye to Issouf, my family, my friends, and my village? This was the gray dread that hung heavy in my chest.

In Bobo, the van pulled to the side of the road and parked under a line of trees that bordered the Grande Mosque de Geredougou. The vehicle would sit here until 1:00 p.m. and make the return trip to Banzon. I waited on the side of the van for my bike and bag to be untied from the roof and handed down. Behind me, under the trees, sat a row of Muslim barbers sitting cross-legged on woven mats. The barbers were busy shaving heads and beards of men sitting down on the mats across from them. They delicately worked with lathered soap and thin, sharp, disposable straight razors.

Once my bike and bag were unloaded, I tightly lashed my bags down to my back rack and began to bike to the Bobo Peace Corps office. I weaved in, out, and with traffic filled with taxis, motorcycles, and a few other bicycles. There were no sidewalks or bike lanes. I passed the large white train station, built during the colonial era of Burkina Faso, which was always deserted unless a rally or protest developed out front. All along the way, the sides of the road were filled with shops and stands selling nearly everything imaginable—purses, drapes, bed sheets, clothing, tires, cell phones, bread, and chickens, both alive and cooked.

I pulled up to the large metal doors of the Peace Corps office and gave three quick knocks. Behind the door, I could hear the guard shuffling as he came to crack open the door and peer out.

"Adance – *welcome*," said the guard while opening the door.

I signed the logbook and parked my bike in line with a group of other volunteers' bikes. Unlike a few days ago in Bobo, I would not be alone in the office. I opened the screen door, entered the main room, and placed my bags in front of two short wooden bookshelves. Given the messiness of the room, several volunteers had been here since I left. A volunteer sat across the room, lounging on his side, wearing a worn tank top and gym shorts, with his legs splayed open as he surfed the internet on his laptop.

Looking up from his computer, the volunteer asked without hesitation, "How was having HIV for a day?"

I paused as my stomach quickly retracted into a knot, then replied, "It sucked."

Everyone knew. The Peace Corps rumor mill quickly disseminated what happened last week. Little did this volunteer and others know, it wasn't over yet. Was everyone going to ask? I didn't know if I could keep it together if I was going to continually be asked about my last HIV scare.

I took my backpack into the back room, hoping to find people who wouldn't want to talk about the previous week. In the small air-conditioned room, two female volunteers were sitting on the couch watching an episode of a TV show that I had never seen. I took a seat in the empty armchair next to them and riffled through my bag for my smartphone and phone charger. The nearly full power strip charged two laptops, a Kindle, an iPod, and two phones. I plugged my phone into the last open spot and connected to the office's feeble Wi-Fi.

As I scrolled through Facebook and updated myself on the current life events and funny video posts of my friends back home, I tried to pay attention to the show the two volunteers were watching. The two girls were recent arrivals to Burkina. They had sworn in and started their service less than six months ago and were in very different places mentally with regard to their time in Burkina.

During our pre-service training, Peace Corps staff members passed around handouts of a graph titled, "Cycle of Vulnerability and Adjustment" that showed a fluctuating line set against a twenty-four month time scale.

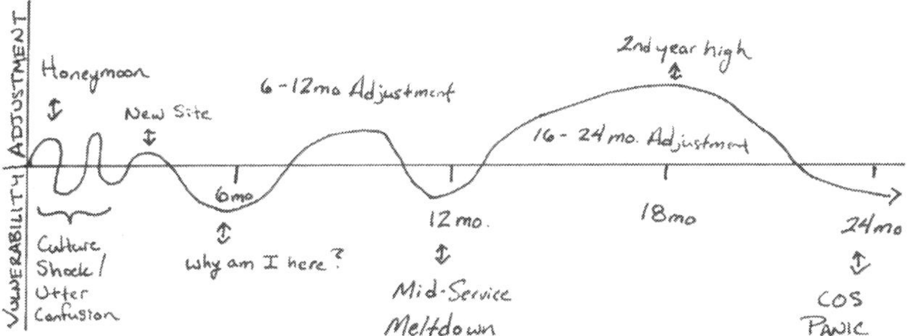

"Your service will be a roller coaster of ups and downs," Peace Corps staff said.

As trainees, many of us glossed over the idea. We knew it would be a difficult two years, but we could never have imagined how well that graph would fit our experience as volunteers. An initial spike in our adjustment or happiness, the honeymoon stage, was followed by a quick series of ups and downs as we struggled to gain a grip on the new country we would call home for two years. Then came swearing in as full-fledged volunteers, followed by the move to our individual sites, when we left our new found volunteer friends and started our careers as volunteers in new villages.

The two girls on the couch were mid-upswing, riding high on the feeling of finally adjusting to their life in Burkina Faso. My training group, however, was reaching down into the vulnerability part of the graph, as our service came to an end. My vulnerability had fallen off the chart.

At no fault of the two volunteers, I was unable to keep a

conversation going. With every exchange, I waited anxiously for them to ask about my HIV test. I imagined them thinking about asking me. Trying to find the right time, holding off long enough to seem organic and compassionate, rather than merely feeding their need for gossip. It was only a matter of time until they asked. I was sure of it, and I wanted no part of it.

I took out my journal and left the room without a word, leaving my phone charging on the table and my backpack wide open at the side of the armchair.

Behind the house sat a walled off courtyard filled with Moringa trees and a small vegetable plot tended to by the guards. Volunteers rarely came back there. I could sit and write without outward distraction.

Slowly, I untied the leather cords that wrapped around my journal. A gold ribbon marked where I last wrote.

09 June 14

"How was having HIV for a day?" asked a volunteer. It sucked to think I was HIV positive. The second time sucks more. I hope I don't. I pray that I don't.

I need to call Caroline and tell her that I'm being medevaced to Senegal Wednesday (today's Monday). Also, I should call Heather, even though I don't want too. She freaked out last time and she asked if the first test could have been a false negative. I should call her. Better than her finding out after the fact. I hope I don't have HIV.

I should have asked to come to Ouaga a day early. I'm in Bobo now. No laptop to watch movies off of. People aren't serving as the greatest distraction. Also, since I'm going to be in the Med-room tonight, it's going to raise some questions.

I may wall myself up in the Med-room. Read. Write. Nap. Those three things seem to define my past few days. Read. Write. Nap. Repeat.

I sat on the ground, a barren patch of earth, alternating between bobbing my pen back and forth and sucking on its end. My mind had been ablaze, yet the thoughts seemed to retreat to unreachable depths once I held a pen in my hand. There was more than what I managed to ink out on the pages of my journal, but the words alluded me.

Maybe it was a self-preservation mechanism. As long as the thoughts stayed in my head, they were simply ideas zipping through the ethos between my ears. Though once written, they were something different—real, validated, brought to life by the strokes of my pen.

I neatly returned the gold ribbon of the journal to where I would pick up next time, and carefully fastened the leather cords around thoughts that had successfully been liberated.

I had been sitting, staring into space for an hour and my legs had fallen asleep. I faltered as I stood and grasped the thin trunk of a tree to steady myself. Once blood and feeling returned to my lower half, I left the courtyard and reentered the transit house. No one had moved from his or her relaxed positions.

Continuing their binge-watching marathon, the two girls remained planted on the couch in the now frigid room. I returned my journal to my bag and took out the 20,000 CFA bill, $40, stashed in an inside pocket.

I was hungry and needed to buy my bus ticket for tomorrow. Rather than invite any of the other volunteers to join me for lunch, I decided to eat alone. I wasn't close with the group at the office and still wanted to avoid any questions about my first HIV scare. I was certain that with time they would ask.

I went to Trois Karite and ordered a plate of rice and peanut sauce. While I waited alone, a man with a wooden caddy moved from table to table. He offered to shine the shoes of men who were dining. When he found a customer, he traded a pair of flip-flops for their shoes and polished their shoes while they ate. A shoeshine cost 150 CFA, or 25 cents. When the man approached me, he looked down to see my grubby sandals and continued walking to another table of men with nicer footwear.

I quickly ate my food and left money on the table.

The bus station was a few blocks away from the restaurant. Rather than walk along the main road, I doubled back toward the Peace Corps office and took the longer, more scenic route. The area, called Petite Paris, was a mix of western affluence and rural village life. Behind tall courtyard walls, cars were parked in driveways next to houses with electricity, running water, and cable. Their homes had tiled floors, painted walls, and plush furniture. Outside in their courtyard, however, chickens still ran loose, laundry was done by hand and hung to dry, and simmering pots sat atop traditional stoves.

Along the way, I stopped into a small store to buy cookies. I was still hungry. For the past few days, I had an insatiable appetite driven by nervousness. Eating provided a momentary escape. I experienced a brief sense of pleasure with each sweet cookie that I ate. Yet, as soon as the pleasure subsided, I was left needing to fill the void, to mask my mental anguish. Thus, I kept eating. One cookie after another.

After enough cookies, bowls of rice, and bread, I would be sick to my stomach. The physical pain of overeating became another form of relief. The tightness of my stomach and nausea were tangible feelings and a distraction from my abstract emotions.

I finished the second package of cookies and tucked the empty wrapper into my back pocket. Later, I would find a half dozen empty wrappers in my pocket and be left to deal with the shame of eating so much junk. But that was a problem for later, so I opened up the third and last package of cookies and began to eat.

The ticketing window was at the back of the bus station. I stood behind a large woman wearing a colorful dress and headwrap, who had grown impatient with the man in front of her at the ticket window. He was trying to ship something across the country to Fada N'gourma, and there was confusion about either the timing of delivery or price. I tried to make sense of the conversation, but could not keep up with the pace that they spoke Dioula.

A line of lost ID cards, wedged into the edge of the acrylic barrier, framed the ticket window. A yellowed printout of the bus schedule, listing destinations, departure/arrival times, and prices hung taped inside the window. I was taking the first bus out of Bobo tomorrow. I would be in Ouagadougou by the early afternoon, in time to meet with the medical staff and Rick, the Director of Management Operations, to finalize the details of my medevac to Senegal.

The woman in front of me quickly bought her ticket and I approached the window with my 20,000 CFA bill and ID in hand. I slid them both under the window, as I said, "First bus to Ouaga tomorrow, please." The ticket woman quickly printed my ticket and passed it to me through the space in the window, along with my change and ID.

Buying my bus ticket was the one thing I had to do today. Calling Heather and Caroline was something I should do.

As I walked back to the office, I started to prepare myself for the two calls. I ran the script in my mind and made sure that I provided only the facts they needed to know. This was a courtesy call. Everything was fine. The follow-up tests were merely procedural, nothing to worry about.

I would call Caroline first, but not before stopping back at the small shop for two more packages of cookies.

I scrolled through my list of contacts to Caroline's name. I hesitated before quickly pressing the dial button. With each ring, I waited with bated breath. She answered. "Hey, Caroline. How are you?"

As succinctly as I could, I told her that I was being medevaced to Senegal in two days for another HIV test. I said it was purely as a precaution and that I would be flown back to Burkina the day after my blood test.

Yet, I wasn't exactly sure that all of this was a precaution. I didn't think Peace Corps would have been so quick to send me back to the U.S. for a precaution, but Caroline didn't need to know the details or my thoughts, especially that I feared I contracted HIV from her.

Calmly, she thanked me for the call and wished me a safe trip. That was it. Caroline didn't seem to think anything of it and I was bothered by her seeming indifference. Very bothered.

How could she not be worried? Maybe it was this kind of apathy for consequences that caused all of this. As much as I tried to stop blaming Caroline for something still speculative, I couldn't. I had no idea if I was HIV positive, and if it turned out to be true I would ultimately have to accept responsibility.

In the distance, an enormous storm front brewed. A wall of dust-laden clouds filled the southwestern horizon. Winds slowly began to pick up and I knew that within the next ten minutes a sand storm would be ripping through where I stood, followed by a torrential downpour. Unhurriedly, I began walking back to the office. I would make it back before the storm hit, and if I didn't, oh well.

I now had to call Heather. As before, I scrolled down to her number. The winds rapidly increased in intensity and people rushed down the street, fleeing into courtyards to take shelter. Slowly, I walked, looking down at her name displayed on my phone. Not far behind me, lightning lit up the red, billowing sky and a sharp crack of thunder popped and resounded through the swirling air. The physical world around me was being hurled into chaos, all the while my mind sat still.

Resolute, I pressed dial and raised the phone to my ear. The wind loudly whorled. I could barely hear the phone ring. I continued to walk as it rang with no answer. Dust filled the air and sharp grains of sand pricked my exposed skin.

Now at the door of the Peace Corps office, I knocked as I continued to press the phone against my ear. The guard opened the door and the ringing stopped with a click—"*The person you are trying to reach is not avail...*" I hung up the phone and it began to rain.

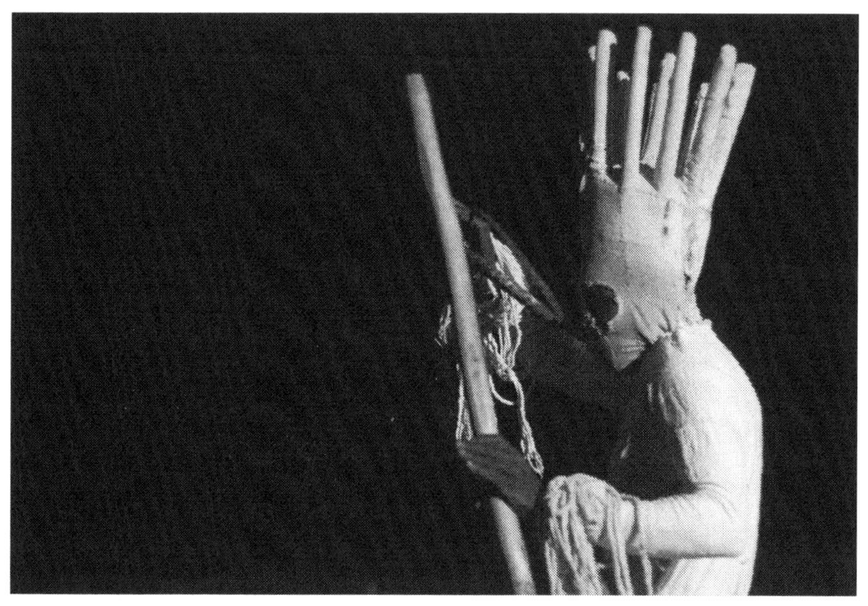

Masked dancer performing at night with staff and whip.

Chapter 18

June 10th – Garden Project

I tossed an empty plastic bag of yogurt into a large metal oil drum turned trashcan as I entered the bus station. I sat down in the waiting area and opened the second part of my breakfast, a package of cream-filled cookies.

On my walk to the bus station, I had stopped at the small corner store to buy yogurt and more packages of cookies. I waited in line behind a woman carrying a small child on her back. She bought bread, packets of powdered milk, and instant coffee. When my turn, I approached the counter and ordered a large yogurt with millet seeds and two packages of chocolate cream-filled cookies. They, however, had only one package of cookies left. Yesterday, in my state of nervous consumption, I had eaten their supply.

At 6:50 a.m., the bus driver honked the horn, signaling to everyone that it was time to board the bus. Each bus company had a different unwritten system for boarding, a chaotic, undecipherable mess to anyone unfamiliar with the particular bus company.

This bus company, Rhamio, was the nicest and most orderly bus company in Burkina Faso. The buses were new, had comfortable seats, and TVs that played local dramas and Nigerian action movies. Tickets could be purchased days in advance and you boarded in the order of your ticket purchase. When buying a ticket, the teller required a form of identification, recorded your name and phone number in their computer system, and printed out a physical ticket. Luggage was taken by an attendant and tagged with the number matching your printed ticket. In a country where you flagged down most transportation on the side of the road, Rhamio stood out.

Yet, even with all the structure, travelers still crowded tightly around the door of the Rhamio bus and pushed their way to the front when their name was called to board. Because of the long pause that preceded my name, I always knew when the bus driver arrived at my name on the list. My name was not Musa, Idrissa, Issouf, or Patrice. My name was Tyler, a name as foreign to Burkina Faso as I was. Following the pause, the driver would look up from his sheet and his eyes would land on me. Tall and white, standing in a crowd of Africans, he knew to whom that name belonged.

I now had an understanding of how it felt to be the student with the foreign name in the U.S., especially Kentucky. Growing up, teachers on the first day of class, or substitute teachers filling in mid-year, would always take pause when certain names were reached during attendance. Kazue, Gaurav, or Mujtaba had their phonetic explanations at the ready, often dumbing down or completely changing the way their name was said to make it easier on everyone else, the ignorant Americans. I spent five years calling my close friend Kanwal, "Con-whal," only to discover from her mother that Kanwal was pronounced "Kaval." I could say her name correctly and would have loved to have known how. Yet, before meeting me, Kanwal had decided she'd have two names. One for her, one for us. I couldn't understand why, until I experienced it for myself.

The bus driver slightly turned his clipboard to the attendant and pointed at my name. Then, for the first time as a Peace Corps Volunteer, I heard him correctly call, "Tyler." I was suddenly filled with joy by the mere fact that someone accurately pronounced my name, a joy quickly stubbed out when the bus attendant corrected the driver, "No, it is Tee-Lur." Unsurprised, I forced my way through the crowd to board the bus.

"I'm Tee-Lur."

Two Nigerian films, three podcasts, and one nap later, the bus pulled into Ouagadougou. I grabbed my bag from under the bus and verified with the security guard that the bag I was leaving with was, in fact, mine.

Outside the bus station sat three taxis and their drivers. Two were helping people load bags into their car as the third looked up to see me.

Damnit. Why him? I asked myself and, from the look on his face, the driver asked himself the same question.

This taxi man, Sie, and I had a mutual dislike for one another and a history to justify it. Without fail, he was always waiting outside the Rhamio bus station in Ouaga when I arrived. Sie knew the location of the Peace Corps house and didn't price gouge me, but the short trip across town rarely happened without problems.

Twice while driving me, Sie ran out of gas. The first time his car cut out and rolled to a stop, we could see a gas station up ahead, so we both got out and pushed the car to the station. The second time he ran out of gas, there was no station in sight. Without hesitation, Sie jumped out of the car and pulled an empty gas can from the trunk.

"I'm going to get gas. Can I have one dollar?" he asked as he stood on the side of the road, looking into the open driver side window.

I handed Sie a dollar coin and he started down the road. I then watched him flag down a stranger on a motorcycle, before hopping on the back of the moto and disappearing down an alley. I was left alone, sitting in a broken down taxi on the side of the road, regretting my decision to drive with him. After ten minutes of debating whether or not I should take my bags and hail another taxi, Sie returned, riding on the back of a different motorcycle.

Once, Sie's taxi completely broke down and I was forced to flag down another taxi, as he yelled at me to stop and wait for him. "I almost have it fixed! Stop, white guy, stop!" he shouted as my extended hand signaled to a second green taxi.

Reluctantly, I approached and greeted Sie, my taxi nemesis. He opened the trunk, held shut by two fraying bungee cords, and took my bag.

"I'm going to the Peace Corps house," I told him.

With a stern, contentious gaze, he looked back at me and said, "I know. Let's go."

Thankfully, I arrived at the transit house without a problem. I handed one dollar to Sie and collected my bags. The house was empty, with only three beds showing signs of other volunteers staying in Ouaga. On the porch, I placed my bags on a bare mattress pushed up against the screened windows and directly under a ceiling fan. As long as it didn't rain, the porch was the best place to sleep.

After grabbing bed sheets and a towel, I walked to the Peace Corps office to meet with Rick to go over my flight details and with Crystal for a final consultation before I left. Tomorrow, I would fly to Senegal, one step closer to answering the question that had been running on repeat in my mind.

Rick was one of five non-Burkinabé staff members, along with the Country Director, Training Director, and the two Medical Officers. I liked Rick. He was a great guy and invaluable to the office. He was the Director of Management and Operations but had also served as the Country Director and Training Director, simultaneously at times, given an unprecedented turnover rate and difficulty finding staff replacements.

Rick's office was on the fourth floor of the Peace Corps office, in a row of other administrative offices. As I walked up the stairs, I wondered what Rick knew. Did he have to be given complete details, know that I need additional HIV tests or only that I needed to be medevaced to Senegal? Even if it was the latter, he was smart enough to figure it out.

Was he going to judge me? Would he talk differently to me? How would he handle the situation? As I moved up the last flight of stairs, I began to grow increasingly anxious. I didn't want to be different. I wanted to be normal. I wanted to be okay.

I neared Rick's office and could hear him talking. His door lay half-open and I looked in to see him alternating between a file on his desk and his checking something on his computer while talking on the phone. I briefly paused before turning around. I would come back in a few minutes. I wasn't ready to talk to Rick.

Down the hall was my Associate Peace Corps Director, Charles, who managed the agriculture volunteer sector in Burkina. He was my primary instructor during training and direct supervisor during my service. Monthly, he would call to check in and see how I was doing and quarterly I would file reports detailing my projects in village. He was a jovial guy, and unlike many other Associate Peace Corps

Directors, he grew up in a rural village rather than one of the large Burkina cities. Charles hailed from a family of subsistence farmers and was at home in the field, swinging a hand hoe and digging through the dirt. He also owed me money.

When I travelled back home for my second Christmas, Charles had asked if I could pick him up something in the U.S. I agreed. Much to my chagrin, he sent a long list of items he wanted: lint roller replacement rolls, three men's deodorants, three women's deodorants, a package of men's disposable razors, body lotion, and Tylenol. He claimed that these things were better in the U.S.

I brought back each of the items Charles asked for, along with the receipt. He didn't have cash on hand when I gave him his goods, and for the past five months had done an excellent job of not being in Ouaga when I was there. Now, I was nearly broke and needed money for Senegal.

I knocked on Charles's closed door, which was followed by, "Hello? Come in," from the other side.

Charles rested behind his desk. The sun shined brightly through the large windows in his small office, filling the room with light.

"Ah, Tyler! So nice to see you. I didn't know you were in Ouaga. Sit, sit, have a seat," Charles recited in his normal cheerful tone.

As I slid my chair out, I asked him how he was doing and quickly followed with, "Oh, and do you happen to have my money?"

He did. Charles pulled out his thick wallet from his front pocket. The leather billfold billowed with receipts and other pieces of paper that were not money. He pulled out a 20,000 and 5,000 CFA note and handed them over to me.

"Taking all my money! It was 25,000, right?" Charles questioned.

"It was actually 26,000, but don't worry about it," I replied. It had taken long enough to get this money. He then shuffled through his desk and pulled out a crumbled 1,000 CFA bill and offered it to me with a smile.

No longer broke, I relaxed back into my chair and began to chat with Charles.

"How are things in Banzon, Tyler? How is Salimata and the rice center? What about Mr. Lega and The Garden School? I heard that you had a graduation for the students. What a wonderful project!" Charles exclaimed.

"They are all good. The Garden School is done for the year, but there are already talks of doing it next year without me," I answered.

The Garden School was my biggest project and accomplishment as a volunteer.

Shortly after arriving to my village, an eager and energetic community member, Rasmané Lega, came knocking at my door. Rasmané wanted to work with me to start a garden, not only for himself but also as a teaching tool for the community.

Gardening was underdeveloped and would benefit Banzon. The project, if successful, would help increase both food security and family income for those who started or improved their vegetable gardening. As it stood, a small number of families gardened during the off-season, while the majority of families elected to only grow cereal crops during the rainy season.

Each day, trucks carried fresh produce to Banzon from more than 40 miles away in Bobo. While cheap to me, the prices were prohibitive to many families. I believed, as did Rasmané, that Banzon could start growing its own vegetables. With a little knowledge and a small, fenced-off portion in their courtyard, families could easily grow tomatoes or squash. Those who had more means could grow large gardens and sell produce in the local market, or even ship and sell their products in Bobo.

Before moving forward, however, I asked Rasmané to calculate the costs of the required materials for starting a garden. I wanted to make sure his eagerness was matched by initiative that would produce results. Making a budget would force him to think through the project, plan the garden, and develop an action plan.

As a volunteer, I had several other community members come to me with project ideas. But in the end, they merely wanted money or material goods. They didn't want ownership of an idea. They wanted a handout and I couldn't blame them for trying. Development projects across sub-Saharan Africa had a long history of imprudent handouts.

What Rasmané produced blew me away. A week later, he delivered a detailed budget, color-coded, including nearly everything we would need. Rasmané had won me over and I began to work with him on a garden and gardening education program.

Rasmané and I took four months to plan out the class schedule, which would last a total of 21 weeks. Until this point, I had held a few trainings with small groups that lasted no longer than an hour. Rasmané and I were setting out to create a comprehensive course that would cover not only agricultural techniques, but also basic business skills.

I had been gardening as a business since I was a child. I, however, knew how to garden and sell vegetables in Kentucky. Burkina is a very different climate and would be a whole new challenge for me. Luckily, Rasmané had recently finished a two-year long training program on gardening. With our experiences combined, in addition to a few textbooks, I thought our garden school would be a manageable undertaking.

Rasmané and I laid out a schedule that would cover everything we could think of:

Week 1: Preparation and start-up of a garden nursery for tomatoes, eggplants, onions, cabbage, and lettuce
Week 2: Maintaining nursery – shade, water, weeding, animals, and pests
Week 3: Preparing the ground for gardening – field selection, grading, shade, etc.
Week 4: Education of garden vegetable needs – soil moisture, watering, shade/sun, nutrient requirements, growth period
Week 5: Vegetable education requirements Part 2
Week 6: Replanting nursery plants in the garden – time of day, watering, considerations for first days after transplant
Week 7: Weeds and water – Recognizing potential problems at the beginning
Week 8: Application of chemical fertilizers, timing, and dosage. Composting and manure utilization
Week 9: Pest control – types of insect pests, parasites and diseases, as well as natural, chemical, and biological treatment options
Week 10: Irrigation
Week 11: Review of Weeks 1 to 10
Week 12: Test One
Week 13: Use and care of animals in both gardening and agriculture in general
Week 14: Marketing of produce Part 1

Week 15: Marketing of produce Part 2
Week 16: Management of a garden as a business – accounting, budgeting, financing, working collectively
Week 17: Management of a garden as a business – Part 2
Week 18: Other potential vegetable crops suitable for Burkina
Week 19: Review
Week 20: Final exam
Week 21: Presentation of a certificate of completion of the "21-Week Garden School"

Initially, we had expected to take on ten students and I decided that the project would be considered a success if half the students completed the 21-week schedule. Yet, community members were eager to join and we had an influx of 35 students show up for the first few weeks of class. After a month, the class size stabilized to 25 students, comprised of both men and women ranging from 14 to 55 years old.

Two months of the project passed by seamlessly. The students continued to return each week and remain active in their participation. We planted a vegetable nursery and began to take field trips to existing gardens. Then the project took a wrong turn, or rather I did when I had the bike wreck that tore my foot open and landed me in the capital for a month.

Further adding to my absence, the bike wreck happened right before a month-long vacation to the U.S. I feared that my garden school project was ruined.

Early on, I had been absent for a week and saw attendance dip. A two-month absence from the project would undoubtedly end everything.

I was wrong.

Given all the months of planning, Rasmané had taken personal ownership of the project and the community members were eager to learn. After my return to village, I found that we had not lost a single student. In the end, 25 students, 20 more than expected, completed the entire 21-week gardening school.

We celebrated the success of the project during a closing ceremony where the Mayor, Village Chief, local Youth Association President, and the local Women's Association President presented each student with a certificate of completion and a manual that covered the material taught over the 21-week garden program. My students even collected money to have t-shirts printed for The Garden School, using a logo that I designed for them.

I was grateful to my students and to Rasmané for all the work that they did because, in the end, this was their project, not mine.

Three weeks after the closing ceremony, The Garden School participants independently held a meeting to form a local gardening association so they could continue to educate themselves and pool resources. They decided to call the association "Wend Pengre," a local Moore phrase.

When I asked Rasmané what the name meant he responded, "It means 'with God's grace.' We want you to have confidence in us, that we will continue to work together after you have left."

The garden school was the iconic highlight of my service as a Peace Corps Volunteer. I had put in the time and effort to build a project that I would be proud of and last beyond my service.

But now I was worried. What if the garden school or the many other great experiences no longer defined my service? An imaginary plaque in my mind read:

Tyler Lloyd, Return Peace Corps Volunteer
Burkina Faso 2012-2014.

*Mr. Lloyd, serving as a Community Outreach Agent under the Environment sector, worked with local farmers and small business owners in Banzon to implement agricultural best practices to increase production and to develop farmers' business skills in order to increase revenues. **

**And, he contracted HIV*

I left Charles's office; no longer having to worry about money, yet with a much larger worry still front and center. Was I going to be defined by a disease? A life lived with an asterisk underscoring my past, present, and future.

Rick was no longer on the phone. I knocked on his door and he invited me in to sit. We exchanged pleasantries as he pulled out a large manila envelope. He wasn't treating me any different than before. The apprehension I held tight in my chest began to subside.

He handed me a printout of my ticketing information, an envelope with a cash advance travel stipend, and my passport, which was kept locked up for safe keeping when not traveling. I would be on an early flight tomorrow, and Sanfo, one of the Peace Corps drivers, would be waiting for me outside the transit house at 6:00 a.m.

Given the short notice, my visa for Senegal had yet to be completely processed, but Rick said that I would be fine. He handed me another piece of paper that he said would show that the U.S. government paid for my visa.

As we talked, it became apparent that he knew why I was flying to Senegal on such short notice with a return flight booked two days later. While Rick never said 'HIV,' he skirted around those three letters when he talked about the difficulties Peace Corps had when trying to find a way to get my blood tested without sending me back to the U.S. They had tried to figure out how to have my blood drawn in Burkina and flown to a lab in France for testing, but that proved impossible. Going to Senegal was the only way I could stay in the Peace Corps and get the testing I needed.

I left Rick's office, but not before thanking him for all the work he did to keep me from being medically separated from the Peace Corps and said that I would see him in a few days.

I was trying to be optimistic. It would all work out in the end. This quick trip to Senegal would be a free mini vacation. I would spend the day reading on the beach. I could go swimming in the ocean. I would find tiny beachfront restaurants with fresh seafood and cold beer. Yes, I would also have my blood drawn, but that was simply a formality, a justification for my jet-setting Senegalese vacation.

Crystal was my last stop in the office. I walked down to the second floor and checked in with the medical secretary, who called Crystal. She was ready to see me. I walked down to her office and pushed open the padded door.

"Good afternoon, Tyler. I hope you're well," Crystal said as I entered her office.

"I am. Went to see Rick and I have all my travel plans ready.

Should be quick and easy," I said with a smile.

"Good to hear. I've been speaking with Dr. Arrat in Senegal, the regional PCMO, to figure out the details. She'll be seeing you in Senegal," Crystal said as she picked up a piece of paper from my file and looked at it.

"Okay. Are those the emails you've been sending her? Can I see them?" I asked. I wanted to know exactly what they had been talking about.

"Sure, Tyler. They are part of your file. Let me print you a copy," Crystal replied as she turned to her computer to print the emails.

As the printer hummed, Crystal detailed what would happen in Senegal. A driver would be waiting for me at the airport in Dakar. They would take me to the Peace Corps office and medical center where I would spend two nights. Dr. Arrat would see me tomorrow, briefly, but my blood would be drawn in the morning the next day. I would have the next day and a half to explore Dakar, before my afternoon flight back to Burkina.

The way Crystal talked about everything, it seemed straightforward and reinforced the narrative I had told myself. This was a simple follow-up test, nothing to be worried about.

Crystal then handed me the printed emails. Quickly, I began to read.

>Subject: TL - Burkina Faso - HIV + screen

I need some confirmation that I am managing a case here in Burkina Faso in the best manner. I would like your input.

Tyler Lloyd is a PCV that came in for a routine COS exam with my colleague. His HIV screening test (HIV Antibody 1 and 2 for Immunoglobulin G, Immunoglobulin M, and Immunoglobulin A) was sent to our Embassy lab. His initial test came back positive. It was then repeated two more times with the second screen coming back negative and the third screen being positive.

The current guidelines state, "If HIV Antibody is repeatedly reactive, the current guidelines are to perform the HIV-1/2 Antibody Differentiation (Multispot) and if that test is negative or indeterminate, the HIV RNA Qualitative Test will be performed."

We sent blood to our HIV specialty lab here for confirmatory HIV tests. They performed the HIV Antigen/Antibody test, which came back negative. Due to government regulations, they will not perform a confirmatory test in country without a positive screening in their lab.

We have been trying to send serum to the U.S. for testing, however logistically this has been a challenge. To send to the USA lab, the specimen has to be at room temperature and arrive within 72hours, which after talking to our Director of Management and Operations is not feasible.

I've been reviewing 'Up To Date' information about the diagnosis of HIV and it is still not clear to me if this current HIV Antigen/Antibody nonreactive result needs a further follow-up. They recommend following up a positive immunoassay test (of which he had two) with a Western Blot (not to confirm infection but to establish timing of infection.)

So- I'm not sure how to proceed at this point. He has had two positive tests and two negative tests.

Please find the attached labs and recent notes.

Thank you for your support

-Crystal

What?

They recommend following up a **positive** immunoassay test (of which **he had two**) with a Western Blot (not to confirm infection but to **establish timing of infection**.)

He has had **two positive tests**. **Two positive tests.**

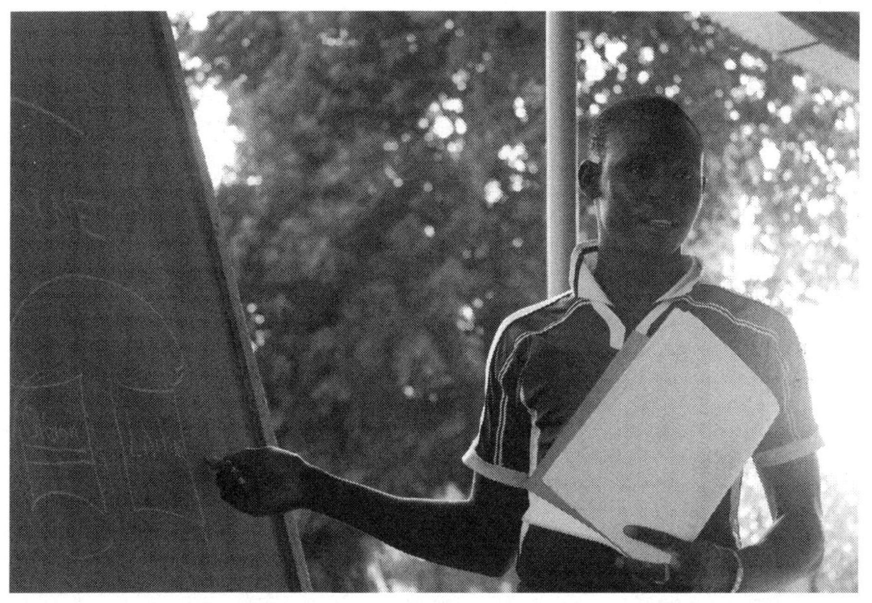

Rasmané Lega teaching a class at Banzon's Garden School.

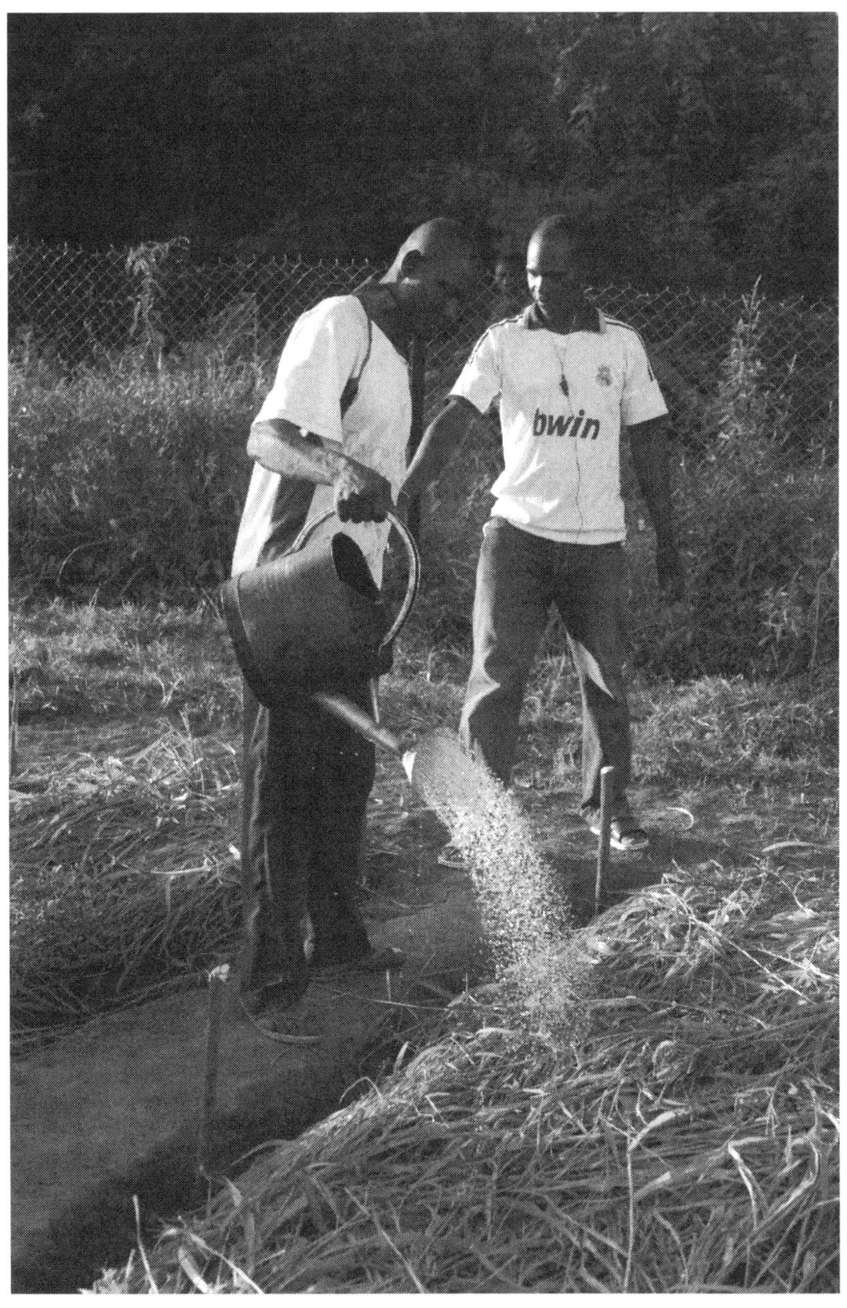

Students watering freshly sown plant nurseries.

Chapter 19

June 11th – Warrior

"Passport," demanded the armed Senegalese customs officer.

I handed over my passport through the opening in the glass barrier to the customs officer, along with the paper printout Rick gave me to show I had a visa. The officer tossed the paper to the side and flipped to my photo. He held my passport up and looked back and forth between the image and me. Back and forth with a discerning scowl. I quickly stood up straight and took off my glasses to match the photo, holding my face still.

The officer flipped through the pages of the passport twice before looking up and asking, "Visa?"

"That piece of paper I gave you, it shows I have a visa. That piece of paper," I repeated while tapping on the glass with my finger in the direction of the printout. The guard wrinkled his brow at my tapping finger, which I slowly lowered away from the glass. He picked up and unfolded the nondescript piece of paper, a printout alleging that a 'Rick' from the Peace Corps of the United States government paid for a Senegalese visa for 'Tyler Lloyd.' The officer picked up my passport again and examined the cheap address label stuck to the front that read 'Peace Corps Passport.' He gently bent the passport and turned it over to inspect the back, before setting it down and turning to the computer in his booth.

The Dakar airport televisions played footage of the recent West African Ebola outbreak. 'Warning' and 'Ebola' appeared again and again on the screen as doctors in hazmat suits cared for dying patients.

"Monsieur Lloyd Tyler, come with me," ordered the guard as he turned to exit his station. He led me to a small room and asked me to take a seat, before leaving and closing the door behind him, my passport still in his possession. I sat alone in the room with my bag slung over my shoulder, scanning the yellowed walls, illuminated by the bright fluorescent ceiling lights. The room felt both unclean and sterile. Nervously, I picked at a chip in the wooden table. *Am I going to be allowed into the country?*, I asked myself.

Another officer suddenly opened the door, carrying my passport and paperwork. Without a word, he walked to the back of the room and rolled a computer cart over to the table.

"Monsieur Lloyd, you need to complete your visa application," said the slightly less gruff officer. "English or French?"

"English, please," I requested.

The officer clicked through several screen prompts before turning the computer toward me. As I completed the questions, he loomed over my shoulder. I finished the form and he took over the computer again. Reaching behind the computer monitor, the officer lifted up a webcam and pulled down a white background behind my head.

"Look at the camera," instructed the officer.

Click.

A small printer spat out my visa, which he affixed to my passport, quickly stamped, and slid across the table to me.

"Welcome to Senegal. The exit is out the door and to the left."

Out the door and to the left, a lone man stood holding a paper sign that read 'LLOYD.' Every other passenger on my flight had already gone through customs, claimed their bags, and exited the airport.

"Hello, I'm Tyler Lloyd, Peace Corps from Burkina Faso."

"Do you need to get a bag?"

"No, this is all I have."

"Okay, let's go."

My face hung close to the passenger side window as we drove to the Peace Corps Senegal office. Dakar was much larger than Ouagadougou, with wide, multi-lane highways and towering buildings.

Colorful billboards displayed advertisements for sports teams, restaurants, and cell phones. I caught a glimpse of the ocean and grew excited by the thought of relaxing on the beach, before quickly remembering the reason for my trip to Senegal.

I started small talk with the driver, asking him what I should see or do in Dakar. He rattled off a list of sights and restaurants, which I paid little attention to. I was busy thinking.

What did the driver think of me?

He knew I was sent here for medical reasons, but I look perfectly healthy.

Is he trying to figure out what is wrong with me?

Maybe I shouldn't have asked for recommendations.

Wait, what did he say?

"We're here," said the driver as he turned off the car.

The driver led me into the building and showed me to the medical office on the first floor.

"Viviane, this is Mr. Lloyd from Burkina Faso. Tyler, it was pleasure meeting you. Viviane will take care of you now."

I shook the driver's hand and he left me with Viviane, the Peace Corps Senegal medical secretary.

Viviane introduced herself and led me across the hall to the apartment where I would stay for the next two nights. One other volunteer currently resided in the apartment. I would have an entire hostel-style bedroom to myself. After placing my two bags on a lower bunk bed, I followed Viviane back to the medical office to meet Dr. Arrat.

Three female volunteers sat with me in the waiting room. I introduced myself and told them I was a medevac from Burkina. They awkwardly paused and I sensed a follow-up question bubbling up in their minds, but they didn't ask for further details. Two of them were picking up medication while in town for other reasons. The third girl waited with her friends.

Where they trying to figure out what was wrong with me? Could they tell?

I grew increasingly paranoid. The more I thought about the HIV test, the more I assumed others thought about the HIV test. It was all I could think about, either the past results or the pending tests and the resultant future before me.

A thin East African woman wearing a white lab coat approached the four of us and extended her hand, "Good morning, Mr. Lloyd. I'm Dr. Arrat. Let's go to my office."

I said goodbye to the girls and followed the doctor down the hall to her small office. She sat down at her desk and opened a file with my name written across the front. She smiled and asked, "How was the flight?"

"It was fine. Short."

"Good to hear. How are you doing?"

I told her that I was fine, a lie, and then tried to figure out what she thought of the situation. Was she concerned? I couldn't tell. But Dr. Arrat could tell that I was worried and run-down.

She kindly walked me through what would happen. Tomorrow morning at 8:00 a.m., she would draw my blood and send the sample to France, after which we would have to wait up to two weeks for results. She, however, thought it wouldn't take more than a few days. Other than having my blood drawn, I was free to explore and enjoy Dakar.

Dr. Arrat pulled out a blank piece of paper and drew a crude map showing me the best way to walk to the beach and where I would find several restaurants and shops. On the top of the page, she wrote her name and phone number.

"This is my personal cell phone number. If you need anything, call me. Suggestions, directions, or anything else, call me, at any time."

I thanked her, folded the piece of paper, and placed it in my pocket. She walked me out of her office and back to the apartment across the hall.

"It is a beautiful day for the beach today, but the apartment also has a TV with lots of DVDs if you want to stay in. You can also make free calls to the U.S. with the phone in the living room. See you tomorrow morning, Tyler," said Dr. Arrat as she walked away, leaving me alone, standing inside the door of the apartment.

I quickly poured out the contents of my backpack on my bed and repacked the bag with my journal, Kindle, and water bottle. I couldn't stay inside. I had to make the most of the situation. Everything was fine and I had a two-day beach vacation to enjoy. Everything was fine.

I left the Peace Corps Senegal office and pulled out Dr. Arrat's map. The beach was close. The paved road in front of the office gave way to dirt as I rounded the corner. The compacted earth looked the same as in Burkina Faso, smooth with a fine layer of light brown dust. I turned back onto another paved road filled with modern stores. Walking down the street, I passed small souvenir shops, cafes, and a grocery store named American Food Store.

I could smell the ocean and soon caught a glimpse of the westernmost shore of the African mainland. I turned down the first street in the direction of the water and moved toward a large restaurant with a thatched roof.

Outside the restaurant, two men selling souvenirs called me over to see what they were selling.

"Come take a look. We have everything you could want, things large and small, all prices, and from all over West Africa," said the heavier-set man.

I walked into their store and began to look for a souvenir. I wanted to bring back something from Senegal that summarized this trip and experience. I scanned through the rows of handmade crafts, searching for an item that captured how I felt, a physical embodiment of fear and strength—and sadness, confusion, and desperation.

"We have bronzes from Benin and masks from all over. This one is from Burkina Faso," said the thinner man, holding up a small bronze statue and pointing to a mask hanging on the wall.

"How much is the mask?" I asked.

"$200."

"Never mind."

In the row of bronze statues stood a man holding a spear and a shield. The skinny six-inch tall warrior thrust the pointed tip of his spear over the top of the round piece of armor held in front of his body. I picked up the heavy metal figurine to get a better look. Was this the souvenir I searched for? Was I this little fearless warrior, fending off danger, alternating between the defensive protection of my shield and the offense of my spear?

No. It didn't feel right. I was not a warrior.

I placed the statue back on the table and wished the men well, promising to come back before I left Dakar.

Inside the restaurant, I sat down at an outdoor table facing the beach. I ordered a plate of fish and a beer and pulled my Kindle from my bag. Scrolling through lists of books, I searched for something to read. On page two, I landed on *Meditations of Marcus Aurelius*, a book I had meant to start.

Quickly, I became lost in the two-thousand-year-old poetic prose of the dead Roman Emperor.

"From my grandfather Verus, I learned good morals and the control of my temper.

From the reputation and memory of my father, modesty and a manly character.

From my mother, virtue and generosity, and abstinence, not only from evil deeds but even from evil thoughts; and further, simplicity in my way of living, far removed from the habits of the wealthy."

Marcus Aurelius continues to list off traits and virtues gained from friends, family, and mentors. One by one, I compared myself against the emperor's list. In what ways could I be better?

My meal arrived and I continued my internal discussion as I tried in vain to concentrate on the delicious fresh fish cooked in yassa sauce, a traditional Senegalese lemon, garlic, and mustard sauce.

Simplicity in my way of living, I thought. For the past two years, I lived well with very little. I was happy but never stopped daydreaming of the things I would buy once I returned home. On a back page of my journal, I kept a running list of all the things I wanted, a list of things to buy as a reward for completing the Peace Corps.

Back home in my parent's basement sat a wall of plastic crates and cardboard boxes filled with my possessions. A mountain of things that I had been happy without. Other than clothes and basic houseware items, I had forgotten what I owned back home. None of it important.

Could I maintain a simple life back in the U.S.? In a country of things, was that even possible? *I want to live a simple life*, I told myself, *value friends and experiences over material goods.*

I paid for my meal and began walking back to the Peace Corps office for a nap. I stopped into American Food Store on the way and slowly weaved through aisles of grocery items I hadn't seen in a very long time. I walked out of the store with a box of pancake mix, fake maple syrup, and a Baby Ruth candy bar that I finished fifty feet from the door.

I stopped at a small boutique along the dirt road and bought bananas for my pancakes and packets of instant coffee for the morning. I also bought a SIM card for a local cell carrier and enough credit for a few days of internet, which all cost four dollars. I slid the SIM card and credit into my pocket and placed the other items in the bag with my pancake mix, syrup, and Baby Ruth wrapper.

Back at the office, I sat my bag of food on the kitchen counter and walked to the living room to sit on the stiff couch. I exchanged my smartphone's SIM card for the new card and scratched away the metallic coating of the cell credit with the side of my thumbnail, like a gas station lottery ticket, to reveal the unique credit code with which to buy minutes or internet. I purchased internet and slouched back into the sofa.

I came back to nap, but couldn't sit still. I picked up my bag, threw it over my shoulder, and returned to the street to stroll through Dakar. I found another beachside restaurant and an ocean-facing table with an umbrella. It took the waiter twenty minutes to notice me, but I didn't mind. I gazed out into the ocean, lost in the horizon, the United States sitting on the other side of the Atlantic.

I ordered a light local beer and started reading again, yet never able to maintain focus. I felt paralyzed by the number of ideas running through my mind. Slowly, I sipped my beer and peeled the label from my bottle. Waves crashed against the rocky shoreline of the Cap-Vert Peninsula. I focused closely on the ocean sounds, light breeze, and cold, sweating glass bottle dripping on my hand—tangible outward sensations rather than the surreal swamp of my mind.

My phone beeped loudly. A message from Medrena. I last talked to her while waiting in the Ouagadougou airport.

Medrena: *Fly safe. Land safe. Be safe. I'll be thinking about you all day... everything will be fine.*

Me: *Thanks. I already went to the beach, had amazing grilled fish, a beer, a Baby Ruth candy bar, and bought pancake mix and syrup for dinner/breakfast. Still scared though.*

Medrena: *Pancakes are the best solution. If you can find berries of some kind, I highly recommend it. In all my years, I've noticed the particularly cathartic power of blueberry pancakes smothered in syrup. Fear is natural. How you handle it is your choice. If you need to, you know you can always call me :)*

Me: *You free today? I get free calling to the U.S.*

Medrena: *Yes! It's my day off!*

Me: A*wesome. Currently out, reading and drinking at the beach. Will call when back at the office.*

Medrena: *Talk to you soon! Enjoy the beach for me!*

I rebounded back to my short-lived, thoughtless stare, interrupted by a beep from my other phone. Heather texted, *Sorry I missed your call the other day. How are you?*

I replied with the latest news but the message was denied. I didn't have enough credit to send a message with my Burkina phone roaming in Senegal. With my smartphone, I typed and resent the message, *This is Tyler on a different phone. I'm in Senegal…*

Okay, be safe. Call me when you get back, replied Heather.

'That's it?' I thought.

On the table, under the empty bottle, I sat enough money to pay for my beer and left the beachside refuge. I was depressed. Deeply depressed.

Before the Peace Corps, I didn't understand depression. In many cases, I had strong doubts of its existence. I thought that depressed people made excuses for themselves and were weak willed. I am ashamed to have ever thought this way.

At times, things suck and you become sad. After wallowing in self-pity, you needed to buck up and move on. You simply had to look at your problems objectively, find solutions, and remove the obstacles in your life causing your problems. Learn from the sadness and move on. This how I thought about depression before the Peace Corps, before I experienced depression for myself.

When I left the U.S. for the Peace Corps, I left a girlfriend. Against my best judgment, we decided to make the long distance work. I had my doubts, but I was in love.

I was single when I applied to join the Peace Corps. As part of my application, I completed a 'Romantic Involvement Worksheet' to declare my relationship status. The first question read, 'How significant do you consider your relationship?' to which I replied, 'I am not currently in a relationship, nor do I predict finding myself in a relationship before leaving that would be considered significant in such a way as to hinder my performance in the Peace Corps.'

That was a month before I met her, a girl I fell in love with and spent nearly every free moment with for 11 months leading up to my departure.

Surprisingly, it seemed to work. I missed her, but it wasn't too bad. Her oldest brother was in the military, so she had experience not seeing a loved one for extended periods of time. It wouldn't be two whole years apart either. Nine months after leaving, I would visit her in Italy where she would be studying abroad, nine months after that I would come home for Christmas, and nine months later I would be done with the Peace Corps.

Given access to internet on my phone, she and I were able to chat regularly. I told her about village, she told me about school. Yes, we were lonely, but we loved each other.

Two weeks before leaving for Italy, she told me not to come. It was over without warning. The previous week she had sent me pictures of possible apartments for us when I returned, and links to castles in Ireland that she thought would be 'perfect for a wedding or honeymoon.' Then, nothing. "Tyler, I don't think you should come visit me."

Quickly, I spiraled into depression. I spent several straight days where I did nothing but lie on my floor and cry. When able to pull myself off the floor, I self-medicated with alcohol, starting my mornings with my village version of a White Russian—instant coffee, sweetened condensed milk, and a packet of coffee flavored whiskey, or two depending on the day.

My entire village knew her name because I talked about her constantly, which led to them asking about her constantly.

On the day it happened, in a state of shock, I walked to Issouf's house. Before I could get the words out to tell him, I burst into tears. He tried to comfort me, but I was inconsolable. I quickly left his house, walking down the main road back to my home, uncontrollably crying. I didn't eat or leave my house for two days.

Breakups are hard. That breakup pulled me down into a very dark place. Every day, I questioned being in the Peace Corps, resenting the choices I made. I begin to question my very existence. Then came the night terrors, fueled by mefloquine, my antimalarial medication known to cause depression, hallucinations, and extreme anxiety, along with a slew of neurological side effects.

For several weeks straight, I abruptly woke up at 3:00 a.m. every morning, dripping with sweat, heart racing, and scared. I could never remember the dreams, but I vividly remembered the profound sense of dread that loomed over me. Then, from 3:00 to 6:00 a.m., I lay in bed unable to sleep; afraid, sad, and lonely. Once I began to catch hallucinations of dark figures out of the corner of my eye during the day, I switched from mefloquine to doxycycline, which caused my skin to breakout in a rash when exposed to the sun for too long.

But the dreams didn't stop and the sadness didn't go away. After a month of crying and self-medicating, I tried a month of trying to buck up and move on. It didn't work either, which caused me to question my willpower and self-worth.

Thankfully, I reached out to Peace Corps for help. They arranged bi-weekly calls with a psychiatrist back in the U.S. Slowly, I worked through my sadness and got better, but I needed the outside help to get better.

Now, the feeling of despair returned. But why? Nothing was final. I had two HIV positive tests and two HIV negative tests. Was I overreacting? I was overreacting. Ignore it. Ignore the sadness. It isn't real. Ball it up and push it to the side until I have answers. Buck up.

I walked back to the apartment and called Medrena. We talked about everything except my tests. We laughed and joked, and made plans for when I came home. It was good to hear her voice, to find solace in the familiar.

Chapter 20

June 12th – Dakar

12 June 2014

In Dakar. Blood was drawn this morning. Soon after, I went back to bed and passed out until 12:30. I might have slept longer if it wasn't for my alarm reminding me to take my malaria meds. Still tired. Depressed? Also dehydrated. The water here tastes bad.

The level of French here is higher than mine. Or different words. Just placed my order at a café. Very hard to understand the waitress.

I'm scared. I think I'm HIV positive. Or my mind has done a good job of connecting facts to make me think so.

- *Unprotected sex at COS*
- *Given the two months, my levels of HIV antibodies would be low, causing uncertain results: the two positive and one negative test by the Embassy and later the negative test at the WHO lab in Ouaga*
- *Caroline also slept with a volunteer who slept with a Burkinabé*

But, Dr. Patel has never had a positive volunteer. He has, however, had 3 false positives. I could be his 4th false positive. Or, Burkina could have its first HIV-positive volunteer. Maybe more… fuck.

Small actions, split second decisions, hedonism, can ruin you for the rest of your life.

Today, at this moment, I'm not in a good place. I don't feel good about my pending results. Or maybe this is fate doing its best to freak me out, get me scared, and value the opportunities I have before me.

"You have to deserve the reward." – Quote from a podcast I listened to earlier.

I've been too privileged.

I'VE BEEN TOO PRIVILEGED.

I'm owed nothing. I've been too carefree and rested mostly on luck or natural talent. I haven't put in the time.

I'm scared.

"Fear is normal. It depends on what you do with it." –Medrena.

Right now I feel low and want to give up. I want to crawl under a rock and die.

What if I wrote a book about this experience? Whether or not the outcome was good or bad. Talk about my service. Life.

Or, will this be another idea that I don't take on? How many of those types of ideas have I had? Hundreds? Thousands? That's my problem. I like to think of myself as an idea guy. But it's time for me to start taking action in my life. Put myself out there to fail. Not how I've failed in the past. My past failures have been like my past successes: passive and left to the ebb and flow of chance.

Chapter 21

June 13th – Baobab

13 June 2014

Took a little nap at Surfer's Paradise after having an espresso. I leave today. The car is coming to get me at 2:00 p.m. I had pancakes for breakfast, finishing off the box of mix that I bought. Today, I'm reigning in the spending. This messed up vacation comes to an end.

Last night, while still in vacation mode, I had Korean food. I've had better. I ordered and ate a ton though - $30 worth. Plate of fried dumplings, bowl of rice, sweet and sour fried pork, and all the sides that usually come with Korean food (dried fish, kimchi, various salads, unknown red spicy things). I was stuffed. Painfully stuffed. I should have stopped myself but I didn't think any of it would reheat well. I paid for it and didn't want to waste it. Today, I'll find rice and sauce somewhere. Go for cheap and simple.

I put down my pen and looked up, out to the ocean. My mind washed back and forth like the tide and crashed against the rocks. I sat for several minutes in a trance before I picked up my pen and begin to write again.

My mind is back on my pending test. Dr. Arrat seemed positive. So has Crystal. Dr. Patel isn't worried because he had never had a truly positive case in his 12-year career. That doesn't mean it couldn't happen. I've already written my thoughts, predictions, laying out a logical link to a positive HIV status as my end result. The doctors don't know all the facts I know. I haven't been 100% transparent. I'm ashamed. I should know better. I was stupid and reckless and now I may have to pay for my actions.

Either way, I'm paying, whether positive or negative, as my mind works and reworks over everything. The past, present, and future. Yet, now I can only wait. Dr. Arrat said results could come as early as a week but could take up to two weeks. Only to wait. Hard to not put my life on pause, not moving forward in life for the time being.

Looking up again, back out to the ocean, my mind continued to run. These ideas would later either be forgotten or remembered as glimmers of dissipated dreams, nonsense verging on insanity. This experience unnerved me and I felt myself slowly coming undone.

I pulled myself from a detached westward gaze. I needed to move and change my environment. It was almost lunchtime and I needed to get ready to leave Dakar.

Walking along the road, I passed by previously visited restaurants as I searched for something new. I wanted to find a tiny hole-in-the-wall place, the kind of place with two or three tables surrounded by mismatched chairs.

A modest wooden shack sitting on a rocky escarpment caught my attention. A subtle stream of white smoke rolled out from one side of the humble building, signs of a fire cooking food. I walked into the building to find exactly what I wanted, three tables, mismatched chairs, and a lone man drinking a Coke while playing on his phone. He quickly stood up and invited me in to sit.

"Do you have rice and sauce?" I asked.

"No, but we have fish. I caught them an hour ago. Very fresh." he replied.

"What kind of fish? How much?" I responded

"Let me show you," enthused the man as he disappeared behind the restaurant's counter and hurriedly returned with two whole, wet fish lying on a plastic tray. The mouth of the larger fish, still alive, slightly opened and closed. "This one is $7 and this one is $9," said the man with an eager smile.

"Do they come with rice or something?" I inquired. That price was more than I wanted to pay for lunch, but this was my last chance to eat fish this fresh for a while.

"Yes, rice," he replied.

"I'll take this one and a large beer," I said pointing to the smaller, slightly deader fish.

I took a seat at a table and watched the man begin to shuffle back and forth behind the counter. He rinsed a glass with a wet cloth before lifting a large frosty beer from a small freezer. The man placed the glass on my table and popped the cap off of the beer with a bottle opener, allowing the cap to fall to the small gray pebbles on the ground. He then turned on the radio and disappeared behind the shack to begin cooking my fish.

I leaned back into the creaky plastic lawn chair and slid my sandals off, burying my feet into the smooth, cold rocks. Beneath the West African pop music playing on the radio, I heard the man banging pots and forcefully chopping. Minus the circumstance, this was my ideal vacation.

Relaxed, I slowly opened my journal to where I left off.

> *Decided on fish and rice by the ocean. $8 with a beer. Not the cheap option but I'm here and can eat good seafood. Should have had seafood last night, rather than Korean. Maybe I should live near the ocean. Are there any ocean front towns in the U.S. that aren't built up, commercialized, bastardized, and ruined? The soil would suck for gardening though, but I could do raised beds and bring in topsoil.*
>
> *Buy a sliver of beachfront land. Maybe abutting a park or reserve. Have my micro house there. Raised beds. Chickens. Or will I live in Kentucky? Now begins the rambling in my head.*

I settled myself into the chair and fantasized about a future dream home. I wanted a simple life, close to nature and my community, like my life in village. I didn't need a lot to be happy. A small home, a garden, a camera or two, and friends. After the Peace Corps and my last year of graduate school, I could end up living anywhere. What would make me happiest?

The restaurant man cut my daydream short as he brought out my food. First, a large bowl of fried rice, followed by three small bowls of different salads. Lastly, the grilled fish on a platter with herbs and lime wedges. My tiny table was covered in food.

All for this for $8?, I questioned to myself. *I bet he is going to charge me more.*

Voraciously, I alternated between the small dishes, onion and mustard salad, macaroni salad, and tangy coleslaw, each one more delicious than the next. The large oily bowl of fried rice, a spiced bowl of carbs, fat, and salt, would have held my attention if it were not for the grilled fish. The fish was crispy on the outside and perfectly cooked on the inside. I freed tender, flaky bites from the fish, which melted in my mouth in a slow ripple of subtle brininess and smoke. I ate every bite, grain, and morsel, and scanned the table of clean dishes and denuded bony scaffolding for one more taste.

I pushed aside my plates and cleared a space for my journal. I still needed to go back and pack for my flight back to Burkina but wasn't ready to leave the beachfront shack, the delicious lunch, and cool ocean breeze. The restaurant owner returned to clear my plates and I praised him for the meal. I handed him a $10 bill and waited to see if it covered my meal. To my surprise, he reached into his pocket and handed me a crumpled two dollars in return.

He left me to reflect on my short time in Senegal. If only I could have enjoyed Dakar more, chosen to come to Senegal. Although, in a way, I did choose when I rejected Peace Corps' plans to send me back home for more testing. Did I make the right choice?

> *Ideas pour out and dance about as I sit. Yet, whenever I try to make something "meaningful" find its way to paper, nothing comes. Likely because I try and force it into a preset mold rather than letting the idea move and take shape for itself. I need to give the idea a place to develop and let it come to me.*
>
> *Yes, first I'll start writing. Maybe it will be disconnected nonsense but eventually, I'll hit my stride and all will fall into place. It will happen. Without trying. The words are inside me, but they're shy.*
>
> *I'm afraid. Afraid of putting myself out there. If I want to really write, I need to get out of my way and let it happen. Will people judge me? Yes. But I want to be judged. And if I am going to be judged it*

should be of my authentic self. I'm Tyler. Following uniform steps and procedures of writing will give me a readable text to work from, but it will have no life. No spirit. It is time for me to release my thoughts. Clear my head and seek peace.

The thoughts never came to fruition. I thanked my gracious lunch host and left for one last attempt to find a souvenir. I kept thinking back to the small bronze warrior statue, but the essence of the tiny effigy did not accurately dovetail with the distorted situation I pained to characterize.

One by one, I stopped into small souvenir shops, searching for a physical thing to encapsulate this period in my life. Again, I found other mass-produced metal figures—warriors, women carrying water, and iconic African animals. Next to a figure of a woman carrying a child on her back, sat a bronze baobab tree…the perfect souvenir.

The oldest, towering, slow-growing Baobabs stand for more than a millennium, weathered by harsh rays and sculpted by drought. Many African cultures tell stories of how the gods ripped these trees out of the ground and replanted them with their roots in the air, or how God allowed the animals to sow the first seeds of all the trees and that the ignorant hyena sowed the Baobab wrong-side up. In my village, Baobabs were revered and believed to be the homes of genies. The resilience and mythos of the Baobab spoke to much more than the past weeks. The Baobab was how I saw Africa, an often generalized enigma, weathered by outside forces, enduring, and beautiful.

I paid for the small, metal tree and hurried back to my room to pack. I found the driver already waiting for me outside the Peace Corps office. I quickly crammed my few days of dirty clothes into my bags and rushed out to meet the driver.

I watched the Peace Corps Senegal office shrink in the passenger's side mirror while my worry began to grow. How long would I have to wait in village for an answer? How long could I keep this a secret from other volunteers? Too many already knew.

The three-hour flight back to Burkina was uneventful. This time, I walked through Senegalese and Burkina security without a problem. Passing by baggage claim, I began looking for the driver who would take me back to the transit house.

"Hey, Tyler. What are you doing here?" asked Christina, another

Peace Corps Volunteer, which caught me off guard.

"I just landed. You?" I replied uneasily.

"Waiting for Abdul. He comes back tonight from Tanzania," responded Christina. "Where are you coming from?"

"Senegal. Just a quick trip. Oh, there's my driver. Gotta go. See you back at the house," I said and quickly walked away—*Shit. Christina now knows. She had to.*

By now, most everyone was aware of my first HIV scare and since Senegal was where Burkina volunteers are often medevaced, Christina had to know why I was in Senegal.

That evening, back at the house, Abdul and Christina approached me.

"Tyler, are you okay man?" asked Abdul.

"No. I'm not ok."

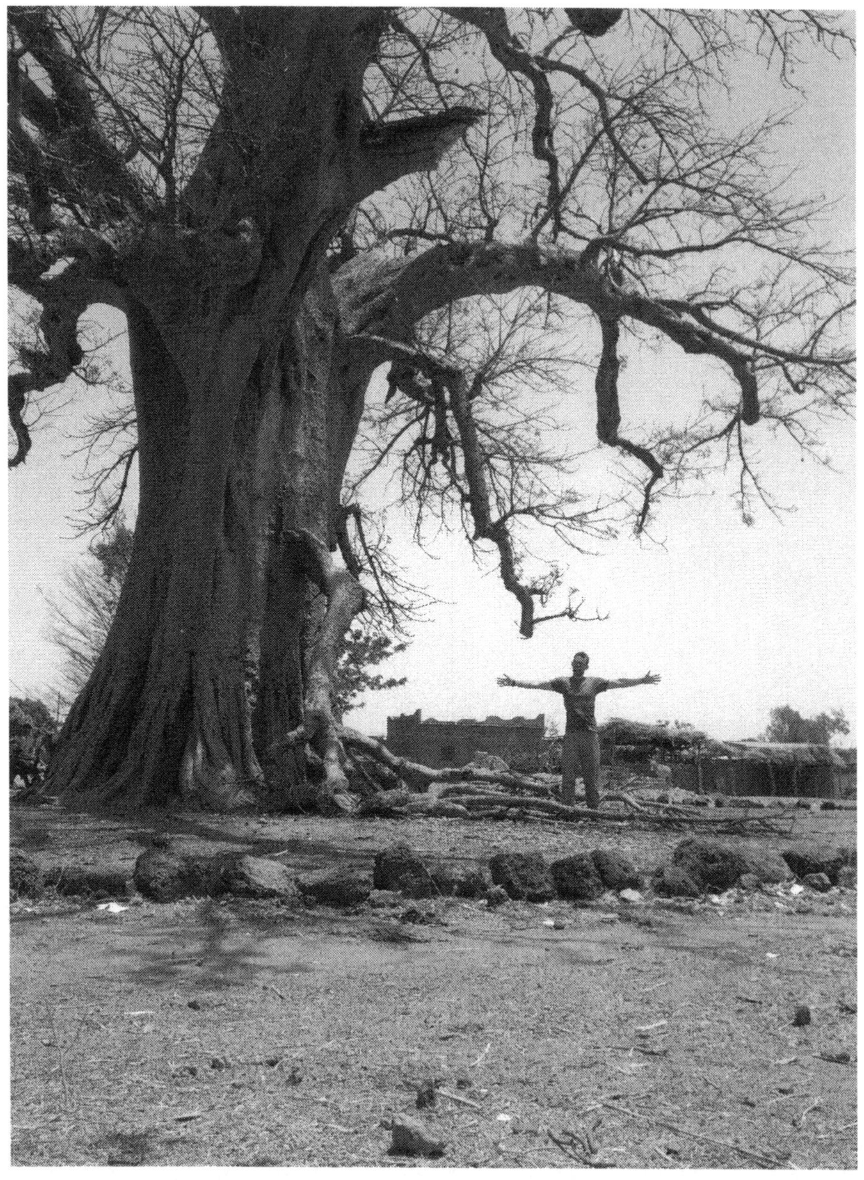

Standing next to the sacred ancient baobab tree of Fada N'gourma.

Chapter 22

June 14th – Cut

A handful of volunteers were staying in Ouaga. Abdul and Christina knew my secret and they did their best to comfort me. I was glad that they had the insight and boldness to ask if I was okay. Last night, as my voice cracked and quivered, I told them everything. It felt good to be greeted with kindness and sympathy upon landing in Burkina. I didn't want to be alone and worried about going back to my village. It was much easier to distract myself in Ouaga.

Rather than wall myself off in the private medical room, I claimed a bed close to others on the porch. With no meetings or special events happening in the capital, the house was calm. I spent the morning bouncing from room to room, striking up conversations with anyone who would indulge me. In the early afternoon, I finally left the house and biked to Le Karite Bleu, a small hotel down the street.

Unique pieces of modern art filled the tranquil inner courtyard of the hotel. A karite tree painted blue, the namesake of the hotel, stood out against the lush tropical garden. I parked my bike inside the heavy metal doors of the hotel and chose a seat next to a small, bubbling fish pond. One other person, a gentleman reading a newspaper, shared the large courtyard with me.

A hotel waiter came out to bring me a menu and to ensure I intended to order something, not merely pilfer free Wi-Fi. I ordered a double espresso, the one thing I ordered at Karite Bleu, because it was fairly priced, good coffee, and their food received below average reviews from my fellow volunteers, which spoke volumes coming from a group of people that subsisted largely off oily spaghetti and tomato paste.

The waiter returned with my coffee, balanced atop a white porcelain saucer, alongside two sugar cubes, a spoon, and a chocolate square. He sat the coffee next to small silver creamer and retired to the hotel. I unwrapped the chocolate and alternated small bites with sips of bitter espresso.

I finished my coffee and sat the small cup down with a clink, when I noticed I was being watched. The hotel's gray-crowned crane, a three-foot tall sub-Saharan bird adorned with a bright red throat and crown of stiff golden plumes, stealthily emerged from a patch of verdant ornamental grass. I looked back at the bird, which quizzically cocked its head sideways. The bird rapidly scanned me up and down twice before dismissing my presence and walking away to patrol another area of the courtyard, possibly to track down the newspaper-reading man who had wandered off.

I opened my laptop and a new word document. The last thing I had written, other than my scattered manic journal entries, was my blog post about testing positive for HIV. Since Crystal's call, I reflected many times on what I wrote and began to regret how prematurely and flippantly I broadcast the experience. Now, in the midst of another episode, I felt compelled to write an addendum and some kind of reconciliation:

> *The past few weeks have been some of the most trying and crazy weeks of my life. I, however, have come out on the other end better, stronger, and wiser after it was all said and done. It all started with the false positive HIV test that I wrote about in my previous post. Although after much reflection, I don't know if writing that blog post was the best idea or rather, maybe it was the timing of the post. Hours after receiving the good news, high on endorphins and life, with the experience as fresh as it could be, I sat down and pumped out a quick summary of what had transpired over roughly 24 hours. I left out some details and concentrated on the heart thumping fact that I had tested positive for HIV. I think it was a great post. In fact, I think it was the best post I've ever written because it came from an organic passion and sense of urgency that's hard to reproduce sans trauma.*
>
> *In the post, I said, "I processed more than I have in months. I discovered*

what was important to me and was surprised by what immediately fell off my radar once I was confronted with a life-altering challenge." And, mind you, I had reflected and realized a lot of things during those 24 hours. Yet, it was only 24 hours. One day. Was it scary as hell? Yes. But, I believe that it wasn't long enough and I turned around too quickly and broadcast the experience out to the world without taking enough time to sort through everything. Maybe if I had hesitated longer, I would have never shared the experience. Maybe I would have written it differently. Actually, I know I would have written a very different story. I likely would have been more calculated, detailed, and written a shitty post that lacked a sense of fear and gravity.

In many ways, I think that I cheapened the experience by writing about it in the manner that I did. I pushed out to everyone what was a life-shaking event, collected several blog follows, a lot of Facebook likes and comments, and scared the crap out of a lot of people. Was I seeking a social media wave of sympathy and support? Yeah, I guess I was and I don't know what that says about me. I wanted to validate the situation via the responses of others as opposed to seeking self-validation (and you could possibly say this post is a continuation of seeking social approval, but I think it is something else entirely).

The day following my post, did I wake up and feel as if I had been granted another chance? That my life has been reset and that I was on a new path towards self-improvement and change? Nope. It was just another day. The days that followed were very much the same. I was off having a great time traveling around Burkina Faso, exploring the sites of the Southwest, and my mindset was unchanged. I hadn't forgotten the experience. No. Testing positive for HIV, even if a false positive, wasn't something I could easily shake. It was there, lurking in the back of my mind, but I was still going through the motions.

Now, all of that has changed as a result of several weeks of additional on-the-edge drama that I am currently choosing to not publicly write about. I am writing this post, however, and I plan to be doing a lot more writing over the next month. Don't worry or speculate though. I'm currently healthy, well, and doing great. I'm going to be writing for myself though, as a cathartic exercise to reflect and work through not only my Peace Corps experiences but also my life as a whole, past, present, and future. Maybe one day I'll publish it all, but for now, I have to be selfish.

I sorta screwed up the first time and didn't make the most of the opportunity that chance had presented me. Yes, that HIV scare was a once in a million (or whatever the odds are of a false positive test) opportunity that I had cheapened and was allowing to fade into a past memory rather than actively taking that energy and focusing it into something great. Luckily, as I now see it, I was given a second chance to have life beat me down, kick my butt, and test my personal resiliency to its core.

I can say, without an inflated ego, that I found several truths during the past few weeks. Now, I hope to take the weeks ahead of me, as my Peace Corps service comes to a close, to follow the faint light of truth and discover where I am to go.

I read and reread the words and hated every single one of them. I published it anyway and found a momentary sense of relief.

I walked my bike back to the transit house, preferring a slow stroll to peddling. Back at my bed and pile of clothing, I looked down with apprehension. I didn't want to pack. Tomorrow, I was scheduled to go back to Banzon, to go back and wait for my results, to slowly pass every second in hopes that my phone would ring and Crystal or Dr. Patel would give me the good news. But what if the news wasn't good? I would have to turn around and come right back to Ouaga, be medically separated from the Peace Corps, and shipped back home, a cast-off, done.

What if my remaining time in village was numbered? Shouldn't this make me want to go back, to make the most of whatever time I had left, be it two months or two days?

No. Staying, wasting time in Ouaga, meant there was no urgency. It meant that I had plenty of time to spend with my village family and friends before my close of service. No need to rush back.

Andy and Kelly were also returning from Ghana tomorrow. It would be good to see them. Andy would ground my thoughts, bring things into perspective, or distract my desperate attempts to find reason in all of this.

I would stay another day. One more day, then back to village. Crystal would understand. I was surprised that she hadn't been checking in or offered for me to stay in the cushy medical room apartment in the Peace Corps office.

I messaged Crystal and asked if I could stay another day in Ouaga. She quickly replied back, *That's fine…*

'That's fine...That's fine...?' What the hell does that mean? I thought. I was worried that I had HIV and trying to keep from spiraling into depression. I wasn't ready to go back to village and I needed another day in the capital. *That's fine? It better be fucking fine.*

I couldn't believe Crystal's response. Was she insensitive to what I was going through? Was I reading too much into her message?

I tossed my phone onto my pile of clothes and walked away. *Whatever.*

I wiped the steamy mirror clean with my towel and examined my four-day-old scruffy beard. During Peace Corps, I vacillated between clean-shaven, scruff, massive beard, and several stints of ironic mustaches that I liked, as did my friends in village, but other volunteers found to be disgusting. My beard grew quickly and I found it easier to let it go feral rather than maintain a clean face. Given my age, relative to the people I worked with in village, I also wanted to appear older and more mature.

Standing in the transit house's men's bathroom, I filled a sink with hot water. I opened my old fashioned 1950's Gillette safety razor and replaced the tarnished blade with a shiny, sharp new blade. This kind of razor was still used all around the world and it was easy to find replacement blades. They were also much sharper than the cheap, yellow disposable Bic razors sold at every Burkina corner store.

I placed my razor into the hot water, allowing the blade to warm, and dipped my shave brush into the sink. Using the brush, I worked up a thick lather from a bar of local African black soap and began to paint a velvety layer of shaving cream across my scruff.

Slowly, I cut away my beard, dipping the razor back into the warm water after every pass. My focus waned and my mind drifted before a sharp slice brought me back to the present. I watched a small red bead of blood form on my neck and slowly trail down to my chest.

Entranced, I watched the blood. What was in that blood? What caused the two positive HIV tests? I took a sheet of toilet paper, wiped away the blood, and finished shaving. I rinsed my face with cold water and dabbed the tiny cut again with toilet paper to stop the bleeding.

I tossed the bloody toilet paper in the trash can and quickly pulled it out. My blood was unsafe. I flushed the bloody toilet paper down the toilet and began to vigorously clean the sink with soap and water. The whole room suddenly felt dirty. I felt dirty.

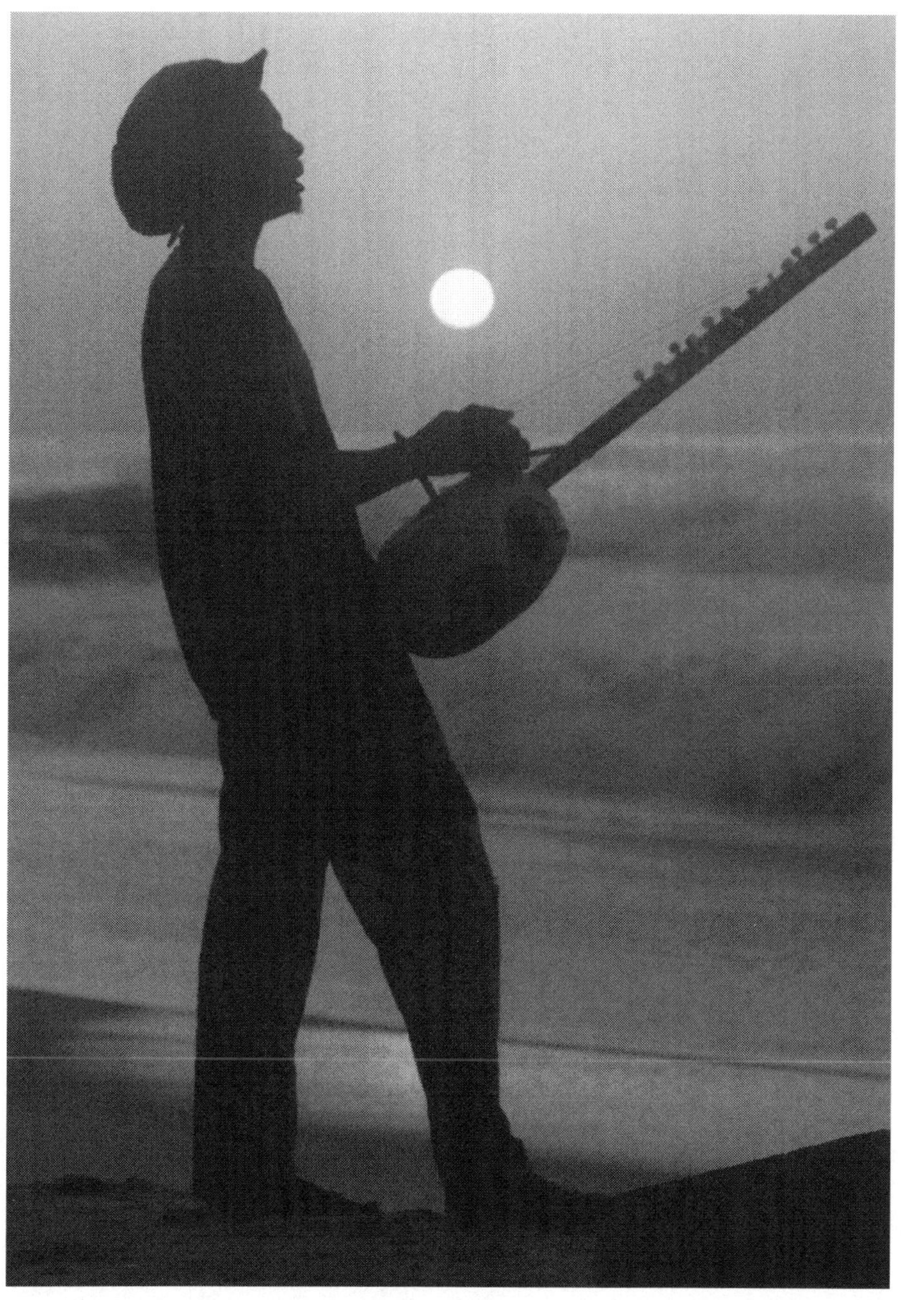

Ghanaian musician and sunset. Cape Coast, Ghana. October 2013.

Chapter 23

June 15th – Next Week

Late yesterday, I received a text message from my mother: *Can't call today, visiting Kyle and going antiquing in Louisville. Call you next week. Love, Mom.*

I was spending another day in Ouaga, a Sunday. My parents were busy and wouldn't be calling today. That was okay.

Other than taking my laundry to be washed, I had nothing to do today. I spent the morning scrolling through news feeds, watching back-to-back episodes of bootleg TV shows, and second-guessing my decision to stay in the capital another day.

Andy and Kelly came back from their Ghanaian vacation in the early evening, tired from the long and bumpy 12-hour bus ride, tanned from a week on the beach, and full of stories.

We were allotted two vacation days a month, for a total of 48 vacation days to use during our two years of service. Given the exorbitant cost of traveling anywhere from Burkina Faso and my meager savings before entering the Peace Corps, I hadn't used all my vacation time. Other than short trips in Burkina and a month trip back home over Christmas, Ghana had been my one real vacation during Peace Corps.

The previous October, I left for Ghana early in the morning with three other volunteers. We boarded the first bus out of Ouaga to Kumasi, a large regional capital in Ghana, where we would spend the night. The following day, our vacation started when we arrived in Cape Coast, a laid-back coastal town where I would have happily stayed for months. In Cape Coast, three days were spent at the beach, exploring the nearby rainforest, and eating. Every meal that I consumed for a week had fresh fish, lobster, or a crepe—sometimes all three.

After Cape Coast, we traveled east to a remote town, Butre, where we spent several nights sleeping in tree houses on the beach. We passed our time in Butre relaxing and exploring the nearby fishing village and a resort town accessible by a steep hike through the jungle. Our trip ended with another day in Kumasi, where we took the day to explore Kejetia Market, the largest market in West Africa.

My trip and memories of Ghana were seven months old but felt distant. Andy and Kelly radiated with post-vacation bliss. I watched them as they unloaded their large backpacks and desperately tried to absorb the tiniest amount of happiness they projected.

Andy was unable to help me, his mind elsewhere and I unwilling to drag my friend down to my level. I smiled and pretended everything was fine. Tomorrow morning, I would take the early bus back to Bobo and catch the truck back to my village.

Village was where I needed to be, back in my home, with my village family and friends. While I wouldn't tell them about my trip to Senegal or pending tests, they would still be there to support me.

This truck, described by another volunteer as "the scariest transport ever taken," was my way in and out of village. I'd travel two hours to Bobo, down a dirt road that often washed out during the rainy season. I grew close to the crew of this truck. They became my friends and were always happy to see me. I was glad to see them too, especially when going back to my village, Banzon, a place that I grew to call home over my two years of service.

Chapter 24

June 16th – Deep

16 June 14

Back in village. Depressed. It didn't take long for that to set in. Maybe I should have COSed early. I have to hope for the best. It's hard to shake though.

Chapter 25

June 17th – Dream

Exiting the staircase, it became apparent that this wasn't the right way back to my room. I was on the wrong hotel floor. Looking for another staircase to take me to my floor, I passed an open door and saw Pat, a Peace Corps Volunteer who served with me in Burkina Faso.

"Hey, Pat. I'm sorta lost and don't know how to get back to my room. Do you know?" I asked as I stood in the open doorway.

"Ha, yeah. I can show you the way. It's no problem. This place is confusing," replied Pat as he exited the room and began leading me down the hallway.

"Really confusing," I sighed.

"Did you already COS? Done with service, pinned and all?" questioned Pat.

"Yep. All done with Peace Corps," I confidently answered.

"Awesome man. Can I see the pin?"

"I don't have it with me. It is back in my room," I sheepishly responded, with both hands buried deep in my empty pockets, wishing I had my pin as proof to show Pat.

"Okay, cool," he said as we reached a door. He opened the door and said, "This is the way back."

I walked through the door as my eyes opened to find myself in my village, lying in bed under my mosquito net, fan blowing on my face.

It was morning, and I had been dreaming.

Ever since hearing, for the second time, that I may be HIV positive, it was nearly impossible for my brain to shut off. The problem now followed me into my sleep. It had been almost a year since I had bizarre and uncanny dreams like this.

The entire dream was a mishmash of past life events. Was there any value in trying to make sense of the dream and decode the symbolism? I hadn't slept well in more than a week. My thoughts, both when awake and asleep, made little sense at this point.

After motivating myself to leave my bed and shake off the dream, I got dressed and headed to Issouf's shop for coffee. Sitting outside Issouf's, on the side of the road, I drank my strong sugarless instant coffee and recorded the past night's dream in my journal.

I can't believe I decided to stay. To leave and come back. I had been given the option of COSing early. I could have been done this week and heading back home, yet I decided to stay.

If you had asked me a month ago, as a theoretical question, "If given the chance to early COS, would you?" I would have instantly responded, "Yes."

This was real now. Given the choice, I stayed. I wanted to complete my service and leave with my friends. I didn't want to believe that I was HIV positive and be ripped from my community, from my Peace Corps service, and thrown back to the U.S. I had to believe that I was okay. That is why I stayed. I was going to be okay. I had to stay positive and make the best of the day. Nothing was certain.

I left Issouf's boutique and returned back to my house where I proceeded to waste the day, passing the hours with a series of naps and watching TV shows on my computer.

Hour by hour, nap after nap, I made my way to nightfall. This sucked. This really fucking sucked. I had an entrenched fear hanging over me.

I clicked my fan on, rested on my back, and stared up at my ceiling. I drifted into sleep for the last time that day, hoping that I would wake up in a different mood. Hoping I would awaken from this nightmare.

Chapter 26

June 18th – Two Years

18 June 14

More crazy dreams. One with a girl who I studied abroad with several years ago and haven't kept in contact with. Forgot all the details though. I didn't reflect on it fast enough. It was there, and then it vanished. Peace Corps is coming to visit tomorrow, to close out my site. Originally they were to come today, in the afternoon, but realized they wouldn't have enough time to do everything. It is also better for me because I really didn't prepare much – clean, tell people they were coming – I've been preoccupied. Today, however, will be filled with working and getting things ready. Time to get my life in motion and back on track.

I couldn't keep it up anymore—the crying, sleeping all day, and binge eating. I had to try and move on rather than wait for Peace Corps to call with an answer. I would throw myself back into routines and projects, stay active, and make the most of my time. This was time I would never get back, no more wasting it.

Tossing my journal to the side, I left the edge of my bed to get ready for a busy day. Peace Corps officials were visiting Banzon tomorrow to have final interviews with my main project counterparts and to close out my site. I would be the last Peace Corps Volunteer in Banzon for many years.

Typically, a Peace Corps site in Burkina Faso hosts three volunteers, one after another, before closing out the site and finding a new village. This way, a community doesn't come to expect volunteers or Peace Corps assistance in perpetuity, nor were new volunteers compared against a long history of former volunteers.

If you weren't the first volunteer in your village, you were always compared to or generalized alongside previous volunteers. I was the fourth volunteer in my village, the result of a special exception and opportunity to work with a newly formed women's cooperative. The volunteer I replaced left a high mark to meet, at least with regard to his language ability.

I came to Burkina Faso knowing zero French, yet I scratched and clawed my way to bare fluency. I then attempted to learn my village's main local language, which I gained a basic understanding of but nowhere near mastery. But I apparently replaced a language savant. He spoke French, Dioula, Moore, and even began to learn Fulfulde.

Every day for my first year, villagers regularly reminded me how well he spoke all the languages. Rather than live up to an unattainable standard, I didn't try to be a master of languages. I devoted my time to seeking out community leaders and passionate people who spoke French, who I could communicate with, and worked through them. Once I began running successful trainings and events, my village didn't care what languages I could or couldn't speak.

I left my house and walked down the wooded path to the Women's Rice Association to find Salimata and tell her that Peace Corps would be visiting tomorrow. Walking through the densely shaded path, I passed a tree Gilbert and I harvested honey from, an old rusted Chinese tractor overgrown with vines, and the concrete pad where I taught karate.

Inside the fenced-in compound of the Women's Rice Association, groups of women were busy working, transforming harvested grains of rice into brown or white rice. When harvested, a thin, fibrous, inedible husk covers rice. The women took the harvested rice and parboiled the grains to expand the rice kernel and loosen the covering. Once boiled, the women spread the rice out across a concrete pad for drying. When the grains of rice dry, the kernel contracts and leaves the husk loosely attached. The women then run the rice through a machine that removes the husk to produce brown rice or the husk and cuticle to yield white rice.

The association's women filled 20kg bags with rice and stored them in their large warehouse. In a given season, the women processed more than 500 metric tons of rice. All of the work that the women put into growing, harvesting, and processing rice gave me a new appreciation for the tiny grains.

In the association's office, I found Sali sitting with Zanibo, the treasurer. They were transcribing records of how much rice had been processed that week into a master ledger. I greeted them and said that Peace Corps would be visiting tomorrow to speak with them and a few other women in the association. They said that they would be here and could set up a meeting.

"What time will they be here?" asked Zanibo.

"They should arrive around 1:00 p.m. Peace Corps will want to meet with a few different groups. Would you like them to meet with you first?" I asked.

"Yes. That would be good. 1:00 p.m. tomorrow," replied Salimata.

Over the past two years, they learned that planning, schedules, and being on time were very important to me. While everyone in my village had phones with clocks, traditional Burkinabé culture was more fluid and less structured than Western culture. In the traditional languages, there were no discrete blocks of time like our hours. They told time in big chunks, a few hours each, that were determined by sunrise, noon, sunset, and the Muslim calls to prayer.

When I went to meetings, trainings, or events in village, I always came prepared with a book to read as I waited. It was not uncommon to wait for more than an hour for people to show up. With time, however, my meetings began to start on time. While not important to them, punctuality was import to me. As I slowly earned their respect, the time I waited shrank.

I walked around the center and greeted the women as they worked. I helped the women load and unload the heavy bags of rice—the one part of the process they trusted me with. After carrying several loads of rice to the warehouse, I said goodbye to the women and left to tell others in my community about Peace Corps' visit tomorrow.

Next, I visited Rasmané, who I worked with to build The Garden School. I pulled my bike into Rasmané's courtyard and greeted the family. Rasmané sat lounging in a chair, playing with his daughter. He rose to greet me and eagerly walked me over to see something he had been working on in the courtyard. Over the past week, he built a large chicken pen with hen houses. Rasmané planned to invest in several chickens and start selling eggs. He told me about his dream of building a larger chicken farm to produce hundreds of eggs a day.

"This sounds great, but will you still be gardening? I asked

"Yes, of course. I took part of the money I earned from gardening this year and invested it in the chickens. Gardening isn't year-round, but the chickens can be. Also, I can use the chicken manure in the garden, which will lower my fertilizer costs and increase my yields," responded Rasmané. He had it all thought out, the reason why I loved working with him.

"Peace Corps will be coming to Banzon tomorrow. Will you be here in the afternoon?" I inquired.

"Yes, I will be here," replied Rasmané.

"Perfect, I'll call you tomorrow and we will visit. Maybe go see the garden."

"That would be great," Rasmané excitedly replied. "Can you stay a while? Have a seat."

"Not today, Rasmané. I have to tell many people that Peace Corps is coming tomorrow. But, thank you," I returned.

I said goodbye to Rasmané and his family seated in the courtyard and made my way to Alu's butcher stand for lunch. I peddled past Issouf's restaurant and waved as he shouted, "TYYY-LURRR."

Alu reclined against the wall of his thatched hut, playing music on his phone.

"Good afternoon, Alu. How is the market today?"

"Slow. Would you like to take a seat and eat?" replied Alu.

"Yes. $1 of meat, please," I said and dismounted my bike.

Alu moved to the grill and began to stoke the faint embers of the fire and slid paper bundles of goat meat off from the side of the grill to the center to reheat.

Alu joined me on a bench and asked, "How have you been, Tyler?"

"I've been good. Getting everything ready to finish the Peace Corps. A few officials from Peace Corps will be here tomorrow to visit and talk to people before I leave. How have you been?"

"I am good. The market has been slow, but I have my health and my family is well," answered Alu. "Wait, you're leaving soon? Done with the Peace Corps? You haven't been here that long. Only a year, right?"

I pulled out my phone to check the date. Today marked two years since I landed in Ouagadougou and stepped off the plane. Today was my two-year anniversary in Burkina and I hadn't even realized it.

"I've been here two years. Two years today," I replied.

"You've been here two years? It doesn't feel like two years, maybe less than one. It's because you're kind. If you're kind, you could be here ten years and it would feel like you arrived yesterday, and if you left for a few days, it feels like a month. Are you sure your two years are over? Can you stay longer? We'll miss you."

"Thank you, Alu. I love Banzon and my friends here. You all are amazing. I will be sad to go," I stammered as I tried to hold back my emotions. Alu and I were friends, but he had never expressed himself like this. He was my butcher and one of the people I talked village gossip with or learned how to swear from in local language. I would miss him too.

I finished my meal and left Alu's butcher shop filled with happiness. The past two years had been unbelievable, very challenging at times, but truly incredible.

Shopping in the market was next on my list. I had been living day to day since being back in village and needed to stop. Waiting for the worst wasn't good for me.

In the market, I filled my backpack with spices, oil, onions, tomato paste, rice, beans, and cabbage—enough food for several days. While waiting for a woman to fill a small bag with freshly ground peanut butter, Noufou, a karate student, rolled up to me on his purple fixed gear bike.

"Good afternoon, Sensei. Welcome back," greeted Noufou with a bow.

I bowed in return. "Good afternoon, Noufou. How are you?"

"I am good. I've been practicing karate. Are we going to start up classes again now that you're back?" asked Noufou.

"Yes. Tomorrow at 5:00 p.m.? Can you tell all the other students for me?"

"Yes. I will tell everyone today. Thank you, Sensei. See you tomorrow. 5:00 p.m. exact."

I biked home, unloaded my groceries, and quickly left again, heading back to the village to surround myself with people. I had kept myself busy thus far today and felt great as a result. I couldn't be tempted to sit around my house and dwell.

I turned into Issouf's courtyard and found a group of children playing.

"Ty. Sanou. Ty. Sanou. Ty. Sanou," they shouted, announcing my arrival as they jumped up and down.

One of the smallest children yelled, "Tubabu!" which was met with a quick smack to the back of the head by one of the older kids.

"His name isn't Tubabu. His name it Ty. Sanou Setile Tyler," the older child rebuked as she waved her finger at the small boy.

"Thank you, but you also shouldn't hit your brother," I interjected.

I took a seat and became engulfed by the group of kids who began to pull on me. They wanted to see one of my hand tricks, hear one of the many funny noises I made to amuse them, or play the game where I treated them like weights, lifting as many of them into the air as possible at one time, or seeing how far I could walk as they all hung off my neck.

Issouf tossed aside the curtain that hung in the doorway of his small house and walked out to see the cause of all the commotion.

"Kids, leave him alone!" shouted Issouf. "Tyler, coffee?"

"Yes please, Issouf."

Issouf ducked into the restaurant and the kids continued to pull on me. They intently watched as I performed several of my tricks, followed by squeals of laughter as my fingers waved back and forth or made funny shapes. Next, I made the funny noises they enjoyed, sounds of bird calls, water drops, rhythmic pops, clicks, booms, and, of course, fart noises, which turned into them screeching, trying to whistle, or shouting as they chased after each other.

Issouf returned with my coffee to the utter chaos unfolding in his courtyard, amused by the absurd scene of a tall goofy white guy trading silly faces with two five-year-old twin girls as a three-year-old sat in his lap, pulling on his ear. Issouf shooed the kids away and handed me the hot, black coffee.

As I sipped the coffee, Issouf retold village gossip and soon slipped into stories of magic and mysticism. Last night he hadn't slept well. When he awoke in the morning, he found a small galette pierced with a stick.

"That was bad magic. Someone was trying to get me last night. I went out this morning to the bush and collected herbs and bark. I'm currently soaking them and will drink and bathe in the water to cleanse my body of negative energy," said Issouf as he reached into his pocket and pulled out a small bundle of herbs. "I'm also using these," continued Issouf as he plucked off a sprig and tucked it behind his lower lip.

"What does it do?" I asked

"It does all sorts of things. Clears away evil. It can fix diarrhea, headaches, malaria, and HIV. Here, try some," replied Issouf as he extended to me the bundle of herbs.

I pulled a small sprig out of the bundle and tucked it against my gum. The herb tasted woody and bitter, but I soon grew used to the taste.

Issouf left me sitting alone in the courtyard while he served other customers. I began to reflect on what he had said. Across Africa, there are many myths surrounding HIV. Some believe that HIV spreads by touch, sweat, tears, saliva, or even the breath of an infected individual, which leads to complete societal rejection of people known to have HIV. Others believe that mosquitoes carry HIV or that HIV is a disease created by white people to wipe out Africa.

As was once largely believed in the U.S., some still allege that only homosexuals can contract HIV/AIDS. Many people believe that they can tell if a person is HIV positive by looking at them, and some consider male circumcision to prevent HIV.

Sadly, some believe that having sex with a virgin can cure HIV, leading to rape and the continued spread of HIV. Across sub-Saharan Africa, many people still rely on traditional medicine, even claiming that it can cure HIV/AIDS. While some traditional medicines do, in fact, reduce symptoms of HIV opportunistic infections, they do not cure HIV. Currently, there is no cure for HIV.

I returned to negotiating my way through the facts. It was very possible that not only was I HIV positive, but that several other volunteers were infected. I wasn't patient zero, but I may be the first person identified. In training, we were warned about HIV. We were shown an old VHS video of former Peace Corps Volunteers who contracted HIV. Some had contracted HIV from locals, others from fellow volunteers.

In the video, each of the volunteers talked about their Peace Corps experience, their choices, and struggles of living with HIV/AIDS. While the video was moving, I shirked it off. These volunteers served during the late 80's and early 90's when HIV was largely misunderstood. Now, we knew much more. I told myself it couldn't happen to me. I was wrong.

Suddenly, my phone began to ring.

PCMO scrolled across the screen. I hesitated to answer.

I quickly pressed the small green phone symbol and raised the phone to my ear. "Hello?"

Crystal responded, "Good afternoon, Tyler. Good news! Your test results came back. You're negative."

I shot up from my chair and replied, "Really, negative? You're sure. 100%? I'm okay?"

"Yes, Tyler. We are sure. It is official. You do not have HIV."

I didn't have HIV.

Pure energy pumped through my veins as a mix of emotions rose up into my throat. I shook with happiness and restrained myself from shouting the good news. I didn't have HIV.

I finished the call with Crystal and quickly sent numerous messages out to everyone who had been waiting to hear my results.

I sat back into my chair and took a slow, deep breath. Everything was going to be okay. Two years after landing in Burkina Faso, everything was okay.

One after another, messages came back.

'Great news!'
'Good to hear. Been thinking about you.'
'Glad to hear it, man. Celebrate.'

When Issouf came back, he could see that my mood had changed. I energetically shifted in my seat, eager to do it all. I wanted to make the most of every second but didn't know where to start. Unable to sit still, I told Issouf that I needed to head home. As he often did, he offered to walk with me part of the way.

Along the way, I tried to tell Issouf about testing positive for HIV, the mix-up, flying to Senegal, and the good news. I faltered as I tried to accurately explain the situation and Issouf struggled to understand what exactly had happened. But he didn't have to understand.

That night, I ate dinner with my family, happily surrounded by people I adored. We ate, joked, and enjoyed each other's company. As the night grew late, family members began to leave the courtyard to go to bed.

Salimata and I sat together in total silence, under the dark night sky. I peered up, gazing into the sea of twinkling stars, unobscured by city lights. A sense of hope and possibility continued to fill my body. Even when staring up into the infinite and expansive universe, I couldn't help but feel significant. Significance in the past weeks, months, years, and in this very moment, peacefully seated next to a woman who couldn't have been more different than me, and who I couldn't have cared more deeply about.

I pushed myself up from my seat and stretched my stiff limbs.

"Time for bed?" asked Sali.

"Yes. Time for bed," I replied.

"May Allah give you a good night's sleep," prayed Sali.

"Amen. And may Allah give you a good night's sleep as well," I returned.

"Amen."

I latched my front door and closed my shutters for the night. Under the breeze of my fan and the thin sheet of my bed, I looked up at the dark ceiling above. I lay there smiling, repeating to myself, '*Everything is ok, thank you,*' and drifted into the first deep, restful sleep in weeks.

A month after hearing the good news, I left Banzon for the last time as a Peace Corps Volunteer. That morning, my host mother Salimata and I said goodbye. When I asked her if she would wait with me at the van until I left, she quickly mumbled that she couldn't, before bursting into tears, wishing me well, and running into her house. This was the one time I saw her cry in my two years and the last time I saw her.

I began to cry as I walked with my other family members up to the village. My host aunt slapped me on the shoulder and told me to stop crying and be a strong man. I smiled and wiped my tears away, as I saw my host sister beginning to tear up.

They unloaded my bags and left with the donkey cart, promising to return to see me off. I headed to Issouf's restaurant and found him making one last extra strong coffee for me.

"I have something for you, Tyler. A song I wrote for you. It says how good you are and wishes you well. I recorded it on my phone," he said.

I took Issouf's phone and sat it next to my voice recorder. I pressed play on his phone and recorded his song on my microphone, carefully listening to Issouf's song. He sang with a soothing voice, mixing in French, Dioula, and Bobo. While I couldn't make out all the words, I could tell the lyrics were filled with love. When the song finished, I looked up to see Issouf crying. Tears rolled down his face. Quickly, I ran around to the back door of the restaurant and gave Issouf a hug. As we both cried, I tried to comfort my best friend.

"This isn't goodbye forever, Issouf. We'll never really leave each other," I said. Unable to speak, he slowly nodded his head.

I left Issouf's place to go to the van. My family and friends had crowded around the van to see me off. I said goodbye to Patrice, Gilbert, Mamou, and many others. I hugged each of my family members and held them tight, the first time we ever hugged.

I took my place in the passenger's seat and looked out to everyone.

"Tyler, wait! Don't leave yet!" shouted Rasmané as he rushed to the van.

For the past several days, I tried to remind Rasmané of my departure. I called, but he never picked up. I stopped by his house, but he was never home. I feared that I would leave without saying goodbye to him.

"Rasmané! I am glad I got to see you before I left," I exclaimed, hanging halfway out the window to give Rasmané a hug.

"Tyler, I didn't get you anything. I'm so sorry. I should have given you a gift to take home," Rasmané anxiously blurted.

"No, don't worry about that. Your friendship is enough," I reassured.

"No, I need to give you something. Here, take this," said Rasmané as he took off his silver wedding ring and handed it to me. "Take my ring."

"I can't take your ring!"

"You've given me so much. Take my ring. You have to," Rasmané insisted as his voice broke. Reluctantly, I took his ring and placed it on my necklace. I held Rasmané's hand tight as the driver started the van. Slowly, I let go of my friend and sat back into my seat.

The van pulled way as two years of friends and family waved goodbye. Issouf stood outside his restaurant, waving and shouting my name, "SANOU SETILE TYYY-LURRR," and my Peace Corps story came to a close.

The road to Banzon, the village where I served as a Peace Corps Volunteer from 2012 – 2014.

AUTHOR'S NOTE

My mom still doesn't know that I flew to Senegal. She doesn't know a lot of the details of my service, but I assume she'll buy this book and read it. Hi, Mom. Sorry.

While writing Service Disrupted, I constantly second-guessed myself. I wondered how people would react to my book, both strangers and friends, some of whom I wrote about. I questioned the level of detail and intimacy I should and could appropriately express. Routinely, I had to check how I projected my interpretation of Burkinabé life and culture, wanting to remain culturally sensitive while not ignoring the fact that I was a foreigner seeing and experiencing something far different from what I knew back in the United States. Most importantly, I felt unsure about using a disease that I ultimately did not have as means to tell my story.

Yet, as evidenced by you reading this, I reconciled each of my concerns and self-doubts and wrote my Peace Corps story. More than reconciling these impediments, I came to terms with them and accepted them as part of my story and me.

Not all my stories were captured during this book's three-week timeline or through the many interspersed vignettes. Some of my strongest memories of Peace Corps aren't even stories at all, but rather minor anecdotes or general feelings that I could not properly weave into this memoir or put into words.

No two volunteers have the same service. Each volunteer comes into the Peace Corps with a vastly diverse background of prior life experiences that shape the way they will see and react to life in their host country. What I have written, however, stays true to my unique service and captures the essence of the two impactful years I spent in Burkina Faso.

The Peace Corps challenged me, nearly defeating my resolve more than once, but I do not regret my service and would do it all again. I say this in all honesty, being acutely aware of our seeming predisposition to look more fondly at past events.

Writing this book provided me with an opportunity to reflect on my service while I reread and reviewed two years of journal entries, photos, and videos. In doing so, I revisited events that I had nearly forgotten—even after only a few years. If for nothing else, trying to accurately put my experiences into words has been highly cathartic and well worth the many months of writing and rewriting.

I sincerely thank you for giving me the opportunity to share my story with you and look forward to your reaction and review.

Best,
Tyler

AUTHOR BIO

Tyler Lloyd served as a Peace Corps Volunteer in Burkina Faso from 2012 to 2014. Originally from Kentucky, he currently calls Washington, DC home. When not serving as a federal employee, Tyler enjoys exploring the city on his bike, drinking strong coffee, and telling stories through photography, video, podcasts, and the written word. Service Disrupted: My Peace Corps Story is Tyler's first book. For more about Tyler Lloyd and his other works, visit www.tyleredwardlloyd.com.

Interested in hearing more stories from Peace Corps Volunteers? Visit mypeacecorpsstory.com and listen to current and returned volunteers tell their story on the My Peace Corps Story podcast.

10% of the profits of this book will be donated to fund HIV/AIDS testing, prevention, treatment, counseling, and care services.

Made in the USA
Columbia, SC
16 October 2017